GETTY

Ticket to ride

MethaneSAT, built to locate and quantify climate-harming methane pollution from the oil and gas industry worldwide, will be ready to launch in late 2022 on a SpaceX Falcon 9 rocket (*above*). It will have the best methane detection sensitivity of any satellite. Public data from the project, led by EDF subsidiary MethaneSAT LLC, will help governments and companies reduce emissions swiftly and transparently. Methane pollution is responsible for at least 25% of the warming we experience today.

A new era for environmental

By Joanna Foster

After facing down a four-year assault on important environmental protections, EDF counsel Vickie Patton and her team are rolling up sleeves and ushering in the next generation environmental safeguards. "General" Patton colleagues call her, answered questions we can rebuild stronger.

Q. Former President Trump took aim at over 100 environmental initiatives. How would you describe the state of affairs that the Biden administration inherited?

A. Thanks to the tenacity of the EDF team, numerous environmental organizations, state attorneys general and many more, Trump's reckless rollbacks were challenged at every turn, and the Biden-Harris EPA has a solid legal foundation on which to carry out the urgent work of protecting human health and the envi-

forced out, and th amount of work t ranks and morale the agency can fu have lost preciou consequences fo neighborhoods t by unhealthy air leap ahead with cleaning up the

Q. What progres in reversing the

AIA **Guide to Newport**

by **Ronald J. Onorato**

Photography by
Warren Jagger Photography

Foreword by
Richard Guy Wilson

American Institute of Architects
Rhode Island Chapter

First edition, March 2007.
Printed and bound in the United States of America.

In 2007, the American Institute of Architects (AIA) celebrates its 150th year,
having been founded in 1857 by Richard Upjohn, Richard Morris Hunt
and eleven other fellow architects. AIA/Rhode Island, founded in 1875, remains
highly committed to excellence in architecture and service to the public. It
offers many programs that enhance the public understanding of design, as well
as the practice of architecture. The AIAri Architectural Forum is a non-profit,
tax-exempt, 501(c)(3) organization, which was established in 2001 by the AIA
Rhode Island to expand our commitment of service to the professional
and lay communities through the granting of educational scholarship and
sponsoring of educational programs. The Rhode Island Chapter of the American
Institute of Architects, The AIAri Architectural Forum and individuals
connected with this publication assume no legal responsibility for the complete-
ness or accuracy of the listings herein or any legal responsibility for the
appreciation or depreciation in value of any premises listed herein by reason of
such inclusion. The analysis and opinions presented in this book are those of
the authors and do not attempt in anyway to represent attitudes of the sponsoring organizations or individuals. Inclusion of a building in this book does
not imply that the building or grounds are open to the public. Users of this guide
are cautioned to observe private property boundaries. We welcome reader's
additions, corrections, or other comments for consideration in the next edition.
Please forward them to the AIAri Architectural Forum at the above address.

Guidebook Committee

Mohamad Farzan, RIBA, AIA, Chair
Paul R. V. Pawlowski, AIA, ASLA
Martha Werenfels, AIA
Kathleen Bartels, AIA
Thomas Cousineau, AIA
Stephen White, AIA

Writing Team

Overview, Chapter Introductions and Entries: Ronald J. Onorato
Foreword: Richard Guy Wilson
Editor: Keith Fleming
Contributing Editor: Dorienne West Farzan
Copy Editor: Antonia Farzan
Index: Stephen Ingle, WordCo Indexing Services, Inc.

Photography

Warren Jagger Photography | Warren Jagger, Robert Brewster
Photo research: Jane Carey

Design and Cartography

Symbio Design Incorporated | Eva Anderson, Colin Murphy

Production

Printers: Signature Digital Offset Printing
Binders: Acme Binding Co

On the cover: A view of Beacon Rock—designed by McKim, Mead & White—as
seen from Brenton Cove. Photograph by Warren Jagger.

Library of Congress Control Number 2007920234
ISBN 13: 978-0-9792727-0-7 and ISBN 10: 0-9792727-0-X

This edition was printed with plant-based inks on 100% totally chlorine-free paper.

TABLE OF CONTENTS

SUPPORTERS

ALLETTA MORRIS MCBEAN CHARITABLE TRUST
CAROL AND LES BALLARD
HAMILTON FAMILY FOUNDATION
PRINCE CHARITABLE TRUSTS
VAN BEUREN CHARITABLE FOUNDATION

American Institute of Architects/Rhode Island
The Felicia Fund
Mrs. John Stephan
Symbio Design
Warren Jagger Photography

The Elms Foundation
The Fleming Charitable Trust II
Vanderbilt Hotel and Residence Club

National Trust for Historic Preservation's Antoinette F. Downing
    Preservation Fund for Rhode Island
The Newport Daily News
Mrs. Howard L. Ross
Subvention Program – University of Rhode Island
    Center for the Humanities
William Vareika Fine Arts, LTD.

Texas Society of Architects

Why an architectural guide to Newport? As an architectural laboratory, the city can be read like a book itself.

On Saturday, June 12th, 1784 Thomas Jefferson arrived in Newport, then a town of 11,000 inhabitants, on a three-day political junket and for the first time faced a perfectly sober example of Palladian architecture on American soil placed before him like a Greek temple up on a hill, with a physical presence more intense, more alive than the rest of town's colonial domestic buildings all painted in their cheerful color schemes so typical in New England. Jefferson would study the façade as he would any of the architectural books in his personal library, analyze and appreciate the divine proportions, the pediment carried seemingly effortlessly by the columns with their subtle curves, the sculptured architrave over the door, the ingenious rustication technique. He would understand the higher meaning behind all these details and recognize it at once, not as a building, but as a piece of architecture. This temple of learning perfectly represented its benefactor's mission of having nothing in view but the good of mankind. The isolation of the Redwood Library up on the hill must have thrilled the young architect of the emerging democratic republic and inspired him to break free from English tutelage. Ironically the Redwood was designed by Peter Harrison, both America's first architect and a fierce loyalist. Nonetheless, both souls must have been touched by the same flame felt by all other architects, and both men must have had far more in common beyond the day's politics.

Like Jefferson, today's perceptive visitor to Newport is inspired by its exuberant architecture, but with the aid of additional tools to decipher the iconographic language of its eclectic architecture. Educated tourists now often consult scholarly guidebooks to better inform themselves about a city which they are about to visit. Since the first AIA guides were published in the 1950's, the American Institute of Architects has produced many editions for countless U.S. cities. The AIA guidebooks differentiate themselves from other books in that they are inclusive of contemporary architecture. This guidebook is the second volume in the series of guides to the architecture of communities in Rhode Island the first volume, the *PPS/AIAri Guide to Providence Architecture*, was published in 2003, in collaboration with the Providence Preservation Society. As the first AIA guide to Newport, this book appears to be long overdue for a city where three of the AIA founding fathers, Hunt, Tefft and Upjohn practiced extensively and left a huge legacy. Hunt, who married, lived, practiced and is buried in Newport, was instrumental in establishing the profession of architect in this country. The first truly original American architect, Richardson, also designed several buildings in Newport, while many of his followers launched their careers (and social connections) in Newport. They followed his path and created that uniquely American architectural style using American materials and technology, the Shingle Style. The main purpose of this guidebook is to inform, but allow room for individual interpretation, it is illustrative rather than encyclopedic, and meant to help navigate the diverse neighborhoods and allow the cultural landscape of each to present itself. It is hoped that it will find a place in the coat pockets of each traveler to the City by the Sea, serving as a sourcebook for both students of architecture and those seeking to expand their knowledge beyond well known works of architecture already documented.

The guide could not have been published without the generous financial support of those individuals, corporations, trusts and foundations that are recognized on the preceding page with our gratitude. The guide benefited from resources provided by the Newport Historical Society, The Newport Restoration Foundation, the Preservation Society of Newport County, the Redwood Library and the Rhode Island Historical Preservation and Heritage Commission. I would personally like to thank Mr. John G. Winslow for sharing his knowledge of many Newport families and their architects, Ron Onorato for taking on the Herculean task of selecting, researching and writing each entry; Richard Guy Wilson for his insightful foreword, Warren Jagger for seeing and capturing each entry with his artistic eye and through his camera lens, Eva Anderson for her splendid maps and layout, Keith Fleming for editing the text, Neal Manchester for waiting patiently before printing the book in the highest quality, my colleagues on the committee, Paul Pawlowski, Martha Werenfels, Kathy Bartels, Tom Cousineau, Steve White, David Prengaman, Pat Germani, Mark Saccoccio; my perceptive friends Michael Abbott, John Tschirch, and Richard Youngken for proof reading the text; my wife Dorienne and my daughter Antonia who provided positive criticism all along; and finally all architects, past or present, whose creative body of work enriches the pages of this book.

Mohamad Farzan, RIBA, AIA
AIA Guide to Newport, Committee Chair

Dedicated to the memory of William H. Jordy

Any book is the result of many contributions and this guide is no exception. Although I knew my experiences as a commissioner on the Rhode Island State Historical Preservation commission, the National Register review board for Rhode Island, and my previous research and publications on Newport and its architecture would provide me with what Mohamad Farzan called my "unique Data base", I also realized that I would have to depend on the generosity of many other professionals to produce the finished text.

After being doubly honored by the AIA in 2004, both by being asked to write this definitive guide and by being given an honorary membership, I quickly came to the realization that this book would provide a novel opportunity to add to what was already well known about Newport architecture. All the significant historical structures are of course included but I decided early on that a guide published by the American Institute of Architects needed to go beyond the predictable and consider the many recent buildings that have become part of Newport's architectural heritage since its justly famous colonial era and Gilded Age.

The leadership of the AIA should be thanked for their vision and foresight in producing this volume and for their support and guidance in seeing it realized. Numerous individuals generously provided me with information, clues and insights into a wide variety of works and I particularly want to thank the various architects who provided me with information on 20th century projects that would have been impossible to obtain in any other way. My friend Mohamad Farzan helped in numerous ways, not only through his considerable knowledge of contemporary buildings but by his ceaseless fundraising to support publication and for being the project's most ardent champion. Keith Fleming, who worked hard to make my drafts much clearer and precise than they otherwise would have been, and Richard Wilson, who wrote the ideal foreword, generously provided the kind of expert assistance that only they could give. Professor James Garman of the Cultural and Historical Preservation Program at Salve Regina University and Bertram Lippincott, the Librarian at the Newport Historical Society, were extremely helpful as they have on many earlier projects. I am grateful to my former student, Elaine Robinson who ably and efficiently field checked the entries and maps. A special thanks goes to Elisabeth Marchi for enduring repetitive readings of my rough drafts and to Jack Onorato who helped map and sequence the tours. Just as importantly, they buoyed my spirits even when I let the pressures of writing spill over into family time.

At the University of Rhode Island, The Center for the Humanities provided a subvention grant to assist with photographs and the Department of Art and Art history chaired by Wendy Roworth and later Barbara Pagh supported my writing through a course reduction in the fall of 2005. I am also grateful to the University for granting me a sabbatical during which parts of the original research for this volume were accomplished, and to Jane Carey and also many former URI students, particularly Caitlin Roseen, Adele Goss and Kimberley Toney who provided special research work or assisted in other ways.

Some of my fondest memories of architecture are of walking around New York City with Bill Jordy many years ago to prepare a walking tour on downtown Manhattan buildings. While there, although he was already a noted professor at Brown University and I was only a lowly doctoral candidate, he continually introduced us both as "students of architecture". A number of years later, I spent many days on the streets of Newport with Jordy to prepare his *Buildings of Rhode Island* volume. Many of the comments he made then, while we stood in front of both little-known structures and well-known monuments, informed my subsequent readings of Newport's architecture. I dedicate this volume to his memory as the dominant architectural historian in Rhode Island, a much-missed mentor and an unabashed enthusiastic and lifelong "student" of architecture.

Notes for the use of this guide:

This guide is intended primarily as a walking guide except for two fairly lengthy sequences that would better be experienced through driving. The West End *(Tour Three)* and Ocean Avenue *(Tour Eight)* probably should be driven but given the complications of heavy traffic, one way streets and a crowded city center, all other sections are best traversed on foot.

Much of the information in this book is based on primary sources in various archival collections like the Newport Historical Society, on reports and nomination papers at the Rhode Island Historical Preservation and Heritage Commission and on interviews with numerous architects who generously shared their knowledge of contemporary architecture with the author.

Finally, there is one important caveat. Many of the buildings contained in this guide are privately owned and residential. Only buildings that can be seen from a public right of way have been included but please be mindful of the rights of property owners and respect their privacy.

For further reading

There are surprisingly only a handful of indispensable published sources which survey the entire subject of Newport architecture:

Antoinette Forrester Downing and Vincent J.Scully, Jr, *The Architectural Heritage of Newport, Rhode Island, 1640-1915*, Preservation Society of Newport County (1952)

The above named book remained the standard work on Newport architecture for almost a half century. More recently a spate of other books have appeared that add to and update their work including:

Richard C. Youngken, *African Americans in Newport*, Rhode Island Historical Preservation & Heritage Commission, Rhode Island Black Heritage Society (1994)

Myron O. Stachiw et al. *The Early Architecture and Landscapes of Narragansett Basin, Volume I, Newport*, Vernacular Architecture Forum (2001)

William H. Jordy, Ronald J. Onorato, and William McKenzie Woodward, *Buildings of Rhode Island*, Oxford University Press (2004)

James Yarnall, *Newport Through its Architecture*, Salve Regina University Press (2005)

by Richard Guy Wilson

"Per square foot, Newport possesses more great architecture than any other American city," is an observation I frequently make about the special charms of this great port city. Certainly some flack ensues with retorts such as what about Charleston? Chicago? or (among the naïve) New York? Well yes, Charleston, South Carolina does have wonderful eighteenth century buildings, and yes, Newport does not have Frank Lloyd Wright, or skyscrapers, but for overall quality, numbers of buildings, and range, from the seventeenth century to the early twentieth century, it can not be beat. Of course everybody knows about the great Newport "cottages" or mansions such as the Breakers, Elms, Marble House, Ochre Court, and Rosecliff, but few people recognize, that although there is no Wright, still it is from houses such as the Isaac Bell and the Watts Sherman that he drew ideas, and without which, no history of modern American architecture can be understood. As far as early architecture, there are few cities that possess buildings of the quality and design sophistication of Trinity Church, the Colony House, Touro Synagogue, the Redwood Library and Hunter house. If one adds onto this the Federal or Early Republic era buildings and then those of the mid-1800s by Russell Warren, Richard Upjohn, Alexander Jackson Davis, George Snell, Thomas Tefft, along with later architects such as Richard Morris Hunt, McKim, Mead & White, Peabody & Stearns, Horace Trumbauer, Ralph Adams Cram and Bertram Goodhue, Irving Gill, and John Russell Pope, the gardens and layouts by Frederick Law Olmsted, Nathan Barrett, and Jacques Greber, the decorative arts contributions by John La Farge, Louis Comfort Tiffany, Ogden Codman, and Allard *et fils*, you are overwhelmed; this is simply the greatest collection of design in the United States, and all in situ!

Of course architecture and design is not just about visual and sensual response, nor just names, but it also has social, intellectual, and cultural dimensions. To have the country's first library, or the first synagogue is significant. The Redwood Library is the first temple fronted structure in the English colonies and helped inspire many American public buildings and the association with classical antiquity. Newport's religious architecture from the Colonial churches and meeting houses through the early twentieth century displays—as in a time capsule—the nation's changing attitudes about worship and acceptance of religious diversity. A subset of this and of tremendous importance is the different burying grounds and cemeteries which contain not only the graves of the famous, but also one of the most significant collections of sculpture and funeral art anywhere on the East Coast. Scattered around the city are a number of colonial burying grounds which are worthy of close study for the remarkable carvings of winged sculls, angels, and even portraits. The Common Burying Ground contains a huge number early markers and of special significance the largest collection of colonial African-American grave markers in the United States. Newport was one of the centers of slave trading and possessed a large black population in the eighteenth century.

In addition to architecture Newport played a major role in the other arts. John Smibert, the first professionally trained artist in the English colonies arrived in 1729 and begat a long line of Newport painters including Gilbert Stuart, Robert Feke, Charles Bird King, and others. In the realm of public monuments Newport possesses significant examples of John Quincy Adams Ward, Augustus Saint-Gaudens, and Felix deWeldon. Similarly, Newport's role in American literature is overwhelming, from Dr. George Berkeley in 1729 through Henry Wadsworth Longfellow, Bret Harte, Harriet Beecher Stowe, Henry James, and Edith Wharton. Newport has been the scenic backdrop for countless historical romances, novels, and poems. That the city is complex is amply shown in Thornton Wilder's *Theophilus North* of 1973, in which the "nine cities" of the town range from the top echelon down to those who wash the floors, carry out the garbage, and tend the shops. Architecture frequently plays a role in Newport fiction ranging from the "Viking Tower" in Longfellow's "Skelton in Armor" to wide friendly porches in James' "International Episode."

Wealth usually begets something—sometimes great buildings, sometimes bombast and junk. From the early 18th century when South Carolinians began arriving to today, Newport has been the place that if you have money, you must be seen. Routinely many of Newport's cottages have been, and continue to be denounced as "conspicuous consumption" and self-aggrandizing monuments. And one does have to wonder whether anybody ever sat down with any comfort in the main hall of the Breakers? Did the Vanderbilt's ever really sit there, or perhaps it was more used by that faceless—nameless—servant from upstairs, or below stairs, and only populated by the owners during a big party. But alternatively, these grand houses show in their bluster the quest and insecurity of many Americans—even the wealthy —to create a history rivaling that of Europe; to be one up on them.

Ironically, the architect of some of these grand houses, Richard Morris Hunt had been trained in France at the Ecole des Beaux-Arts to design great public buildings. Unfortunately, Hunt seldom got the great public commissions and with a few exceptions his well known designs are for private houses. However, time passes and these houses such as the Griswold, Ochre Court, Belcourt, and the Breakers have become public buildings.

Newport is not just about the great mansions and the Colonial remains but it also contains a huge collection of more modest wooden cottages that go under various names: Gothic, Stick, Swiss, Queen Anne, Colonial Revival, Olde English, Shingle, Bungalow, and Arts & Crafts among many. One can argue that in the design of these houses a new and genuinely American approach was developed that marked a significant break with the old world. Yes, the style was important, but equally they contained the rudiments of the American "living room," and the open plan. These houses for the most part were on lots with a lawn in front, gardens or some space to the rear, and were not attached. In embryo one can see the development of the American suburban house type. Similarly, the great street—Bellevue—and many other streets which were summer vacation streets became the prototype for American suburbia.

In addition to "greats" of American architecture Newport had its own cast of locals who provided much of the context of the town. Builders and architects such as Seth Bradford, Dudley Newton, John Dixon Johnston, and the father and son team of George Champlin Mason, designed many notable buildings. Although a local, Dudley Newton was able to invade high society and designed a number of buildings for the out of town elite. The Mason team is especially important since they promoted the Colonial remains and along with Charles Follen McKim and his book entitled *Old Newport Houses* (a collection of photographs) helped make the city one of the centers of the Colonial Revival from the 1870s to the 1920s.

Time has not stood still in Newport and modernists will be thrilled by the International Style buildings at Salve Regina University by Maginnis, Walsh & Kennedy, or the Post-Modern designs by R.A.M. Stern and the Newport Collaborative. Equally important is the examples of adaptive reuse and Newport as a center for historic preservation.

Of course Newport is more than houses but a real city with many different neighborhoods and a reason why this guide book by Ronald Onorato is very important since he has gone beyond the well known and included neighborhoods out along Broadway and the various wards. This is the unknown Newport but well worth an examination to see how people really lived and where one can discover many treasures.

Ronald J. Onorato has taught art and architectural history at the University of Rhode Island for many years. He took his Ph. D. at Brown University and has researched and written extensively on Newport architecture. Together with William McKenzie Woodward, he edited and completed the late William H. Jordy's guide to the state, *Buildings of Rhode Island* (2004). This book is a considerable expansion of Jordy's volume and presents new materials and many more buildings. Enjoy!

Newport and Its Architectural History: Building, Neighborhood, Place

by Ronald J. Onorato

Newport holds many claims to historical significance. Its colonial history of religious toleration, a part in the early history of slavery *and* in the abolition movement, and its prominent reputation as a maritime and yachting center are all important to Newport's character. But, first and foremost, its unique sense of place resides in its architectural heritage. Given its relatively small population and restricted landmass, Newport has, per capita and per acre, arguably the densest collection of notable architecture — representing the widest historical span — of any American city. Several hundred buildings are remarkable for their vernacular uniqueness, their historical associations with important values, events, individuals and institutions, their architectural significance and authorship, or for some combination of these factors.

Founded in 1639, Newport was part of the separatist ethos of the English colonists who settled New England in the seventeenth century. A year earlier, a group of schismatics had followed Anne Hutchinson from Boston through Plymouth Colony to a new home at the northern end of Aquidneck Island, today known as Portsmouth. The founders of Newport, about 30 in number, wanting to split from the Hutchinson group, explored the shoreline further south until they found a promising site with a fresh water spring and adjacent to a deep, well-protected harbor. Newport quickly became a successful seaport, with numerous wharves, marine enterprises, specialized artisans, well-connected merchants and a group of structures built of stone, brick and wood clustered around the original settlement. The desire to escape from the religious hegemony of the Massachusetts Bay and Plymouth Bay colonies formed the basis for Newport's settlement. This impulse toward religious tolerance allowed for the followers of religions as varied as Baptists, Sabbatarians, Anglicans, Congregationalists, Moravians and perhaps most surprisingly, Quakers and Jews, to settle, contribute, and thrive in the city's economic and cultural development.

The eighteenth century saw this development come to fruition in Newport's first "golden age" in the decades between the 1730s and 1770s. This economic development was fostered by Newport's continuing success as a port, its production of luxury goods by scores of artisans like the famous Townsend-Goddard family of furniture makers, and its role in the matrix of slave trade. Slavery drove the commercial engine of the town, providing a captive labor force and also bringing wealth to those involved in the sinful and highly profitable triangular trade in which, in essence, Africans were shipped to the Caribbean, sugar cane to distilleries, and rum to England for monies that could be used to start the cycle of slave purchase all over again. But the horrific fact of slavery did nonetheless bring to Newport a large African community that would go on to add its talents to the city's and create a vibrant, varied culture of its own. Remarkably, Newport's Colonial architectural heritage includes numerous sites that can be identified with that African American community—neighborhoods, homes, workplaces, churches and graveyards—as well as evidence of the role that African Americans played in construction and artisanal activities. From the architectural evidence we can deduce the living patterns of this important community both before and after the period of manumission occurred in the 1770s.

More than in most American cities, the Revolution drastically affected the fortunes of Newport (the city was occupied by British troops for almost three years: between 1776 and 1779). Although the city fell without a shot being fired, half the island population left town and Newport went into decline: its maritime commerce ground to a halt, bringing about severe shortages of food and supplies. While other cities like Providence and Salem, Massachusetts fared well after the Revolution, Newport took much longer to recover economically, and the period between the 1770s and the 1830s saw little of the architectural ebullience of the pre-war decades. There were a few Federal-era structures built in Newport, including a few fine brick residences, like Robert Lawton's house on Mill Street and even an Asher Benjamin designed Bank building on Thames Street (no longer extant) but these are exceptions to the rule of this era.

Newport revived its architectural heritage when nineteenth century residents began to build large-scale hotels (such as the no-longer-extant Ocean House) to attract summer visitors. Such communal living arrangements could be enjoyed elsewhere but Newport had something unique to offer. A prominent local architect, George Champlin Mason, along with others, marketed Newport as a cottage colony, emphasizing its historical heritage of small colonial buildings, some of which could be rented for short-term visits. Newport's old picturesque streets, somewhat frozen in time, became part of its appeal as did its cool island climate and proximity to the rustic pleasures of a rocky coastline and up-island glens. These qualities were the antithesis of what was occurring in other older cities which were undergoing modernization and growth through industrialization. Lacking river power to run mills and railroad connections to ship manufactured goods, Newport never industrialized and thus again became a refuge—not from religious persecution but from the unsightly stacks, mechanized noise, and noxious smells of grimy "Brown decades" industry which affected so many other American towns. Newport's architecture imaginatively came to reflect residential comfort and social ambition rather than pragmatic mass production.

Happily, this shift to a summer colony brought outside influences to bear on Newport's architectural development as a wealthy clientele from elsewhere built their second homes on the outskirts of the small, still colonial-sized town. By 1851, New Yorker Alfred Smith and others envisioned a new street leading south from the town to the coast over a mile away—this became the artery today known as Bellevue Avenue, which allowed previously un-built-upon pastureland to be developed into residential lots. The character of this area changed rapidly between 1875 and 1900 as those made rich from industrialization began to build dozens of large-scale summer homes, many in eclectic, European-inspired revival styles, some with palatial airs, but all creating a fantasy backdrop against which their summer revels could be played out. This conspicuous consumption resulted in Newport's most publicly appealing architectural artifacts, the mansions of its second Gilded Age replete with tapestried ball rooms, gold plumbing fixtures, liveried coachmen and even entire interiors taken from great houses in Europe and shipped directly to Newport.

What with the weight of Newport's colonial past and its more recent quotations from European architectural history, the twentieth-century phenomenon of modernism never became a major factor in the city's architecture. The combined economic pinch caused by the 1929 stock market crash, the Depression, and the creation of income taxes served to suppress the elaborate Beaux-Arts architecture of the mansions. What was built in the years up to World War II does, however, form a remarkable group of largely civic and institutional structures, such as the Central Fire Station, The County Court House, The Main Post Office, the Seaman's Church Institute, the Nursing School and the Hotel Viking all done in a brick, Colonial Revival style. None of these designs use the materials or the vocabulary of progressive forms associated with modernism, but many of these were important to the business life of the town as it faced the social and economic challenges of those years.

This same weight of Newport's considerable architectural heritage channeled whatever architectural energy there was at mid-century into preservation. Early and important preservation institutions and grassroots efforts were initiated after World War II, including the Preservation Society of Newport County (1946), the publication of *The Architectural Heritage of Newport Rhode Island* by Antoinette

Downing and Vincent Scully (1952), historic district zoning (1964), Operation Clapboard (1964), and the Newport Restoration Foundation (1968). The city may not have embraced modern architecture but it did presage and parallel the timely historic preservation sensibility that led to important federal and statewide programs enacted in the 1960s to protect our architectural legacy.

With the construction of the Newport Bridge in 1969, the virtual departure of the U.S. Navy, and the advent of mass-tourism, the town's dependency on and attitude toward tourists underwent a sea change. Overcrowded neighborhoods, rowdy visitors, parking and traffic issues, noise pollution, and (sometimes) insensitive design and re-development have all served to create tensions in the historical and social fabric of Newport. While many of these issues are beyond architectural solutions, the particular challenges facing professionals today are the need to maintain the historical fabric of the town, to insure that development occurs as tastefully and thoughtfully as possible, to allow for water access, and achieve a balance between business interests and the quality-of-life concerns of the resident population. To that end, several agencies and activities—such as the Historic District Commission, special planning projects often supported by both public and private means, and most recently, the hiring of an historic preservation officer at City Hall, together with the many architects who live and work in the town—are working toward achieving this precarious balance of old and new that defines Newport's architectural milieu at the beginning of the twenty-first century.

In the pages that follow, the reader will find entries covering hundreds of individual buildings as well as mention of larger architectural examples, such as intact streetscapes and road patterns, urban redevelopment schemes, and the character of individual neighborhoods. While proper attention is paid to the famous structures from Newport's history—such as a seventeenth-century meeting house, an eighteenth-century library, or a nineteenth-century Gilded Age cottage—that are central to the town's character and reputation, I have also occasionally wandered far from those well-trod trails to consider other areas of the city that are seldom discussed: the spine of Broadway and its side streets, the large institutional, industrial, and commercial tracts in the West End wedge, and the modest buildings clustered between Spring and the harbor known as the Fifth Ward and Southern Thames. In addition, groups of buildings like the cluster of early twentiety-century civic structures done in a Colonial Revival style (mentioned above), as well as contemporary designs by living architects reflecting a new revival phase of breaking free from earlier traditions, are considered here for the first time. These are all key to understanding Newport as a small city that, world famous as it is for its cultural heritage, is affected by both typical urban issues of budgetary constraints, quality of public education, poverty rates, and housing costs, as well as by the more atypical opportunities of historic preservation and the challenges of seasonal tourism.

When Thorton Wilder wrote his novel *Theophilus North*, he found it useful to think of Newport as being nine different cities that were all present simultaneously. This multiple perspective may indeed be the best way to view a place as richly complex as Newport and it is in keeping with such a "layered" approach that I have highlighted different neighborhoods or districts that fan out from the original core of the early settlement now centered on Washington Square *(Tour 1)* and its immediate environs. Beginning to the northwest of the square, and proceeding around it clockwise, these are: Easton's Point *(Tour 2)* , The West End *(Tour 3)*, Broadway/North End *(Tour 4)*, Historic Hill & Harbor *(Tour 5)*, Kay-Catherine-Old Beach *(Tour 6)*, Bellevue Avenue & The Cliffs *(Tour 7)*, Ocean Avenue *(Tour 8)*, The Fifth Ward & Southern Thames *(Tour 9)*. Most of these would be familiar to local residents, but many are outside the bounds of the usual tourist or visitor. Nonetheless, each of these districts has its own character and most were developed during specific eras in Newport's history. Some preserve a strong sense of a coherent historic era (such as Easton's Point) while others (such as Washington Square) contain a variety of types and styles; still others (such as the West End) are the subject of more recent development and urban planning. This neighborhood-by-neighborhood approach points up the fact that the full range of architectural treasures that make up the true sense of Newport are not confined to the rare examples created by architects of national repute but can be found in the many buildings, sculptures, and sites created by thousands of individuals from varied backgrounds who, over generations, have lived and worked in Newport for over 350 years.

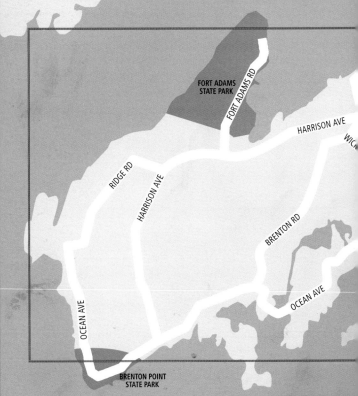
JAMESTOWN

FORT ADAMS
STATE PARK

FORT ADAMS RD

HARRISON AVE

WIC...

RIDGE RD

HARRISON AVE

BRENTON RD

OCEAN AVE

OCEAN AVE

OCEAN AVE

BRENTON POINT
STATE PARK

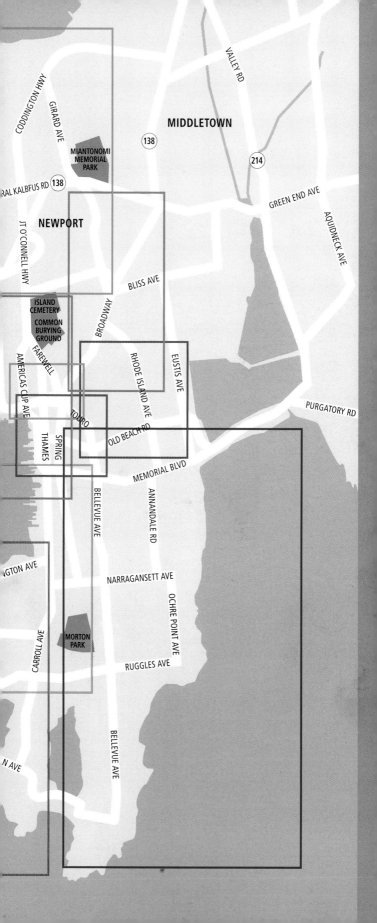

1. WASHINGTON SQUARE

Washington Square is a good starting point for getting a sense of Newport's history and architecture. A Square that is more trapezoidal than square, its present-day form was not achieved until the nineteenth century—with some of the major buildings dating from the early years of the twentieth century. Even so, this area has always been the geographical and historical heart of Newport. The first group of Anglo settlers—who included William Coddington, John Clarke, Henry Bull and others—each clustered their house lots of about 10 acres close to a fresh water spring and a short distance uphill from the shoreline. The spring itself still flows (though its course is now subterranean due to numerous grade changes) and is marked by a plaque adjacent to the gas station on Spring Street across from Barney Street. One of the original settlers' houses, that of Henry Bull, still existed on the corner of Spring and Stone Street up until 1912 when it was destroyed by a neighboring fire.

While most of the other architectural artifacts of the first settlement town are gone, what remains are a few street names (Coddington, Bull, Clarke) and the street layout. Vectors leading along the hill and harbor (Thames Street, Spring Street), up island (Broadway) and northwest, out of town, toward a burial ground established by the 1660s (Farewell Street), don't quite converge but instead enter at various points a street pattern that bordered a small open space flanked by residential and institutional buildings. By the nineteenth century, this spot came to be known as "The Parade." That this urban space continued to be thought of as Newport's civic center was made clear during the 1884 reunion of Newport residents when a monumental triumphal arch was erected near what is now the junction of Broadway and Meeting Street to welcome an entire generation of Newporters from near and far.

From Newport's earliest days other important civic structures also stood nearby—meeting houses, inns, a jail, churches and later banks, theaters, and stores. Anchoring this sense of civic identity, then as now, are two key eighteenth-century structures—the Colony House

continued on page 298

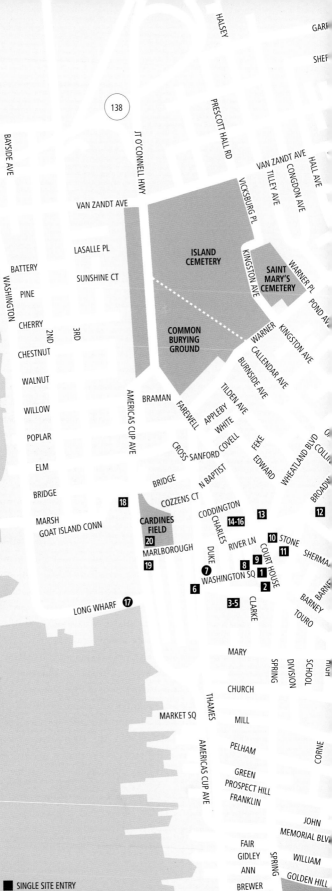

■ SINGLE SITE ENTRY

● MULTI-SITE ENTRY

1

COLONY HOUSE (1739) RICHARD MUNDAY

Washington Square

While more than a few towns on the east coast can boast of numerous colonial-era residences, Newport's most important structures from this period are not just private houses but also a unique collection of public buildings built prior to 1776. Two of these civic structures can be found at either end of Washington Square: the Colony House by architect-builder Richard Munday and the Brick Market by Peter Harrison. Although separated by smaller structures and streets when they were originally built (the Square had not yet arrived at its current configuration), today we can fortuitously compare them with a simple shift of our head. Each of them represents a different era of architectural knowledge and taste.

When Munday was commissioned to design the Colony House, his charge must have been not only to replace the modestly house-sized wooden structure that stood on the site, but to represent the stability and success of the colony—particularly since it coincided with the centennial of the town's founding. Munday (who had had an earlier role in the design of other Newport buildings including notably that of Trinity Church) here creates an idiosyncratic provincial masterpiece, concocting a medley of details that his overall composition never quite brings under control. Consider, for example, the wonderful array of geometric shapes he uses to outline his principal masses and openings. Circles and scrolls, octagons and rectangles are joined by truncated triangular gables, lunette dormers, and the diamond grid of the roof balustrade. Munday uses aspects of this array to focus attention on his entryway. The superimposed stone stairs and doorways reach a crescendo in the heavily carved pediment of the balcony doorframe. It was from this elevated balcony in 1776 that the Declaration of Independence was read to the crowd below, one of many such proclamations made from this rostrum. Much has been made of the wonderful broken pediment above the door

2   3

with its fancy carved-wood pineapple, a symbol of hospitality in the port city, but it was actually a later addition carved by Jim Moody in 1784.

As we might expect, however, from a talented "housewright" (one of the ways that Munday referred to himself), he relies heavily here on sources from earlier buildings and probably from printed material as well. While others such as Henry James have noted its "Dutch dignity," the closest and most obvious reference for Munday was probably the renowned John Hancock House completed just two years earlier in Boston (now destroyed). It seems likely that Munday made the trip north to see Hancock House first hand, as the composition of his main elevation as well the entrance carvings, quoining, and other façade details all echo the Boston model.

2 NEWPORT COUNTY COURT HOUSE (FLORENCE KERINS MURRAY JUDICIAL COMPLEX) (1925-1926) WILLIAM CORNELL APPLETON & FRANK A. STEARNS

Washington Square

Despite the common critique of this Court House that it demonstrates both an insensitive placement next to the venerable Colony House and a pale reflection of the latter's provincially bold design, it nonetheless instructively reveals the difference between early twentieth-century revival style and its colonial referents. Where the Colony House is sculptural and dynamic in its massing, composition, and shaped decoration, the Court House is more restrained, relying on a kind of modern planarity that confines its ornament to a shallow veneer. A decent representative of its revival era between the World Wars, it is more graphic than sculptural, and more intellectualized than the intuitive design of its eighteenth-century neighbor.

4

3 **JANE PICKENS THEATER (ZION EPISCOPAL CHURCH)** (1835) RUSSELL WARREN, ALTERED (1976) **& OPERA HOUSE** (c. 1864), FAÇADE RESTORATION (2003) NEWPORT COLLABORATIVE ARCHITECTS

49 Touro Street & 21 Touro Street

Although it would be hard to tell now, this revival house movie theater was once a temple-fronted church by the idiosyncratic Bristol-based architect Russell Warren. Today, all that is left of his original elevation are a few Ionic capitals embedded over the interior proscenium arch framing the screen. Down the block, the Opera House Theater, c. 1864, had for much of the late twentieth century a false front of random stone work and painted out details but now shows a recently restored façade of rhythmically arranged arched windows. Perhaps just as important as their architectural history is that these buildings help maintain a sense of Washington Square as the quintessential public space of the real (i.e., non-tourist) Newport — replete with banks, courthouses, public sculpture, a fountain, and marqueed movie theaters.

4 **ST JOSEPH'S RECTORY (INN AT WASHINGTON SQUARE)** (c. 1893) J.D. JOHNSTON

39 Touro Street

A peculiar late-nineteenth-century addition to the Square whose architect designed and built this frame structure with roof line, window trim, and trefoil screen to compliment a brick and masonry Gothic-styled school building that once stood behind this property on what is now the site of the municipal parking lot. It currently houses an inn.

5

5   **BULIOD-PERRY HOUSE** (c. 1755), **JOSEPH ROGERS HOUSE** (c. 1798), **WILBOUR-ELLERY HOUSE** (c. 1801), **& OLIVER HAZARD PERRY MONUMENT** (1884) WILLIAM TURNER, SCULPTOR

29 Touro Street, 33 Touro Street, & 51 Touro Street

Originally a residence, this handsome block became a bank, as its impressive rusticated wooden front might suggest, before being purchased by Oliver Hazard Perry in 1818. Now referred to as the Buliod-Perry House in honor of that famous local son, it clearly shows the influence of Peter Harrison's sensibility, translating the classical grandeur of masonry forms into indigenous materials. The Harrison idiom stands out particularly in the context of two other houses on the south side of Washington Square: the Joseph Rogers House, c. 1798, and the Wilbour-Ellery House, c. 1801, both rather predictable clapboarded Federal town houses, although the latter has a wonderfully framed entryway taken from another house in the 1970s.

Today, the Perry connection is reinforced by the nearby dramatic sculpture of the youthful commander (by Newport sculptor William Turner, 1884) as he heroically exhorts his crew to fly his battle flag and consequently engage the British just prior to his remarkable victory on Lake Erie.

6   **BRICK MARKET** (1772) PETER HARRISON, ALTERED (1842) RESTORED (1928-30) NORMAN ISHAM, RENOVATED (1993) IRVING B. HAYNES AND ASSOCIATES

127 Thames Street

Where Munday's earlier Colony House is intuitive and colloquial, Harrison's Brick Market is intentional and sophisticated—both buildings reflecting the spirit of their respective designers and eras. No hodgepodge of quirky shapes and details here; instead there is balance and sophistication in the way Harrison works his patternbook knowledge into a coherent hipped-roofed, rectangular

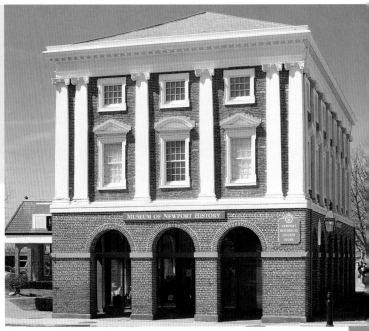

6

block. This simple mass is divided by the regular placement of monumental engaged Ionic pilasters (in wood) superimposed on a basement course of arches. In this arrangement we can see what Harrison took from seventeenth-century echoes of Inigo Jones Banqueting House at Whitehall and even from sixteenth-century precedents like Michelangelo's Palazzo del Senatore in Rome, all of which he filtered through such printed sources as Colen Campbell's *Vitruvius Britannicus* of 1716.

Built to serve as a town marketplace and granary, the storage spaces on the upper stories were perched atop an open arcade—a configuration that succeeded both functionally (a kind of sheltered market open on all sides to pedestrian traffic) and aesthetically (a reduction of fussy detail). Subsequent alterations filled in several arches and changed surface finishes, notably covering the bricks with several layers of paint. But in 1928 Isham began restoring the arcade, revealing the brick surface once again but also adding revival details that were not original. Happily, some sense of what Harrison intended is apparent now that Isham's Colonial Revival windows have been removed from the front bays on the ground floor. The building has seen diverse uses as a market, printing office, theater, and city hall, and now as the home of The Museum of Newport History that serves as an excellent introduction to the 350-plus years of Newport and its cultural heritage.

7

7   JOHN RATHBURN-GEORGE GARDNER-ABRAHAM RODRIQUES HOUSE (CITIZENS BANK) (c. 1722), ALTERED (c. 1740, 1950) & BANKNEWPORT (1929-30) THOMAS & JAMES

8 Washington Square & 10 Washington Square

The eye-catching ornamentality of what currently houses Bank Newport, replete with a monumental Corinthian colonnade, cast bronze doors, and carved marble moldings was surprisingly called "purely colonial" by a local newspaper at the time of its dedication. Given its date, many of these carefully included details are industrially mass produced rather than individually crafted but they still show a remarkable sense of the little things that, when combined, make for a visually pleasing whole. The scale of these elements is another matter—a somewhat retardataire ambition (for the early modern period) to evoke status and stability using a monumental classical idiom. The interior is worth a visit, as a virtually intact, double-storied banking room with mahogany fixtures, plaster reliefs, and massive vault doors behind the grilled tellers counter.

When built, the then named Savings Bank of Newport replaced a modest wood-frame grocery store and must have stood out, particularly in contrast to the smaller, gambrel-roofed structure across Duke Street, originally the John Rathburn-George Gardner-Abraham Rodriques House, c. 1722, but subsequently altered (the wonderful pedimented dormers seem mid-eighteenth century) and since 1804 used as a bank. It was restored (re-colonialized) in 1950. Whatever their function, colonial frame buildings were often all but indistinguishable from private residences until form started to follow function in the nineteenth century.

Today, the date of the Bank Newport's 1929 building may seem a bit strange, coinciding as it does with the onset of the Depression, but the colonnaded building is one of over a dozen civic masonry structures employing a revival idiom and constructed in Newport between 1916 and 1940. Such a concentration suggests how

8   9

important "brick and mortar" projects were to Newport's economic survival during those lean years.

8 MERCHANTS EXCHANGE BUILDING
(c. 1865), REBUILT (1936), RENOVATED (2005)
NEWPORT COLLABORATIVE ARCHITECTS

38 Washington Square

The 1936 Colonial Revival skin of its main block belies earlier origins as a wood-frame, mansard-roofed building with numerous arched windows dating from the third quarter of the nineteenth century. All of its inhabitants, from an 1890s bank (whose vault façade still exists within) to a social club for businessmen chartered in 1905 (and replete with second-story Colonial Revival club rooms), have been engaged with the economic vitality of Newport. The same holds true today as an architectural firm, the Newport Collaborative, is the current civic-minded occupant, having inventively reconfigured its interior spaces with a blend of industrial and high-tech stairwells, free-standing glass walls, and other new elements that are a surprisingly effective complement to the multipaned windows and moldings of an earlier era.

9 ARMY & NAVY YMCA (1911) LOUIS E. JALLADE,
REMODELED (1988-89) NEWPORT COLLABORATIVE ARCHITECTS

50 Washington Square

This large Renaissance Revival block seems to misunderstand the nature of Newport's urban core. Its four-story size, irregular plan, and polychrome glazed details, while consistent with function and its revival idiom, are flamboyantly out of place in close proximity to the wood and brick of its predominantly colonial Newport neighbors and may be just a case of an off-island architect rarely making a site visit. Despite its insensitivity to context, this was also one of the first cast concrete structures in Newport, an innovative method of construction that was much remarked upon as "strange" by dubious "sidewalk superintendents." Although no

10

longer affiliated with the armed services, it continues to serve an important urban function as it was reconfigured in the 1980s to accommodate social agencies and low-cost housing by J. Michael Abbott of NCA.

10 BROADWAY BLOCK

Between Farewell & Marlborough Streets (north side)

At first glance, there may not be much that leaps to the eye here architecturally, except for the urban vitality of different store fronts, but what you see in Newport is not always what you get. A closer look at the upper stories reveals that several of the structures (numbers 2-6, 14, 22, 26-30) along this hodge-podge street, date back to late seventeenth-, early eighteenth- and nineteenth-century Newport. While the gambrel or monitor roof-lines and window placements give us some clue as to dates, it is primarily through an archaeology of their interior framing that the antiquity of these much changed buildings can be confirmed. Regardless of date, these compact forms, butted up against each other, still suggest a kind of dense seventeenth-century streetscape of the kind found most often in older European cities.

11 WANTON-LYMAN-HAZARD-HOUSE (STEPHEN MUMFORD HOUSE) (BEFORE 1700), ALTERED (c. 1765), RESTORED (1927) NORMAN ISHAM

17 Broadway

The Wanton-Lyman-Hazard House, although known more for its succession of later owners, was built by Stephen Mumford, a missionary to Newport in the 1670s. As one of the earliest professionally restored houses in Newport, Mumford's house combines an early house form with evidence of later enlargements, alterations, and restorations. As it appears today, it does not look representative of late seventeenth-century forms, nor does it appear typical of a Georgian dwelling of the eighteenth century, although it carried aspects of both eras. Widely studied by such

11

preservation luminaries as Norman Isham and Antoinette Downing, it has, since the early twentieth century, been considered one of Newport's significant historical houses; although its dating has been debated, most scholars now agree that it was built by the mid-1690s. Its steeply pitched roof, massive, pilastered chimney and exposed, chamfered beams and braces (both hand-hewn and mill-sawn), all suggest its late medieval English sources when first built.

Rarer features, its impressive plastered cove under the front eave as well as the front pedimented door, might have been added slightly later by Mumford or his son, updating the more traditional Jacobean forms of his "goodley" house with a newer London-derived classicism (à la Sir Christopher Wren). The interior layout reveals two main rooms on each floor, with ells and additions added throughout the eighteenth century; another attached shed and a large rear structure had become like the rest of the house—ramshackle—and were removed by Isham in the 1927 restoration. One other marvelous artifact on the interior is the broad brick arch in the basement supporting the chimney stack above. There is much we don't know about the house's architectural history—for example, its original window pattern, the dating of interior finishes, and when the "kickout" changing the slope of the roofline to meet the new cornice was created. More recently archaeological field work outside the house, led by James C. Garman, has uncovered many features and much artifactual evidence for building and lot changes or uses in and around the property.

*City Hall anchored the
identity of modern Newport
at its historic core.*

Few historic houses remain intact from the period of their construction. While Mumford's house has several wonderfully preserved features ranging from its tall, quirky roofline to the decorative detail of lambs tongue stops on its chamfered beams, its importance today is as an on-going study site of architectural history. Like so many of Newport's earliest buildings, it has been much changed by the utilitarian needs of its owners and the decisions of its preservationists. As interpreted today by its current owners, the Newport Historical Society, it retains a strong sense of its past and is a wonderful, well-documented example of how preserved buildings evolve into their current forms.

12 NEWPORT CITY HALL (1898-1900) J.D. JOHNSTON, INTERIOR & TOP FLOORS DESTROYED BY FIRE, REBUILT (1925-27) W. CORNELL APPLETON

43 Broadway

Built at the end of the nineteenth century and sited at the edge of the civic district defined by Washington Square, the combined public use and elaborate image of this building served to anchor the identity of the modern city of Newport at its historic core. It seems telling that City Hall was built at a time when almost two centuries of governmental activity in the elaborate Colony House was being replaced by the new State House in Providence. Here, in a commission that capped his career, local architect J. D. Johnston created another visually memorable, monumentally decorative masonry edifice. Replete with mansarded tower surmounting a second-floor porch, the roof punctured by too-elaborate dormers and topped by a filigreed-iron grill work, it was both conservative and decorative at the same time, as much influenced by recent Second Empire design as by its immediate historic surroundings (the original design can still be seen in a watercolor hanging in the first floor hall). In 1925 a disastrous fire destroyed much of the interior and upper stories and caused the first recorded death of a Newport fireman in the line of duty. W.C. Appleton, a Boston architect who was working at the same

12

time on the new County Court House at the top end of Washington Square, emphasized in his post-fire renovations the centrality of the cupola and the classicizing trim of windows and moldings. This results in a building that reflects a loosely based Colonial Revival vocabulary tinged with both conservative and progressive elements. On the exterior, Appleton's efforts are clearly demarcated in the modern planarity of a flush block wall atop Johnston's rusticated surfaces, as well as in the new revival detailing of central tower and the arched windows on the corner pavilions. Where Johnston's design was retardataire and quirky, Appleton's renovation projects a strictly business-like demeanor.

City Hall is still the center of nearly all civic activity in Newport and is the meeting site of numerous commissions and departments, including the Zoning Board and the Historic District

13

Commission, so important for the survival of Newport's architectural heritage.

13 FRIENDS MEETING HOUSE (1699), ADDITIONS (1705, 1729, 1807), ALTERED (1858 ,1867,1922), RESTORED (1967) ORIN BULLOCK, JR.

Corner of Marlborough & Farewell Streets

The barn-like bulk of this building is one of the earliest surviving religious structures in New England. How it looked originally is the subject of much conjecture, as what we see today is the result of many additions and deletions that have occurred during its more than 300-year history. The Quakers, who had flourished in the religious toleration of Newport since their arrival in 1657, constructed the original section (centered on the large double doors) in 1699, later flanking it by additions to the north (1729) and south (1807) as their need for yearly meeting space grew. Some important features of that earliest meeting house in its late-medieval form still remain, at least in part: the great field stones used as a foundation (to the left of the central entrance); the rare, diamond-paned, leaded windows (on the second-story rear elevation); and a few archaeological traces of accordion lath, interior surfaces, and fragments of its timber-framing system.

Through the early eighteenth century, amidst mostly one- and two-story residences, the vertical rise of the meeting house (with an ornate cupola topping its hipped roof) would have been the most prominent building in town. Even today the interior of the main chamber, spanned by a massive grid of structural hewn timbers, remains visually impressive, although its sadly truncated below a newer gabled roof. The nearly Gothic verticality of the

interior space was lost in nineteenth-century alterations, so that the exposed structural elements of the medieval-scaled beams and braces now read as being more haphazard than systematic, more jury-rigged than rational.

As the attendance of the yearly meeting waned, the meeting house — along with its land — passed through a succession of owners, both public and private. Ringed by smaller buildings from its earliest years, these were razed or moved in the twentieth century to give a false impression of an open, park-like lot. In the late 1960s one of the most prominent mid-twentieth-century restoration architects, Orin Bullock, was brought in (from his home base in Maryland) to stabilize and restore the venerable structure. During the restoration, a tentative plan to return the buildings to their original core was abandoned. This was largely due to the discovery of a unique system of moveable walls or shuts that made the interior space expandable for the mass attendance at yearly meetings. Replete with its ancient pulley mechanism, this wall system, created sometime after the eighteenth-century additions, is another aspect of the building's pragmatic rationality and was considered too unique a feature to be lost if the demolition of the southern addition were allowed to proceed. Any notion to restore the building's original plan was put off indefinitely. During these same years, the meeting house was given to the Newport Historical Society, which today presents it as an important site and also uses it for special events and conferences.

Although it is now a structural pastiche and abbreviated by its numerous alterations, the central sanctuary still hints at what must have been the greatest of early Newport's religious spaces. It remains a testament to the special status achieved by the Society of Friends in colonial Newport.

14   15

14 WHITEHORSE TAVERN (BEFORE 1673), EXTENSIVELY ALTERED & GAMBREL ROOF (1780), RENOVATED (AFTER 1952)

26 Marlborough Street

A building as remarkable for its numerous owners and uses as for its architecture, this is one of the few seventeenth-century buildings (along with the Friends Meeting House across the street and the Wanton-Lyman Hazard House nearby) whose interior is accessible to the public. William Mayes, the earliest owner, acquired the lot from that of one of the first settlers, William Coddington, and we know a tavern was operated here as early as the 1680s. On the interior you can still see the spaces of the original house — a two-room structure with a central pilastered chimney, framed by bulky timbers.

Owned by the prominent Nichols family in the eighteenth century (one Jonathan Nichols II was a successful merchant and lieu-tenant governor of the Colony), the building was employed as tavern, meeting hall for the town council, and a residence for, among others, a silversmith and a pirate. After the Revolution, it was updated by a later Nichols family member to reflect more contemporary tastes in keeping with such grand mid-eighteenth-century houses as the Nichols House on Washington Street built by the same family. For us today, the result is similar to that of many of Newport's earliest buildings: rudimentary seventeenth-century lines are all but obscured by the more refined Georgian-Federal sensibility of pedimented doorways, classical moldings, and sash windows. Despite these alterations, with its low ceilings, dim lighting, and fireplaces ablaze, it is still one of the best places in Newport to experience some of what an early domestic space would have been like.

16

15 ST PAUL'S METHODIST CHURCH (1806), ALTERED (1842,1881,1930, C. 1960)

18 Marlborough Street

To a new congregation in 1806, this church must have seemed like an impressive achievement with its geometric forms rising from street to bell-capped tower, evoking the then-current style popularized by Charles Bulfinch and Asher Benjamin. Later in the century, extensive alterations raised up the building to allow for a basement. This inadvertently changed the proportions of the building and necessitated a reconfigured entryway. The light, crisp classical and Palladian details of its upper stories are compromised at street level by the subsequent opacity of the entryway, giving it a closed, boxy appearance.

16 THE NEWPORT JAIL (JAIL HOUSE INN) (c. 1772), ENLARGED (c. 1800), ALTERED (1965) & STEPHEN DECATUR HOUSE (c. 1725)

13 Marlborough Street & 19 Charles Street

A jailhouse has stood on this site since 1680 (an earlier wooden structure was moved and demolished when this more substantial brick building was erected, under the construction supervision of George Lawton and Oliver Ring Warner, just prior to the Revolutionary War). On the outside, it evokes genteel "house" as much as impenetrable "jail," since it intentionally retains the rooflines, detailing, and some sense of the scale of nearby domestic colonial architecture (until much of that was cleared in the later twentieth century for use as parking lots). During the decades of housing prisoners and not tourists, it served as both a local detention center and as one of the five county seat jails in the statewide system, a configuration that was eventually supplanted by the construction of a State Prison in mid-nineteenth-century Providence. Although never compared to it, the jail is essentially a smaller version of another Newport building constructed around the same time, the Alms House on Coaster's Harbor

17

Island (now Founders Hall, Naval War College). Both masonry structures have the same central cross gable, fanlighted pediment, broad front porch, and long extended wings whose regular window patterns reveal their common function: to house large numbers of unrelated residents.

Just behind the jail, across tiny River Lane, is the small gambrel-roofed wood-frame house at 19 Charles Street, which was probably built in the first quarter of the eighteenth century. Commonly referred to as a "half house" form because of its size, off-center entry, and room plan, this is one of the earliest survivors from this period in the Washington Square neighborhood. Its history gives clear evidence of the local penchant for moving houses around, having been dragged from its original site next to the Colony House in 1833 to make way for the Levi Gale House (which was itself moved up the hill when the County Court House was built in the early twentieth century). On its original site, it was once the home of French Naval Lieutenant Etienne Decatur, grandfather of Stephen Decatur, a hero (along with another Newporter, Oliver Hazard Perry) of the War of 1812.

17 LONG WHARF (c. 1680), REDEVELOPED (1967), NEWPORT MARRIOTT HOTEL (1988) DONHAM AND SWEENEY, FAIRFIELD RESORTS (1995) NEWPORT COLLABORATIVE ARCHITECTS, & THE INN ON LONG WHARF (1982) DAUGHN SALISBURY ARCHITECTS

25 America's Cup Avenue, 5 Washington Street, & 142 Long Wharf

Stretching behind Harrison's Brick Market, and essentially continuing the path of Broadway some 2,000 feet toward a deep water harborage, is Long Wharf. Capitalizing on the smaller wharves that had been built from the first year of settlement, this was one of the first "public works" improvements in the seventeenth-century settlement and is characterized by the mercantile ambitions that defined colonial Newport. Hardly recognizable today

for the active commercial wharf it was for 300 years, it underwent urban redevelopment in 1967—which shifted its focus from marine and industrial concerns to the retail and tourist trade (hence the change of name from Long Wharf to Long Wharf Mall on its inland block). The low, shed-like buildings that flank the one-block shopping mall that stretches from Thames to America's Cup Avenue might represent an attempt to echo the mostly wooden utilitarian buildings that once defined the harbor side. But this reference is obscured by the buildings' incongruous mansarded-roof lines and the banal homogeneity of their design, which ultimately surrenders itself to the retail mania for large glass windows.

The westernmost section of Long Wharf, which borders the inner harbor, was developed a bit later but has fared little better. The 1987/88 design of the Marriott Hotel, with its front entrance facing the city along America's Cup Avenue, manages to reach onto Long Wharf with a streetscape of smaller gabled pavilions. Unfortunately, the lower streetscape, backed by an out-of-scale main block, makes an ill-advised attempt to mime the architectural texture and variety of the old chandleries and shops that were razed to make way for its construction. More visually appealing are the plan and detailing of Fairfield Resorts. Inspired by Newport's love of the late nineteenth-century Shingle Style, and demurely screened back from the corner of Long Wharf and Washington Streets to create its own Casino-like inner space. Even this seems a bit out of place as refined and residential, more "uptown" than the still-workaday character of the surrounding wharf area with its nearby pumping station, boatyard, and state fishing pier. Worst of all, at the Bay end of the wharf, the banal monolith of the Inn on Long Wharf is a big, opaque wall perched atop stilts, overshadowing boats and buildings alike and selfishly obstructing any visual connection Long Wharf once had to the outer harbor, Goat Island, and the Bay beyond.

18

18 HUMPHREY "HARP" DONNELLY III NEWPORT GATEWAY VISITOR & TRANSPORTATION CENTER (1988) PHILEMON STURGES

23 America's Cup Avenue

An earlier scheme for this tourist center, by a rival architectural firm, envisioned a twelve-story tower at the corner of Washington Street and Long Wharf. What was eventually built is happily more modest in size but still stands apart from the abutting streets of the Point Section. Together with the newer hotel and parking structures clustered around Long Wharf, the brick-and-glazed block trim of the Gateway Center creates, without transition, a visually impenetrable wall of buildings between the older residential neighborhood and the harbor front to the south. The all-but-blank face of its three-story brick tower, whose shape may allude to the kinds of industrial structures that once inhabited this former rail yard site, is jarringly contrasted with the rows of white fabric canopies extending along America's Cup Avenue and toward the parking garage that act as an ineffectual covered walkway. This streetscape could have given a dignified sense of arrival to visiting tourists (much as a train station platform performs this function, for example), but what we have instead is overwhelmed by the bright material and peaked forms. Intended to read like ocean waves, it instead sadly suggests to many a somewhat comical rendition of undergarments strung together and blown up to the scale of circus tents.

19 CENTRAL FIRE STATION (1931) TRAFICANTE & NIEBUHR

21 West Marlborough Street

Another of Newport's Georgian Revival buildings from the era between the World Wars, this replaced an earlier, all-brick station nearby. The main block has a gabled roof running along the street axis and four main vehicle doors forming an arcade across the first story of this primary elevation. Carved limestone trim is used

19

≥ 20

to frame these doors against the brick-wall surface. This, along with the bold quoining, doubled end chimneys, and other classic details, derives from and is more reflective of Newport's grand eighteenth-century past than its twentieth-century modernity.

20 BERNARDO CARDINES FIELD (1937)

Corner of West Marlborough Street & America's Cup Avenue

Though the wooden bleachers and stone field house were constructed in part under the auspices of the federal Depression-era agency, the Works Progress Administration in 1937, this ball park is by some accounts one of the oldest such inner-city fields in the country. The land on which it was built, filling in the old Cove, had been earlier developed with small industrial buildings and a railroad yard (the terminus of a line that ran down the western side of Aquidneck to Long Wharf from Fall River, Massachusetts via a connection across the Sakonnet River in Portsmouth). Ball games might have been played on the site even before the land was purchased by the city from the railroad in the mid-1930s.

The exterior of rough masonry and thin-wood sheathing are contrasted with one of Newport's most inviting civic spaces — a park-like greensward whose outfield fences barely define the baseball diamond from surrounding small-frame houses. Despite late twentieth-century pressures to develop this civic open space, today the human scale of the park is a visual relief and a kind of throwback to an earlier era, particularly when seen against the oversized buildings that were put up nearby during the late twentieth century. There is an almost nostalgic, nineteenth-century air about the place, with its single ticket-taker, its seats close to the field, and the sounds of downtown traffic still happily mingling with the sweet crack of a bat during the baseball season when the semi-pro team that plays here is at home.

2. EASTON'S POINT

Referred to by locals as just "the Point," its more formal name alluded to one of the town's founders, Nicholas Easton, who established a farm here in the seventeenth century when its original shoreline more closely resembled a projecting "point" of land (centuries of erosion and landfill have softened its shape). Passed on to Quaker proprietors after Easton's death, it was by 1725 subdivided into house and garden lots with the streets named, per the Quaker fashion, either numerically (America's Cup Avenue was originally called Fourth Street) or in reference to nature (Water Street was Washington Street's original name). By the eighteenth century this was a Friends-populated neighborhood, set between an active harbor and the great Friends meeting house a few blocks away. On its streets lived wealthy merchants and numerous craftsmen, among them the famous Townsend and Goddard family of furniture makers. It was also a relatively tolerant culture, symbolized by free blacks such as the stone cutter and mason Zingo Stevens who lived here with his family. Merchants' mansions stood close to their owners' counting houses, artisans lived close to their workshops, the workshops surrounded warehouses or yards for materials and kitchen gardens for food, and all were in the proximity of the docks so that the local products could be shipped near and far. Even one's final resting place lay close at hand, for when Point residents died, Newport's municipal graveyard, the Common Burying Ground, was only a few blocks away.

Quite a few remnants of this world are still around today. If many dependencies and sheds are now gone, the eighteenth-century streetscapes are mostly preserved, with few additions after the nineteenth century. This was a compact community, close to the old town center and within walking distance of daily needs. Even today the Point is less affected than other sections of town by the crowds, traffic, noise, and clutter of tourism, and its relatively quiet grid of streets lined with historical buildings makes it one of Newport's most desirable residential neighborhoods.

◀ WILLIAM HUNTER HOUSE

138

ROSE
ISLAND
18

NARRAGANSETT BAY

CAPELLA S

GOAT
ISLAND
18

DEFENDERS ROW

AMERICA

■ SINGLE SITE ENTRY
● MULTI-SITE ENTRY

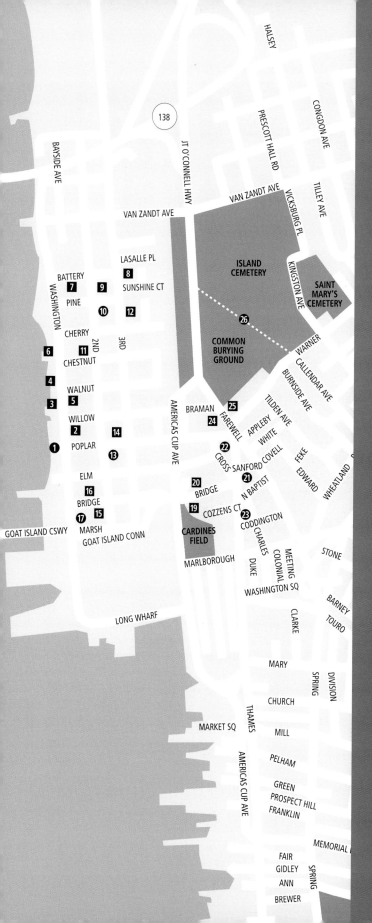

1   **WILLIAM HUNTER HOUSE (JONATHAN NICHOLS-COLONEL JOSEPH WANTON HOUSE)** (c. 1720), ALTERED & ENLARGED (BETWEEN 1748 & 1758), RESTORED (1952-53)

54 Washington Street

CAPTAIN JOHN WARREN HOUSE (HENRY COLLINS HOUSE) (BETWEEN 1736 & 1758), ENLARGED TOWARD THE GARDEN (BEFORE 1775), DOOR & PROBABLY DORMERS (c. 1795-1800)

62 Washington Street

THOMAS ROBINSON HOUSE (c. 1725), ENLARGED & REMODELED (c. 1760), OLD KITCHEN REMODELED AS REAR SITTING ROOM (1872) CHARLES FOLLEN McKIM, GARDEN PORCH & PART OF NORTH ELEVATION (LATER)

64 Washington Street

Of all the many historical streetscapes in Newport, Washington Street best reflects the most distinguished architecture of the pre-Revolutionary era of large eighteenth-century mansions. These impressive homes echoed the wealth and status that developed here in Newport's first golden era thanks to artisanal production, maritime industries, and commercial trade. Three of these grand houses on the water side of Washington Street—the William Hunter House, the Captain John Warren House, and the Thomas Robinson House—reflect these fortunes in their size and refined ornament.

The Hunter House, now owned by the Preservation Society of Newport County and open to the public, is the southernmost of these three, which all essentially employ variations of the same template: a five-bay, central entry-design with gambrel roofs. All started as smaller buildings in the 1720s and '30s with a central chimney and a small entry hall. Within a generation, the wealth of their owners was such that enlargements were made to expand the plan into four rooms (on each floor), flanking a central hall or passageway. All three also had a commercial dock (one was over

400 feet in length!) jutting into the Bay, so that each house wore, in essence, two "front" elevations (connected by that hall extending through the house) — with one entry facing the town and the other for approach by water, a scheme that was at once both practical and ostentatious.

One of the most ornate aspects of the exterior is the wonderful cornucopic carving of pineapple, sunflower, pomegranate, and foliage that is framed by the broken scroll pediment. Some take such imagery to symbolize the exotic produce made available by Newport's international trade back in its maritime heyday. Whatever its meaning, it was probably carved by Newport craftsman Jim Moody (but has not always been over the Washington Street entrance). Taken from the waterside entry in the nineteenth century, when the mansion had become a rooming house, it was installed on two different entrances at the Dennis House across the street. When the Hunter House was restored by its present owner, the Preservation Society of Newport County, the original carving was returned to the Washington Street entry of the Hunter site and the Dennis House got a carefully crafted replica.

The Hunter, Warren, and Robinson Houses vary in composition and detail, such as the particular combinations of decorative details on doorway surrounds. More subtle distinguishing features are in the composition of the entry elevations. Where the Hunter House, in its enlarged state, has windows clearly paired on either side of the central door, the Warren House windows are more casually arranged, with varied spacing, and the Robinson House stretches the spaces between each window to accommodate its wider street front and also doubles the second-story fenestration above the entry. What might at first seem like a very limited vocabulary is here given visual richness by the craftsmen who created these handsome houses over a number of years.

The interiors of these houses are justly famous and in the Robinson House an early experiment in Colonial Revival design can still be found. Charles Follen McKim, who had strong personal ties to the

Point neighborhood, remodeled a room in 1872 using details derived as much from furniture as architecture. His local ties, Quaker background, and interest in colonial architecture probably prompted Benjamin R. Smith, a descendant of Quaker Tom Robinson, to hire him for the remodeling of the old kitchen on the water side. An early photograph of this hearth commissioned by McKim around 1874 still exists and was intended for publication in a collection of photographs documenting the colonial style in Newport for other architects. This project must have gotten the young architect another commission, the Dennis House across the street, for a short time later McKim added what he called a living hall to the rear of the Dennis House. Today McKim's hearth for the Robinson House, framed by spindled turnings, seems too attenuated and cluttered to be colonial but these early efforts would eventually mature into the Colonial Revival style for which his later firm of McKim, Mead & White would become famous.

2   ST JOHN THE EVANGELIST EPISCOPAL CHURCH (1894) F.C. WITHERS

Washington at Willow Streets

This is clearly meant to evoke an English parish church, informally composed with entry porch at one corner and bell tower on the other. The rough-faced granite, trimmed with darker sandstone makes the church seem more massive than its actual size, as does the siting of the tall tower so close to the side street. The interior is also worth a visit with wonderfully crafted woodwork throughout.

3   M.H. SANFORD HOUSE (EDNA VILLA) (1869-70) WILLIAM RALPH EMERSON AND CARL FEHMER

72 Washington Street

We might initially be attracted to the water views from the simple stick porches wrapping around this summer house built for a business partner of Commodore Vanderbilt. What looks like a fairly typical mid-century mansarded summer cottage, however,

4

holds a delightful surprise inside. A spectacular array of Victorian decorative finishes in wood and stenciled plaster awaits the visitor who enters this unique environment. Elements and patterns from a panoply of exotic sources are employed here (often described as "Pompeian" at the time). No single stylistic term can hope to adequately convey the scheme but Margery Deane, a nineteenth-century Newport journalist, enumerated for the *Boston Journal* some of the elaborately crafted woodwork just after the building's completion: "*...floors from top to bottom are laid in hard wood, in fancy patterns, no two rooms alike...oak, ash, cherry, hard pine, maple and black walnut.... The woodwork of the parlors is butternut, with ebony trimming and panels of mottled wood. The dining room is...the only room in the house papered...(in) green and gold, in the imitation of leather.*"

The elaborate entry hall rises more than three stories, its grand staircase incorporating different inlaid wood patterns on each landing. Projecting balconies, stained glass, and bronze gas-light fixtures add to the sumptuous quality of this space, which ascends to a special aerie at the top used by Kate Field, a writer and the niece of Sanford. Here, from the rich, dark interior of bamboo furniture and oriental rugs, she could enjoy the unimpeded views of harbor, bay, and beyond as she gazed out the window or at reflections in mirrors carefully positioned so the panoramic view was still visible even if reclining on a couch.

4 CAPT WILLIAM FINCH HOUSE (c. 1770)

78 Washington Street

This large gambrel was built just before prevailing styles changed toward more federal lines. Little-altered since its construction, it sits end to street but still hints at the influence of Peter Harrison's classicism with a pilastered and pedimented entry door and heavy lintels over the front windows. Maritime and craft interests are mingled here once again (the owner was the commander of a privateer in the Revolutionary War who made his living as a house joiner).

5   6   7

5 PITTS-SOUTHWICK HOUSE (c. 1757), REMODELED (LATE NINETEENTH-CENTURY)

71 Washington Street

Another case, among many on the Point, where a late-nineteenth-century version of the colonial is layered over an authentic mid-eighteenth-century structure. The form of the porch, shaped windows, and too-ornate moldings give the later facelift away.

6 JOHN TRIPP HOUSE (c. 1725)

88 Washington Street

This rare, small stone ender is also unusual because of its cobbled oven projecting from the exposed masonry wall. But this is not, strictly speaking, a Newport house (it was moved from an original site and reconstructed on this bayside lot). There is a thrifty Yankee tradition, still occasionally seen today, of houses being raised and carted around town — this one, however, was unusual in being barged all the way down Narragansett Bay from Providence.

7 16 BATTERY STREET (c. 1932) ALBERT GARDNER GROFF

This is a modest house by a lesser-known Newport architect whose massing and pergola porches gently echo earlier idioms — a midwestern Prairie style wrapped in East Coast shingle work. Groff, who was born on the Point and lived at 76 Third Street (and thus known in local parlance as a "Point Hummer"), was trained in the 1920s at the Pratt School in New York. In the 1940s he started a long architectural career at the federal agency that later became the National Aeronautic and Space Administration better known as NASA.

8   9

8   SOLOMON SOUTHWICK HOUSE
(MID-EIGHTEENTH CENTURY)

77 Third Street

Although grandly sited at the head of Battery Street, this large, handsomely proportioned house with gambrel running along the street was probably moved from the inland side of Washington Street sometime in the nineteenth century. It was privately restored in the early 1950s when the Point was still considered a rough-and-tumble neighborhood close by the Navy Base. The same post-World-War-II wave of preservation also saw the establishment of the Preservation Society of Newport County, which now maintains Hunter House and a number of nineteenth-century mansions.

9   JOHN & THOMAS GODDARD HOUSE (1741)

81 Second Street

Typical in form and composition (four bay, two and a half stories) for a house owned by successful artisans in the eighteenth century, its reticent modesty is even more striking when compared to the elaborate scale of the wealthy merchants' houses on Washington Street (where this house once stood with its now demolished shop attached as a large rear ell). On the interior, there is an unusually elegant curved stair within; but little on the outside suggests the level of craft we might expect from a house belonging to such famous cabinet makers.

10

10 JOHN ALLAN HOUSE (1859) & 41 SECOND STREET (c. 1833)

67 Second Street & 41 Second Street

Since the Point section was so heavily built out in the eighteenth century, there are comparatively fewer mid-nineteenth-century houses here than in other sections of Newport. The formulaic Greek Revival conventions of the period used on the Allan House stand out more than they might elsewhere. A slightly earlier example of the style is 41 Second Street, with its "paneled" pilasters and triangular pediment window. Although this panel treatment is rare for Newport, it is found in other nearby seaports (Nantucket and Martha's Vineyard, for example). Could the owner have been influenced by visits to other ports of call?

THIRD AND WALNUT STREET MARKET, c. 1920.
SOURCE: *Collection of the Newport Historical Society*

11

12

11 WM S. CHILD SCHOOLHOUSE (1875)
CHARLES FOLLEN McKIM

11 Chestnut Street

A little-known early work by the architect Charles Follen McKim, now converted into a residence. In the mid-1870s, before his famous partnership with William Rutherford Mead and Stanford White, McKim was very familiar with the Point section of Newport because of his courtship of Anne Bigelow, whose family lived there. He completed several projects in this neighborhood, each of which presages some later interest of the partnership, including the sculptured variety of shapes and forms on the Fairchild Barn at 79 Second Street (now remodeled) and the early Colonial Revival additions to the Dennis House at 59 Poplar Street. For 11 Chestnut, McKim's design is all gable, with the bold, sheltering roof slope a forerunner of the firm's justly famous (but no longer extant) Low House built in Bristol about a decade later.

12 SCHOOLHOUSE (EARLY NINETEENTH CENTURY)

71 Third Street

What survives from previous centuries often gives us a skewed sense of what was built. The typical vernacular of two-and-a-half story, three-bay eighteenth-century houses (or for that matter, the gable-to-street classical overtones of the mid-nineteenth century), today suggest homogenous historical streetscapes when the truth is that pre-twentieth-century Newport was sprinkled with small, atypical, utilitarian structures such as this. They add variety and dimension to otherwise regularized street elevations but are seldom the buildings deemed worthy of preservation. Not much to see here architecturally, except to note that this is the only surviving one-room schoolhouse in Newport, now converted into a small residence.

13

13 JOHN FRYE HOUSE (BEFORE 1777), ADDITION (MID-NINETEENTH CENTURY), RESTORED (1968), JOSEPH BELCHER HOUSE (c. 1740), JAMES DAVIS HOUSE (c. 1731), & GEORGE FOWLER HOUSE (JOSEPH GARDNER HOUSE) (c. 1725)

35 Second Street, 36 Walnut Street (at Second Street), 42 Second Street, & 32 Second Street

An interesting collision of forms and centuries, with the original one-and-a-half story gambrel roofed structure on the corner, the John Frye House is flanked by a later and larger gabled addition to the south. Framing suggests this might have been an extant building, moved and butted up against the earlier house. The addition, which served as a store into the twentieth century, almost seems to be subsuming the eighteenth-century structure as it crowds and towers over the smaller building that still manages to hold its own by the dramatic vertical extension of its chimney. Rather than creating a unified whole, the two parts remain articulated by different foundations, offset window levels, and the outline of the gambrel traced in moldings on the street elevation.

Along with the Frye House, other nearby houses along or just off Second Street show a multitude of early eighteenth-century variations on gambrel forms and entry designs. The Belcher House (Joseph Belcher was a noted pewterer) has a steeply pitched gambrel front and a saltbox to the rear, while the other two (originally owned by James Davis and Joseph Gardner) use the three-quarter house form. The Davis House focuses on a full-pedimented, transom-lit doorway, while the Gardner entry has a broken pediment interrupted by a portal fanlight. The earliest of these structures, Gardner's house, is now known as the George Fowler House after a nineteenth-century owner.

14

14 ZINGO STEVENS HOUSE (MID-EIGHTEENTH CENTURY), ENLARGED (LATE NINETEENTH CENTURY)

51 Poplar Street

In its original, unassuming one-and-a-half story form, this house was the home of Zingo Stevens, an African American and freeman who had been owned by the John Stevens II family prior to 1772. Zingo is almost certainly the same man who had formerly been known as Pompe (or Pompey) Stevens but who, after manumission, had abandoned the eighteenth-century Anglo conceit of a classical name and taken back his own West African birth name. Zingo (as Pompey) worked in the nearby Stevens shop, cutting gravestones (one from 1768 for his brother, Cuffe Gibbs, is in the Common Burying Ground), but probably did other work as well since he is later listed as a mason. We know a fair amount about the life of Zingo — including, notably, his leadership in Newport's early African Union Society (one of the earliest such community organizations in the country, established in the 1780s). He owned and lived in this house on the Point amongst other tradesmen and artisans (of both races) and, like many people, had a nearby kitchen garden lot for which he diligently paid rent to Quaker proprietors. We have documentary records of Zingo's religious activities, his interactions with the Anglo community, his marriages, his friends, his will, and an inventory of his property at the time of his death around 1816. The inventory lists varied possessions that would likely have been in this house (including a bedstead, a wheelbarrow, tools, and even silver shoe buckles), many of which he left to his daughter, Sarah Rodman, who lived here into the 1860s.

Zingo Stevens and his family occupied the two rooms and loft spaces that now constitute the second story of this structure. Its awkward proportions and odd window arrangement are due to alterations necessitated after the house was raised onto a new first story in the nineteenth century.

15

This is one of a number of frame houses that are documented as owned and/or lived in by African Americans in the eighteenth and early nineteenth centuries. While some early African American enclaves were disrupted by later urban developments (such as the construction of Columbus Memorial Boulevard), others—like the Pope Street neighborhood across town *(see Tour Nine)*—still boast several historically black-owned buildings similar in scale and simplicity to the Poplar Street structure.

15 CHRISTOPHER TOWNSEND HOUSE & SHOP (c. 1725)

74 Bridge Street

While the gambrel-on-hip roof, pedimented door, and even the eccentricities of entry or chimney placement are typical of early eighteenth-century Newport, the survival of a shop structure from that period is not. Here, we are lucky to have the daily living and working arrangements for a colonial craftsman who specialized in ships' cabinetry (and who was a member of an illustrious cabinetmaking family at that!). It is worth noting that relatively small, one-story shops were not unusual in this era but were not always attached to the artisan's residence *(see, for example, Entry 21 of this Tour, the later John Stevens shop and residence situated across Thames Street from each other).*

16

16 PITT'S HEAD TAVERN (c. 1726, c. 1744)

77 Bridge Street

This is another of the many old Newport houses that has led a peripatetic existence. It was built by 1726 on the old Parade, now called Washington Square, at its northeast corner with Charles Street. In 1877 it was moved farther east on Charles Street to make way for an Odd Fellows Hall and stood there until it eventually relocated to its present site on Bridge Street in 1965.

Called an "upright" house form by earlier historians, this is essentially a broad gambrel residence that sat along a dense wall of houses on its original site. That it was enlarged several times after the house changed owners in the 1740s and 1760s is suggested by the slightly eccentric layout of entry door and windows. Early paint analysis suggested that it was originally painted a light, creamy tone of white. Some of its trim, including the alternating shapes of triangular and segmental dormer pediments, the correctness of details and proportions of the entry surround and its cornice of modillion blocks, suggest similarities with other Newport buildings by Peter Harrison, including the Redwood Library and the Vernon House. Despite what may be Harrison's alterations in the mid-century, many features survive from its earlier state including the massive framing around hearths, the small central entry hall, its tightly wound stairwell, and the flat, sawn balusters of its railing.

We know little of its designers but more about many of its inhabitants, including its first two owners, John Clarke and Jonathan Chace, both mariners, and Henry Collins, who bought the house from Chace and was often called the "Lorenzo de Medici of Rhode Island" as a wealthy merchant, art collector, and patron of culture. Ebenezer Flagg, a founder of the Redwood Library, and his wife, Mary Ward, the niece of Collins, might have been given the house as a wedding present by Collins after their marriage in 1741. John Stevens II, the well-known stone cutter and mason, did a lot of work for the Flaggs, including setting paving stones

17

and entry steps, altering the chimney, and notably setting what were probably fashionable Dutch tiles in the decorative fireplace surround. After 1765 it was sold to Robert Lillibridge, jun. who turned it into a much-frequented coffee house and tavern under the sign of the "Pitt's Head" (an exterior signboard, no longer extant, which held a likeness of the "Great Commoner" William Pitt). During the Revolutionary War, while still a tavern, the Hessians were headquartered here, the British used it as a kind of recruiting station, and eventually our allied French troops were billeted within its rooms. Once owned in the mid-twentieth century and partially restored under the aegis of the Preservation Society of Newport County, it is now again a private residence.

17 JACOB DUHANE/CAPTAIN SIMEON PORTER HOUSE (BEFORE 1749), ANN WEBBER HOUSE (c. 1794), & ISAAC DAYTON HOUSE (MID-EIGHTEENTH CENTURY)

37 Marsh Street, 33 & 35 Washington Street

These are three houses in proximity to each other that show the vernacular variety of eighteenth-century design. If we take five window bays as the typical front elevation, we can see here its full form in the Ann Webber House, a "three-quarter" variation on the Duhane-Porter House, and on Dayton's gabled building next door the smaller "half" house configuration. Much of the original material on these three has been replaced or changed: the doorways on the Webber and Dayton houses are replacements, and the Porter House has recently undergone extensive restoration. The Porter House once served as a free school for the poor, the first such in Newport, opening its doors in 1814 as a gift from Captain Porter.

18

18 GOAT ISLAND & ROSE ISLAND

Looking out toward the west from this corner are Bay islands that have always played a part in Newport's history. Although originally used as pasture land, much of what was of architectural interest on nearby Goat Island is now gone (for example, the military complex of large brick buildings that housed the Navy Torpedo Station). This was all demolished when the 1965 causeway opened the island to residential and tourist-centered development. The sloped rise of the brick hotel tower on its north end dates from the 1970s, a faint visual echo of the razed factory buildings that were for a time, in the mid-twentieth century, the largest industrial plant in the state (staffed by some 5,000 workers).

While Goat Island's architectural history has been almost entirely rebuilt in the last few decades, the over 18 acres of Rose Island sited about one mile off the Newport coast in the East Passage of Narragansett Bay is accessible only by boat and therefore its historic features have suffered less redevelopment. Although today best known as an environmental education center where you can book quiet overnight stays in the 1869 Lighthouse, it also contains a treasure trove of military ruins and features. The mansard-roofed lighthouse itself was abandoned after the construction of the Newport Bridge but restored by Newport Collaborative Architects to an early-twentieth-century appearance, relit in the 1990s, and revived as a destination. A stay is filled with rustic charm as there is no running water (although there is an old iron hand pump in the pantry) and little in the way of twentieth- century electronic distraction. The lighthouse also serves as the main facility of the wildlife preserve that seasonally limits access to large areas of the island to protect nesting birds. Off shore to the northeast is a small outcrop, Citing Rock, where harbor seals can been seen basking from October through April.

The lighthouse was built right on top of an old bastion, one of many such artifacts from the island's military past. There are

19   20

located here a sequence of fortifications including: a 1778 British Battery, a rare 1780-81 Revolutionary War fort constructed in collaboration with French troops under Rochambeau to guard the mouth of Newport Harbor, a major First System Fort begun in 1798 (Fort Hamilton), and numerous structures, barracks, and buildings from the late nineteenth century through World Wars I and II. From 1883 until the mid-twentieth century, the island was used for explosive storage, a torpedo station, and other ordinance work. While some of these historic elements are not accessible for conservation or safety reasons, there are plans to interpret these features and make them more available to the public in the future.

19 CALEB CLAGGETT HOUSE (c. 1725)

22 Bridge Street

Everything is slightly askew in this eye-catching early gambrel, probably due to expansions and the addition of a rear lean-to. Its off-center door divides eccentrically arranged windows; the massive chimney, with its four "smokes" — or flues — sits to one side. Most prominent of all is its one brick wall (facing west), a rarity for such an early Newport house that is made even more striking by the decoratively sinuous irons that tie it to the timber frame.

20 CAPT PETER SIMON HOUSE (c. 1727), ENLARGED (MID-EIGHTEENTH CENTURY), RESTORED (c. 1950, 2007)

25 Bridge Street

When Peter Simon acquired an already standing small house on this site in 1736, he enlarged it into the two-and-a-half story gable-on-hipped-roof building that we see today. Much early interior detail remains, including ornately turned balusters and paneling from as early as the 1730s. The ornate doorway dates from around 1800, and comes from a house in Bristol.

21

UPPER THAMES STREET

21 JOHN STEVENS SHOP & STEVENS HOUSES (MID-EIGHTEENTH CENTURY), JOB BENNETT HOUSE (C. 1721), & CAPT WILLIAM REED HOUSE (MID-EIGHTEENTH CENTURY)

29, 30, 34, 36 Thames Street, 44 Thames Street, & 58 Thames Street

This three-block stretch of Newport's early thoroughfare is a remarkably intact streetscape of colonial houses. Anchored near the street's northern end by a group of buildings related to the stone cutters John, William, and Philip Stevens and their families, this phalanx of buildings fitted cheek to jowl along small city lots allows us to experience the same streetscape that one of the Stevenses' clients might have known around 1750. Adding to this effect is the Stevenses' shop, a later eighteenth century structure located, like their houses, a short distance from the Common Burying Ground that was destined to be filled with generations of their crafted stones. Today it houses one of the country's oldest continuous businesses. Walk up to the intersection of Thames and Farewell Streets, stand under the replanted Liberty Tree (where patriots once gathered to discuss Revolution), and look back toward Washington Square to get the full experience.

Toward the center of town, the early Job Bennett House is a large, hipped-roof house, preserved by the early Point-based grass roots preservation effort Operation Clapboard, which began in 1964. At 58 Thames Street another tall, gambrel house dating back to the mid-eighteenth century is that of Captain William Reed (unfortunately, it is not shown on the Ezra Stiles map of 1758 that allows us to date so many colonial structures). There is here the

dignified uniformity that one might expect of wood-frame Anglo-American buildings—the clapboard siding framed by simple moldings, the small-paned windows surrounding modestly emphasized entryways. But imaginative individuality is also evident here in the varied rooflines of the buildings' gables, gambrels, and hipped roofs. Some have flattened facades, others deep overhanging eaves. Some have their long sides to the street, others use an end gable as their entry elevations. The post-and-beam technology was little changed, but it allowed for a broad range of tastes and images to vary the townscape.

Such antiquity made this neighborhood of architectural interest to the nineteenth century as well. In 1874, Charles Follen McKim commissioned a portfolio of photographs documenting Newport's old houses and several of these are of buildings along this stretch of Thames or nearby.

11 **CROSS STREET** under restoration, 1968.
SOURCE: *Early Homes of RI*. IMAGE BY HELEN MASON GROSS.

22

Finally, two houses here also provide a visual caution for those seeking authentic colonial structures. Numbers 9 and 31 Thames Street (1979, c. 1990) were built in the late twentieth century to mime the characteristics of earlier American residences. Though these are modern structures cloaked in colonial dress, they too help retain the human scale, street elevations, and textures of this eighteenth-century neighborhood.

22 GOVERNOR GIDEON WANTON HOUSE (EARLY SEVENTEENTH CENTURY)

11 Cross Street

This diminutive gabled house, originally owned by seventeenth-century governor Gideon Wanton, was moved by the Newport Restoration Foundation from land that lay close to the Coddington family burial ground on Farewell Street. Like many of the Restoration Foundation properties, its interior has been substantially renovated and modernized. Nevertheless, its placement amongst other early colonial structures (such as the similar house next door at Cross Street and, across the way, the gambrel-roofed Spooner House, c. 1740, at 1 Elm Street, whose wider window spacing lends it a grander appearance) helps this neighborhood retain an appropriately dense urban streetscape.

NATHANIEL CODDINGTON-THOMAS WALKER HOUSE (KING'S ARMS TAVERN) (c. 1706-1713)

6 Cross Street

Larger than most surviving residences of its date, this too was moved by the Newport Restoration Foundation from nearby Coddington property to its current site. Here the roof line is a hybrid—hipped toward the street, the opposite elevation gabled. The wide planes of its roof, which stretch from the heavy projecting eaves to the massive pilastered chimney, lend this house a commanding scale clearly signifying the social status of the owner and his family heritage.

23

23 REVEREND DANIEL WIGHTMAN HOUSE (c. 1694) & 6 CODDINGTON STREET (c. 1721)

2 Coddington Street & 6 Coddington Street

Here we find two houses connected to the Reverend Wightman, a housewright-trained minister who came to Newport from South County (across Narragansett Bay) in the early 1690s. Thick, chamfered beams, gunstock posts, a small stairwell, and a massive chimney stack on a stone foundation all reflect the early date of 2 Coddington Street. Unfortunately, later renovations have replaced roofline, doors, windows, and sheathing and altered its notably early character under a nineteenth-century makeover.

Next door, at 6 Coddington, is a remarkable survivor that is probably a house that stood on the property that Wightman gave to his daughter and son-in-law in the early 1720s. The small story-and-a-half house, clustered with additions and ells, gives a good sense of what such tiny, unadorned houses for the "middlin'" population must have looked like. It is based on a seventeenth-century form found more commonly in northern Rhode Island and Cape Cod than in Newport. Given their diminutive size and ad hoc additions, few of these have survived untouched by later elaborations.

24 ALMY-TAGGART HOUSE (c. 1720)

56 Farewell Street

Here we find an early gambrel-roofed house, set end to street, whose most remarkable feature may be its horizontal, beaded-edge siding painted a deep blue. The house was probably enlarged in the mid-eighteenth century and owned by Job Almy, who advertised it (somewhat disingenuously) in Newport's newspaper, *The Mercury*, as being "A large, commodious, new dwelling, House, well finished and painted blue" that possessed "A Stable, Garden, good Well, a fine Cellar, and other Conveniences." Much of this is now gone but the house as restored still has its interior

24   25

staircase, the massive step-topped chimney with seven hearths, and the blue siding that was protected for many years by a skin of shingles (which was removed during restoration).

25 JOSEPH & WILLIAM COZZENS HOUSE (c. 1765)

57-59 Farewell Street

Two brothers built this colonial duplex, a rare form in Newport. Its is essentially two gambrel-roofed half houses, each a reflection of the other so that the entry doors sit toward the center and the chimneys are at either end.

26 COMMON BURYING GROUND (c. 1660) & ISLAND CEMETERY (1851)

Bounded by Farewell Street, Warner Street, Kingston & Van Zandt Avenues

For over 200 years, until later suburban cemeteries were opened in the nineteenth century, this neighborhood contained all five major burial grounds for Newport. Notable among them is the ancient Common Burying Ground, which possesses about 5,000 markers, the earliest dating back to the 1660s. Scores of early death head slate stones by the noted John Stevens Shop are here as well as markers by other noted artisans of the colonial period (including John Bull, the Tingley Shop of Providence, and William Mumford of Boston, whose works allow us to trace changes in taste and attitudes about commemoration and death from that early period). One of the unique aspects of the yard is an African American section at the north end whose earliest extant stone dates back to 1720. This is sited at the farthest reaches of the cemetery from the colonial town (in those days no one would have approached from the rural countryside to the north) and was originally referred to as an "outsider" section. In the nineteenth century, the African American community gave it another name, God's Little Acre. Here, in what now constitutes a national treasure, lies what may be the most extensive collection of

12

grave markers for colonial African Americans. In it we find an unparalleled record of that community's experience of slavery, subsequent freedom, and its on-going relationship with the rest of Newport since the eighteenth century.

Wrapped around the old burying ground, and designed in response to its shabby condition in the mid-nineteenth century, is the Island Cemetery—Newport's version of a garden cemetery. In actuality, however, with its essentially flat topography and lack of natural amenities such as ponds, groves, or hillsides, it is hardly garden or park-like and it is hard to imagine Newporters strolling or picnicking on its grounds in the way residents of Cambridge used Mt. Auburn or those in Providence used Swan Point (two other progressive cemeteries that predate Newport's version by a few years).

Rather than landscape design, our interest in Island Cemetery instead lies in the number of monuments it possesses by important nineteenth-century architects and artists. To find these, proceed straight along the road leading from the Warner Street entry. Just to your left, and about five blocks in, you will come to the large circular Belmont plot. Within easy walking distance of this circle are many graves of Newport's social elite, including two by Augustus Saint Gaudens (the King Monument, 1876, in collaboration with John La Farge; and the Smith Monument, 1884) about a block to the right of the Belmont plot. Also to be found here are a number of distinguished tombs and markers by Richard Morris Hunt. One, for George Peabody Wetmore, 1873, is a gable-topped stele with oak leaf swag (it's located to the right, just beyond the circle). Also to the right of the circle is a Hunt-designed tomb in dark-grey granite inspired by ancient catafalque forms for the Ledyard family in 1882-1893. Also on the right, just before one reaches the Belmont circle, is Hunt's diminutive temple-like mausoleum for the Marquand family, 1885.

By far the most striking of the Island Cemetery's tombs was conceived for Augustus Belmont and his family and echoes the shape of that family plot. It features the sweep of a classical excedra as a backdrop to caryatid figures by Hunt's office sculptor, Karl Bitter. These standing, draped females stand watch over a central pink granite tomb (similar to the Ledyard design) and are said to be modeled on Belmont family members. The entire crowded ensemble of multiple graves sits before the gothic sandstone shape of the Belmont Chapel, today in derelict condition but originally designed by George Champlin Mason, Sr (who had just built Belmont's now razed seaside Villa By-The-Sea in 1860). A generation later, in 1891, interior renovations were executed by Hunt.

Given Hunt's resident status within the social elite of Newport, it should be no surprise that his own family plot is here, nor that it lies close to the graves of his prominent patrons in the northern boundary of the cemetery. After an 1895 funeral at Newport's Trinity Church, which included Charles Follen McKim as a pall bearer, Hunt was buried beneath a severe, polished, dark-granite slab. While later family burials have largely retained this form, those for the architect and his wife are distinguished by being elevated on a single step and with text carved across their longest dimension. Also in this plot is the marker for Hunt's son, Richard Howland Hunt, who carried on running the Hunt business until his death in the early 1930s. The Latin inscription on the elder Hunt's tomb reads *Laborare Est Orare* (To Toil Is To Pray), a fitting epitaph for a man who designed scores of buildings and monuments, established the American Institute of Architects, and influenced the architectural language of a generation.

3. THE WEST END

This area of town covers an irregular wedge of land whose narrow point is close to the Pell Bridge overpasses and whose sides are bounded by the Bay, the outer Broadway neighborhood, and by Newport's town line on the north. Throughout much of the city's history, this sprawling district was the rural end of town where a few large estates and farms lay scattered along a ridge of land sloping down to the water and to one of the town's alms houses, which stood on an island just off the coast. Of these establishments only the alms house survives as Founders Hall on the Naval Base. In fact, when the Navy established its training site on Coaster's Harbor Island in the 1870s it began to bring development to the west side of Newport, as did the railroad tracks leading into the town itself. This eventually developed into Newport's late-twentieth-century industrial zone (water treatment plant, electrical substations, public transport garages, town waste facility, bridge ramps, factories). Add to this large gas stations, car dealerships, fast food franchises, a streamlined diner, and even the town's very own Wal-Mart and a visitor can't be blamed for thinking that the West End could pass for the usual commercial strip found on the outskirts of so many American towns.

Although the slick commercial clutter and acres of asphalt parking lots still visually separate it from the rest of Newport, the West End has other, more interesting distinctions—both historic and contemporary. Coaster's Harbor Island, for instance, probably served as one of Nicholas and Peter Easton's landing sites as they explored the perimeter of the island looking for a place to establish their settlement. And much later, in the mid-twentieth century, the first Newport music festivals were held overlooking this same Bay island on the hillside below Miantonomi Park. Today, for all its utilitarian brutishness, the West End is often the first glimpse of Newport to greet the thousands streaming into the city via the Pell Bridge. Happily, more recent urban redevelopment has led to the construction of innovative public housing designs here (replacing earlier, less hospitable attempts), as well as to a few wonderfully lively Post-Modern educational facilities.

◀ WAR MEMORIAL TOWER, MIANTONOMI PARK

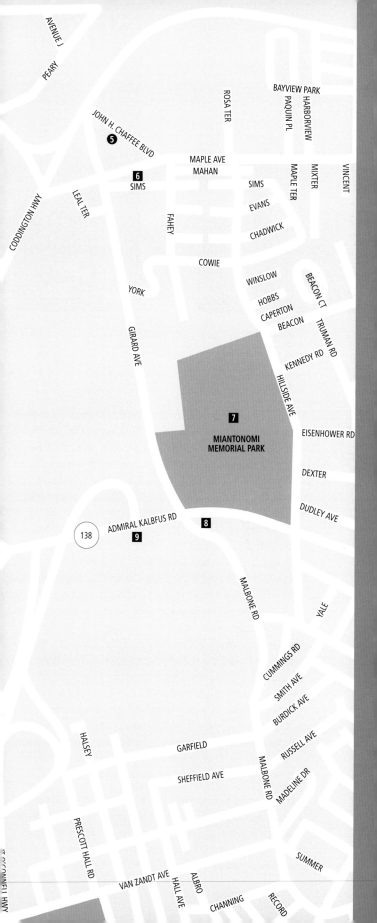

1

1   PELL BRIDGE AND APPROACHES (1966-69)
PARSONS, BRINCKERHOFF, QUADE & DOUGLAS
ENGINEERS/DESIGNERS

With the memory of the disastrous 1938 hurricane still fresh in the public mind, and over the west passage, the Jamestown Bridge, having just been completed, planning began for a bridge to connect Jamestown with Newport over the east passage of Narragansett Bay. After the hiatus of World War II, and after having won the Navy's approval (in 1950) to construct such a bridge, the state legislature created the Rhode Island Turnpike and Bridge Authority four years later. This agency eventually commissioned the New York engineering firm of Parsons, Brinckerhoff, Quade & Douglas, which had successfully engineered the earlier Jamestown project, to design the new span. The result, a suspension bridge almost 3,000 feet long, was one of the longest in the world when finally completed in 1969. Several technical innovations were incorporated into the fabrication of the bridge: novel construction methods for the 15$^{1}/_{2}$-inch steel cables, the application of a glass-reinforced acrylic coating to protect the cables, and the earliest use of an anchorage where the cable load is borne against the rear of the anchorage block and grouped in a configuration known as a "rocket launcher" for its resemblance to a piece of military hardware. The two main 400-foot-tall towers—with their utilitarian construction, attenuated proportions, and Gothic arches—hold the graceful swag of cables that in turn suspend the roadway about 200 feet above the water.

Despite the engineering innovations and what some considered the beautiful lines of the design, there was much controversy surrounding the erection of the Newport Bridge (as it was originally named). Preservationists were concerned that the scale of the bridge would visually destroy the character of the nearest historic

2

neighborhood, the Point; worse, it was feared that the construction of adjacent entry roads and ramps would entail the literal demolition of historical structures. Pressure from prominent activists such as Antoinette Downing and Esther Fisher Benson, along with the support of other heavyweights such as Governor John Chafee and Senator Claiborne Pell, made the planners aware that the finished designs needed to limit the demolition of extant structures. Today the span, renamed the Pell Bridge after the prominent United States Senator from Newport, is the most recognizable artifact of Newport's built environment and has even become a kind of unofficial logo for the state, appearing on the reverse of the Rhode Island quarter dollar when it was minted in 2001.

2   **THE COMMON SENSE GUM FACTORY** (1912)

221 Third Street

Some architectural types are rarer than others in Newport. Although warehouses and manufacturing once clustered along the harbor, the railroad tracks, and the railyard (now the site of the Gateway Center), few turn-of-the-century manufacturing buildings have survived. Even more remarkably, the long industrial block here is accompanied by small cottages along Third Street, some of which were developed at the time for workers' housing in what amounts to Newport's own version of a modern mill village.

On the horizontal rectangular brick of the factory itself, the orderly window treatment of horizontal openings and knee walls, framed by monumental pilasters, would seem typical except for the numeral "5" fashioned at the top of each shaft. The mystery is solved when one realizes that this was originally a gum factory whose products sold for a nickel. More recently, this old industrial building has been put to new use as an office complex.

3

3   ## ADMIRAL'S GATE TOWER (1985)
NEWPORT COLLABORATIVE ARCHITECTS

221 Third Street

Projecting up behind the early-twentieth-century industrial form of the Gum factory is this late-twentieth-century commercial office tower. It's another rarity in the city—and surprising for its context until one realizes that its upper floors afford desirable views of the bridge and Bay beyond. As designed by Glenn Gardiner, the planarity of its gridded outer surfaces of pre-cast panels and window forms read as a paper-thin skin except toward the top of its six stories, where there is an unexpected visual collision of glazed corner pavilions flanking the central motif of twin gabled sheds.

4   ## UNITED STATES NAVAL WAR COLLEGE

The Naval War College is centered on Coasters Harbor Island, a small island north of the harbor reachable by causeway from the mainland. It has an array of interesting historic—and, perhaps more surprisingly—modern buildings. The earliest of these, Founders Hall (c. 1819), was built as one of Newport's early charitable alms houses. Its masonry walls, central gable, and porch recall another early institutional building for Newport, the Jail on Marlborough Street. Founders Hall has been used by the Navy since it took over this site in the late nineteenth century. The other prominent historical building on the base, Luce Hall (1892), houses the Naval War College. Designed by George Champlin Mason, Sr, it borrows the cupola, peaked gables, and horizontality of Founders Hall but stretches it out along the waterfront, adding smaller classical porches to define entryways and a rusticated stone surface in place of the brick. A later, identical western wing was added at a right angle to the original Mason building in the early twentieth century.

4

Nearby, the brick buildings of the Naval Hospital (including a small industrial gem, the steam plant along Third Street) date from the 1920s (only one or two other large-scale buildings were added to the War College campus itself before the 1970s). In the '70s, when few local patrons were commissioning institutional buildings in a contemporary idiom, the Navy built three substantial buildings for auditorium and classroom space. Grouped around three sides of a plaza that opens toward the Bay, the trio of Spruance Hall (1972), Conolly Hall (1974), and Hewitt Hall (1976), while not distinguished individually, are intentionally composed to make a monumental ensemble of brick planes and pre-cast-concrete elements in a vaguely Modernist vocabulary.

Unfortunately, because of new security restrictions, the War College, so important today as the heart of Newport's long standing Naval community, is no longer readily accessible. Visitors must make special arrangements for viewing these buildings, although Founders and Luce Hall can be seen clearly from afar by looking north while leaving Newport on the Pell Bridge.

5

5 COMMUNITY COLLEGE OF RHODE ISLAND NEWPORT COUNTY CAMPUS (2005) & EAST BAY COMMUNITY ACTION PROGRAM BUILDING (2005) NEWPORT COLLABORATIVE ARCHITECTS

John H. Chafee Boulevard

The anchor of Newport's West End urban redevelopment plan is a quirky juxtaposition of two dissimilar buildings by the same design firm. The Community College of Rhode Island Newport County Campus is the local satellite facility, designed by J. Michael Abbott where three functions have been integrated into a single three-storied structure: a classroom wing with laboratories, rooms for student services, and a large auditorium. The long shed splays open into two wings spread in a wedge shape; closing off the open end is a rotund tower with an overhanging conical roof. These forms help identify the functions of interior spaces and connect the building to localized historical forms. You wouldn't have to look far for specific sophisticated sources such as the coupled gables, engaged turrets, and surface patterns of McKim, Mead & White's Casino or scores of late-century shingled houses. At the same time, this teaching complex, with its masses enlarged into broad, relatively unadorned shingled planes, also reveals stylistic roots in barns and other humble, utilitarian structures.

The other social services building across the street, East Bay Community Action Program, houses Head Start. Glenn Gardiner obviously designed this for a much younger clientele with its bulk masked by a series of scrim-like projections sheathed in multicolored corrugated metal. The top edges of these are cut into undulating wave forms interspersed with stretched fabric awnings, further suggesting the architecture of childhood: carnival booths, circus tents, bathing pavilions, and other playscapes. No entry signage is needed here; the entire building says "step right this way!"

6

7

6 NEWPORT HEIGHTS (2005-2006)
ICON ARCHITECTURE, INC

Maple Avenue & streets south

A variety of traditional forms—porches, gables, turned posts, and patterned shingles — enliven these mixed-income housing units. They partially replaced (and stand in remarkable contrast to) the grim monotony of the barracks-like housing dating back to World War II that served an earlier generation of residents in the same neighborhood. Designed mostly as row houses, with some units grouped into separate apartment blocks, they cleverly evoke the different rooflines, massing, and scale that give many urban streetscapes their visual appeal.

7 WAR MEMORIAL TOWER (1929) McKIM, MEAD & WHITE, LANDSCAPE (1915-1921) OLMSTED BROS.

Miantonomi Park

This largest of the city's parks (at some 30 acres) is associated with important colonial sites, including the supposed seat of Miantonomi, a Narragansett sachem during the earliest years of English settlement, as well as with the later remains of a British fortification hastily constructed during their occupation of Newport in the Revolutionary War. The 80-foot tower— and the park within which it is set on a high ridge—were intended, however, to be memorials to the 72 Newporters who died in World War I. With its cylindrical arcade in random fieldstone, its form inescapably alludes to the city's most famous tower, the famous seventeenth-century stone mill in Touro Park. Although the project was not realized until after the death of the firm's last remaining principal partner (Mead in 1926), its form is clearly influenced by the kind of knowledgeable historicism that made McKim, Mead & White a success from its earliest days. Here, however, the tiered, crenelated shape is more watchtower than mill in the way that it conflates Newport's colonial farm structure with the timely symbolism of *semper vigilans*.

8

8 NEWPORT DAILY NEWS BUILDING (1969)
CHAS T. MAIN, INC

101 Malbone Road

This building—with its unadorned brick and plate-glass panels set beneath a heavy horizontal masonry band—was the antithesis of what architecture meant to most Newporters in the mid-twentieth century. Given such prevalent conservatism, the low, abstract slab of this combined printing plant and office complex was a brave, albeit late, attempt at corporate Modernism commissioned at a moment when Newport's economic and architectural fortunes were about to shift with the opening of the new bridge. It best expresses its modern roots in the cantilevered section jutting out over the rocky slope of the hill that looks toward the Bay—a glass pavilion floating on cast-concrete support struts dimly recalling the master language of Wright, Johnson, and others.

9

9   NEWPORT GRAND (1976), RENOVATED (1996)
NEWPORT COLLABORATIVE ARCHITECTS

150 Admiral Kalbfus Road

Constructed as a Jai Alai fronton with a cavernous interior for the ball court and viewing stands, this huge shed has morphed into a different kind of gambling facility. The live game is gone, replaced now by the virtual thrills of electronic betting. So too, what originally looked like a big, unadorned, metallic shed was gussied up by architect J. Michael Abbott in a kind of mansion makeup — including pediments, stucco rustication, balustrades, shutters, and a row of graphically flat cypress trees. All this is a rather tongue-in-cheek attempt to mask the barren, utilitarian character of the original outsized building whose presence nevertheless stubbornly persists.

F.W. ANDREWS HOUSE, 1872 by H.H Richardson, Maple Avenue, demolished in the 1940s.

SOURCE: *Collection of the Newport Historical Society*

4. BROADWAY/NORTH END

Broadway, one of Newport's first streets, already appears on Henry Bull's 1641 sketch map as Broad Street, a wide clearing leading from the small settlement up island toward outlying farmlands and toward Portsmouth, then called Pocasset. It was first called "the big highway" and was true to its name—its width extending from its current path over to West Broadway (now named Dr Marcus Wheatland Boulevard). While some of Broadway's length may have traced native paths, natural features, or animal tracks, it quickly became a significant thoroughfare for the Colony. It originated at the point where Long Wharf crosses the axis of Thames Street, thus establishing a pipeline from productive farmlands, through the town, and to the water. Broadway developed into one of the two main business routes of the town (the other being Thames Street at the head of the harbor). By the nineteenth century, Broadway had clearly become the locale for the majority of the city's civic and religious institutions. Extending northward from the businesses lining Washington Square and nearby City Hall, the lower part of Broadway boasted shops and stores, schools and churches, and was served by one of the trolley lines established in the city after 1891.

The subsequent history of upper (northern) Broadway was entwined with this trolley line as it opened up residential development on many smaller streets crossing the major road. This "North End" was a roughly wedge-shaped district that was built as a trolley suburb upon former farmlands. The other major factor in this area was the construction and growth of the Newport Hospital. After its establishment in 1873 about a quarter mile north of Washington Square, the hospital's growth brought with it the need for housing, street access, and other services to this part of town. In addition to its large physical plant, this neighborhood's hospital connection can also be seen in some of the local street names (Ledyard Street, for instance, was named after Henry Ledyard, a prominent intellectual, Newport resident, and founder of the hospital) as well as in the kind of multiple family housing found more frequently here than in other parts of town.

continued on page 298

◀ GARDNER S. PERRY HOUSE

SINGLE SITE ENTRY

MULTI-SITE ENTRY

1   2

1   THOMPSON MIDDLE SCHOOL (1894) JAMES C. FLUDDER, (2002) HMFH ARCHITECTS

39 Broadway

An earlier junior high school building stood on this site for about a century before it was torn down to make way for the wing built in 2002. This was part of a comprehensive plan to renovate the older Townsend Industrial School Building (built by Newporter, James Fludder) and then extend it with a modern addition to the east that would stand as a distinct building. Connected to the late-nineteenth-century structure by the communal space of a two-story stairwell and atrium, the new extension contains classrooms, offices, and a "cafetorium." In its general siting and composition as well as in the rhythmic details of window placement, mullions, and polychromed brick patterns, the new facility (by the Cambridge-based firm HMFH Architects) acts as a visual transition between the small-scale detailing of the old Townsend School and the broader, tan-colored forms of the church next door, maintaining and even strengthening the streetscape of downtown Newport.

2   ST JOSEPH'S ROMAN CATHOLIC CHURCH (1904-1912) CREIGHTON WITHERS

Broadway and Mann Avenue

This imposing church structure was built over a number of years as the parish gradually raised money for its erection. Withers (who in the early 1890s had supervised the building of St John's Church on the Point for his father, the architect F.C. Withers) was contracted to build a new church to replace the patchwork of buildings this congregation occupied on Washington Square. He chose to wrap this naved structure in Italianate-Romanesque forms that are executed in buff-colored brick with terracotta trim. Its ornate interior contains mosaics and a Carrara marble altar. The classical geometries of the triumphal arch entryway, round windows, and interior arcades separating the central space from

the aisle all help to create a sense of monumentality and grandeur befitting a church with a seating capacity of over one thousand (making it still one of the largest meeting spaces in the city). When it was completed in 1904, furnishings from the old church on Touro Street (including altar rails, statues, and the sanctuary lamp) were re-installed in the new lower chapel. The church was used immediately after its completion but was not consecrated until 1922, when the building debt was at last retired.

3 POLICE STATION (1985) THE ROBINSON GREEN BERETTA CORPORATION

120 Broadway

The old jail on Marlborough Street served as the municipal lock-up for almost 200 years until this new structure was designed in the mid-1980s. The projecting gabled entry portico and mullioned windows pedantically recall the earlier brick jail but the larger size of the windows and their twinned grouping are particular to the new design. So too, unfortunately, is its placement off the line of the sidewalk, which makes it among the first buildings along this stretch of Broadway to disrupt the coherency of the traditional streetscape in favor of strip-mall-type parking.

4 TISDALL BLOCK (c. 1900)

150 Broadway

Situated along what is still a retail stretch of Broadway, this is one of the few architecturally intact survivors of what was once a relatively common commercial form: the glass-fronted store block below with apartments above. Its gentle bays, undercut porches, and shingled surfaces tentatively conform to an urbanized Queen Anne style.

5

5   NEWTOWN & KERRY HILL

While the streetscapes running to the south off Broadway reflect the large-scale late-nineteenth-century and early-twentieth-century styles of the Kay, Catherine & Old Beach neighborhoods, the neighborhoods to the north date from an earlier period. These streets are worth a visit as they are filled with many structures from the eighteenth and nineteenth centuries that housed a population of craftsman, laborers, and their families who lived, worked, and worshiped here. The residents included a large number of African Americans, centered in the area known, since the late eighteenth century, as Newtown, as well as a later community of Irish immigrants in what came to be called Kerry Hill.

While the earliest development of a street grid here dates to the 1770s, a number of streets in the Newtown blocks off Dr Marcus F. Wheatland Boulevard (the former West Broadway) were opened around the Civil War era — hence names like Vicksburg and Burnside. Others, like Tilden Avenue and White Street, are much earlier and contain a number of buildings from the first half of the nineteenth century, some of which were moved, like many houses in this neighborhood, from other locations in the city. An even earlier eighteenth-century house stands at 28 Kingston Street: the tiny one-story gambrel house that appears on the famous Blascowitz map of 1777. Others on Warner Street date from the last quarter of the eighteenth century, such as the early Federal house at number 12. Structures in this neighborhood reflecting the historically vibrant African American enclave include the Old African American Episcopal Church (currently used as a private home at 3 Johnson Court) and the Community Baptist Church on Dr Marcus Wheatland Boulevard.

Moving farther out on Broadway, the grid of streets bounded by Broadway, Van Zandt Avenue, Pond Avenue, and Malbone Road — and called Kerry Hill — has later buildings, erected in the last decades of the nineteenth century. Some blocks here, such as the yoke-shaped configuration of Tilley and Congdon, were envisioned as a single development: a road pattern was laid out

6

through former open land on which small, pattern-book-style workers cottages were built, a few of which still retain their jig-sawed trim. Pond Avenue also retains a number of these small one-and-a-half-story porched houses, such as the nearly identical twinned Patrick Horgan cottages, c. 1873 (numbers 2½ and 4), and the more elaborate trimmed and restored house a few doors away decorated with patterns of vertical boards (number 18). Toward Malbone Road, larger shingled houses with turned porch posts and with Queen Anne flourishes (such as at 102 Warner Street) can be found despite many having been stripped of interesting trim and re-sided. What may be the most inventive instance of decoration on such houses is at 18 Bayview Avenue, where the porch posts suggest cart axles and the dentil work under the over-hanging eave is replaced with small wooden cannons. Might this have been the house of an artillery man?

Broadway came to provide a service corridor for these neighbor-hoods, functioning as a transportation route and as a street containing numerous churches, retail shops, a branch post office, and other amenities where the residents of Newtown and Kerry Hill could shop for their daily needs.

6 COMMUNITY BAPTIST CHURCH (1983) MAURICIO BARRETO (URBAN DESIGN GROUP)

50 Dr Marcus F. Wheatland Blvd. (formerly West Broadway)

A number of buildings along this street attest to the African American community in this neighborhood. The Stone Mill Lodge, a fraternal society founded in 1895, and the Martin Luther King Community Center, originally built about 1944 as a USO for African American servicemen, are both still active but the newer, purpose-built edifice completed in 1983 for the Community Baptist Church houses one of this neighborhood's most active institutions. Its simple clapboarded exterior carefully fits into the scale and texture of nearby modest homes and businesses, but

7   8

what sets it apart is its main block running along the length of the lot and recessed from the lot line with a projecting gabled entry-way reaching out to the sidewalk. Its bulk is also adjusted to its surroundings by the low sloping line of its roof, terminating the eave edge at the first-story level. Its church function is further distinguished by the nave-like shape of its meeting hall, topped by a long row of continuous clerestory windows projecting up from the roof ridge and filling the interior worship space with light from above.

7   FIRST PRESBYTERIAN CHURCH (1892)

J.D. JOHNSTON

167 Broadway

For this design, Johnston borrows a rather later Richardsonian idiom of Romansque gables and squat turrets centered on the grandly oversized stained glass window dominating one end of the worship space within. Johnston, who began his career as a carpenter-builder, had become by 1892 one of Newport's most prolific architects. It may be telling that he was later fondly remembered by members of the Presbyterian Church building committee as "a very fine artist who drew plans, paid his own expenses when going about with the committee to inspect church buildings and in many ways contributed time and ability without remuneration to the enterprise."

9

8 GARDNER S. PERRY HOUSE (1890-91) J.D. JOHNSTON
280 Broadway

As a well-regarded builder-architect, Johnston designed and constructed numerous houses in the Broadway-North End area, its greatest period of development coinciding with the most active years of his career. This one, which replaced the owner's earlier house on the same site, is typical Johnston: rough granite base supporting somewhat predictable massing (corner tower, big gable over entry porch), clapboarded and individualized with ornate mill work, in this case foliate reliefs. Could this predictability be due to Johnston's reliance on published designs that he could then alter for his clients? Such printed sources continue the earlier tradition of pattern books but in the late nineteenth century, they were accessible to many in the building trades through professional journals. For even later, smaller pattern (or possibly catalogue and prefabricated) houses in the area, see the twinned examples across from each other at the corner of Bliss Road and Fowler Street or the mirrored duplication of 115 and 113 Kay Street with a third iteration of the same house at 376 Broadway.

9 NEWPORT HOSPITAL (1873), ALTERED & ADDITIONS (LATE NINETEENTH CENTURY), VANDERBILT PAVILION (1903) WILLIAM ATKINSON, NURSING SCHOOL (c. 1926), BORDEN-CAREY WING (c. 1930), TOWER (1967-1970) DONALD RITCHIE, ADDITIONS & MAIN ENTRANCE (2001) TAYLOR AND PARTNERS

Not much to look at here architecturally except for the accretion of over a century's worth of buildings, alterations, and in-fill additions all driven by the pressing need for space and specialized functions more than architectural sophistication. Although the earliest domestic-scaled wood-frame structures that the hospital inhabited are long gone, there are still remnants of the 1903 classicizing surgical wing that was incorporated into the most recent

10   11

Post-Modern alterations. An earlier attempt at visual unity involving the Georgian-styled Nursing School (note the wonderfully decorative embellishment of the pedimental relief) and the slightly later Borden Building ended up producing two major brick-walled public facades. But it is the late-1960s tower, a novelty in low-rise Newport, that today defines the image of the hospital. More than later attempts to rework entrances or add glitzy touches of glass and steel, its checkerboard verticality (while not exactly inspired design) does overwhelm the disparate elements around it and, ironically, gives the hospital a kind of recognizable architectural identity.

10 COMMERCIAL BUILDING (EARLY TWENTIETH CENTURY), RENOVATION (2006) JAMES ASBEL

311 Broadway

Sited on this acutely angled corner, this building started life as an early-twentieth-century service station and was later turned into a bakery. In its most recent incarnation it has become a playful deconstruction of traditional forms. An earlier tall clock tower has been "defaced," capped by a small hipped roof and turned into a picturesque turret, while new mullion-less windows have opened up the shingled mass. The most emphatic gesture of the recent renovation, however, is the separate wall plane pulled off the main mass that forms a new interior space between the resulting trellis-like screen wall and the main block of the building.

11 342 BROADWAY (c. 1895)

One of the largest houses in the neighborhood, its size suggests that this part of Broadway was no stranger to the social ambitions that created grand residences in other parts of Newport. Grandness here in the late-nineteenth-century idiom of the Queen Anne Style is accentuated by the twin entry doors, the doubled gables that face Broadway, the ornate double curve of its elaborately layered turret cap and, not least of all, its hilltop site, one of the highest lots in this part of Newport.

12   13

12 CAPT JOHN W. DOWNING HOUSE (FAIRVIEW)
(1873-74) DUDLEY NEWTON

34 Malbone Road

Perched on a hill with rear elevations looking toward bayside sunsets (as its name suggests), this is a good example of the summer cottage style prevalent in the 1860s and 1870s. Here Dudley Newton, a well-known local architect, predates the Queen Anne, shingled, and Colonial Revival idioms made popular only a few years later. As usual he "overdoes" it with large elements—such as big dormers crowded into a busy composition. Many of these features, such as the decoratively trimmed hooded windows and porch work, suggest bucolic summer shade. For as it happens, when this house was built Malbone Road was not yet a busy city street but a rural lane running out of town through a more open landscape.

13 MALBONE (1848-49) ALEXANDER JACKSON DAVIS

Malbone Road

From Davis's own drawings, we know that in the 1840s this was an open site with a commanding view of the Bay. Clearly intended to be picturesque in both its design and its country setting, this sandstone house echoes an earlier English taste for the medieval —although here it reads rather more staid than fanciful, with crenellated towers at either end, a few projecting bays, and a fairly regular roofline. More remarkable for us today, perhaps, is the proximity of this country estate to the town itself.

Equally significant are the house's historical associations. Its pink sandstone was reused from an earlier residence on the site that gave its name to both the current house and road. Malbone Hall was built in 1741 as a country retreat by wealthy merchant Godfrey Malbone (built with stone from his own quarry in Brooklyn, Connecticut). It may have been one of the last designs of Richard Munday (who died around 1741, having been associated with the design for Malbone's town house). We only have

14

written descriptions of Malbone Hall today, however, as it burned to the ground in a spectacular blaze in 1766 while Malbone entertained dinner guests. The host, realizing he couldn't save his elaborate mansion, had his servants move the festivities nearby and is purported to have said to his guests: "If I have lost my house that is no reason why we should lose our dinners." Malbone may not have left Newport with an architectural treasure but he certainly set a high standard of hospitality and *sangfroid* for posterity.

14 JOHN BLISS HOUSE (c. 1680-1715), ALTERED (EIGHTEENTH AND NINETEENTH CENTURY), RESTORED & REAR ADDITION BUILT (SECOND QUARTER TWENTIETH CENTURY)

2 Wilbur Avenue

Where Bliss Road first diverges from Broadway it is lined with a dozen or more late-nineteenth-century houses that reflect the form and flourishes of the Queen Anne and Shingle styles. These are crammed into lots that suggest a different clientele for the housing in this area — the kind of people who, while aware of contemporary architectural styles, had less wealth than those Newporters who were commissioning larger versions of these houses in the nearby Kay, Catherine & Old Beach neighborhood.

The rarest treasure in the North End, however, stands a few blocks farther along Bliss Road and is from a quite different era. John Bliss, a Quaker Elder, owned this property and probably built his

*The rarest treasure
in the North End is the
only surviving stone
ender house in Newport.*

house sometime in the late seventeenth or early eighteenth century. The last surviving stone ender house in Newport, this is a good example of what was a relatively common form in this area at that time (a form that is preserved today in only a few other locales, mostly in the northern part of Rhode Island).

The picturesque wall of mortared rubble stone has a bulbous projection that is an oven in the back of the rear fireplace—a feature found infrequently in surviving stone enders. The stone wall reaches neither front nor rear elevations nor to the roofline, but this does not necessarily suggest alteration since the gambrel roof is probably original and a very small entry hall is squeezed between the stone wall and the entry door at the left corner. This last feature is similar to the original plan (since altered) of the contemporaneous Eleazar Arnold House in Lincoln, Rhode Island. Other houses dating from the 1720s that also sport gambrel roofs — such as the Israel Arnold House in Lincoln and the John Tripp House (now on Washington Street but moved from its original site in Providence) — show similar, though smaller, sections of stone hearth wall exposed on the outside. Added to these elements, the large first-floor room dominated by the hearth and the heavy exposed beams all reveal the John Bliss House to be one of numerous Rhode Island houses that were built using common traditions of construction whose source was Jacobean England. There are alterations here — interior additions, window placements, and the classical surround of the entry door—but many of them occurred early in the house's eighteenth-century history, something that usually signals a change in ownership or a family's rising wealth and status.

The John Bliss House sits with its hearthside to the axis of Bliss Road because the house predates the street pattern. As late as the beginning of the twentieth century, this colonial house still sat on open farmland.

PHOTO SOURCE FOR ENTRY 14 JOHN BLISS HOUSE: *John Hopf, courtesy of the Newport Historical Society*

15

16

15 450 BROADWAY (c. 1870)

The ornamental quality of this gabled house, with its board-and-batten surface and stickwork porch, became typical for the kinds of modest single-family houses put up in this outer neighborhood during its transformation from small farms to city streets in the last third of the nineteenth century. Some of these houses were labeled "Swiss cottages" at the time. This probably referred to the sawn trim and tracery patterns under the eaves and stick-framed porches on display here as well as in another altered example at 3 Bedlow Avenue a few blocks away. It also could have referred to the turrets and bays of others in the area (such as 2 Thurston Avenue, also altered). Such language, appearing in the local newspaper, is actually an early attempt at realty hyperbole that sought to equate this far end of town with an even more exotic locale. In fact, the architectural image makers were very busy in this neighborhood as just about every fashionable architectural style can be found along these North End streets, from mid-century Gothic houses (2 and 12 Summer Street), to large, elaborately gabled and ornamented Queen Anne-style residences (7 and 9 Rhode Island Avenue) and even rare apartment blocks (171 Broadway). These compete for space with craftsman bungalows (24 Brook Street) and small cabin-like shingled cottages of 1900-1920 (5½ Ledyard Street) and Dutch Colonial or other revival styles from the next two decades. This mélange of fashionable styles, aimed largely at the middle-class population that came to live in this streetcar suburb, makes this neighborhood more architecturally varied than any other in Newport.

16 ST PETER'S LUTHERAN CHURCH FIRST PHASE (1959-60), WORSHIP CENTER (1973) HERBERT MCLEISH

Broadway

Before this congregation moved from an earlier site on Corne Street in 1960 and erected the rear block as a servicemen's center, they had dropped the word "Swedish" from their original name

17

(Swedish Lutheran Zion Congregation). Despite the new name of St Peter's and the confused layout of phased construction, the vertical sheathing of natural (stained) wood and the polygonal shape of the worship center at least managed tentatively to evoke Scandinavian sources. Given Newport's conservative patronage in the mid-twentieth century, this church remains one of the few examples in Newport of a 1960s vernacular-naturalist Modernism, best exemplified locally by Pietro Belluschi's memorable work of a few years earlier for the Portsmouth Abbey School a few miles away at the northern end of the island.

17 BIRD'S NEST (MID-EIGHTEENTH CENTURY), ALTERED (c. 1845)

526 Broadway

The charming nickname of this small cottage, which sits at an odd angle to the street and all but turns its back to the nearby traffic-clogged intersection, ironically reminds us that this crossing was originally the site of a small rural community, an offshoot of Newport proper, situated about a mile from Long Wharf (hence the nickname still used locally of "One Mile Corner"). The vaguely classical trim of the house suggests it dates from the 1840s — with Gothic details on the lattice work porch added later. But both of these were fairly early alterations to the original farmhouse, which was built in the mid-eighteenth century. This property was rented by civil engineer Colonel George Waring, who was instrumental in establishing water and sewer systems in both New York City and Newport during the third quarter of the nineteenth century. The Bird's Nest became a familiar address among the intelligentsia of mid-nineteenth-century Newport, for here were held early meetings of the intellectual group with strong ties to Boston that would come to be known as the Town and County Club under the leadership of Julia Ward Howe.

5. HISTORIC HILL & HARBOR

Like the Point Section to the north of Washington Square, the hill rising from the wharves and streets to the south of the Square is a neighborhood densely packed with early architecture. The area can be understood by dividing it into two sections: the commercial zone along Thames Street at the base of the hill closest to the harbor itself; and the mostly residential irregular grid of streets running off either side of Spring Street parallel to Thames about halfway up the hill.

Along the harbor the commercial interests of the town grew rapidly. Banks and the Customs House shared these streets with chandleries, lumberyards, and other dockside operations. In the eighteenth and nineteenth centuries, this was often the first glimpse that outsiders would have of Newport—a working waterfront whose rising backdrop included narrow streets built up with houses and churches. Laborers and seamen, mostly single and male, comprised much of the population clustered near the waterfront and this demographic resulted in numerous rooming houses for workers, as well as the kinds of businesses that would cater to their desires, such as saloons and "social" clubs. So many of these establishments were in business by the early twentieth century that this central section of Thames Street came to be known as "Blood Alley" for its rough-and-tumble ambience. But since the departure of the Navy in the 1960s, little of this Newport remains. Where there were once services for residents —clothing stores, the newspaper, the utility companies, service stations, and dry cleaners — there now can be found a more generic resort commerce selling T-shirts, trinkets, sunglasses, and ice cream.

Changes in the urban fabric also occurred here. The last quarter of the twentieth century saw the insertion of the four-lane America's Cup Avenue between the hill and the harbor, as well as the outdoor mall-type development of Brick Marketplace with its adjacent parking lots and consequent disruption of street patterns and traffic flow. This area, once so important to Newport's residents, is now devoted to the economic vitality of tourism and avoided as much as possible by locals during the high season. Ironically, it has now become somewhat isolated from the day to day life of Newport.

1

TRINITY CHURCH (1725-26) RICHARD MUNDAY, SPIRE DESIGNED AND ADDED (1726, 1741), TWO-BAY ADDITION AND SPIRE REBUILT (c. 1762), RESTORATION (1991) IRVING B. HAYNES AND ASSOCIATES

Off Spring Street between Church and Frank Streets

In 1702, a few years after the Church of England began to organize in Newport in 1698, the Anglicans erected a simple house of worship. By the early 1720s the congregation grew enough so that a more substantial church was needed. Although we know little about the builder of the new structure, Richard Munday, before his work on Trinity, he must have had considerable experience to be chosen for such an important commission.

What we see today on Trinity is a gable-roofed body with double rows of arched windows and a steepled square tower abutting its western, gabled elevation (this vertical ensemble was designed at the same time by Munday but built and rebuilt later in the eighteenth century). Originally five bays long, with double rows of arched windows, it was later enlarged to seven bays.

Munday creates a church that is one of the first to be built in the colonies in the tradition of Sir Christopher Wren, the architect who rebuilt London after its disastrous fire a generation earlier. Only Boston's Old North (St Stephen's) Church, built in 1723, predates the use of Trinity's Wren-inspired forms and composition, including its steepled entry tower, the original five-bay length, and the tiers of compass-topped windows. Most emphatically, it abandons the older tradition of the meeting house form, with entry on the long wall, for a naved building whose entrance is on one of its shorter ends, a configuration that was also in keeping with Anglican conventions.

For a time it was even suggested that William Price, the Boston print dealer who sold and possibly reworked engravings of Wren's designs, be credited with the design of both churches, but the

*Whatever his inspiration,
Richard Munday reinterpreted
his sources into his
own unique vision in wood.*

inspiration for Trinity could also have come from directives issued by the Church of England's Society for the Propagation of the Faith as such building activity was seen in large part as missionary activity. There is also evidence that Munday had direct knowledge of other Boston buildings—for example, his later Colony House seems based on a famous Boston residence, so the builder could well have had direct experience of the earlier Old North.

Whatever his inspiration, Munday has reinterpreted his sources into his own unique vision in wood. The double remove of Munday from his Wren models—London to Boston to Newport —gives his design a greater sense of individuality and inventive energy than the more sedate Old North. You can see it in the strangely arranged forms on the tower with broad expanses of wall between certain elements, while others seem jammed together. Other forms, such as pilasters, finials, and socles, are stretched and exaggerated, perhaps to emphasize their verticality. At least one unusual shape might also be symbolic: the double arching of the uppermost shuttered tower windows—possibly echoing Commandment tablets. Even the pediment above the side tower entry doors is broken in a novel way with a semi-circular notch. The result is not naïve but intuitive, delightful, and ultimately memorable, as with his later Colony House *(see Tour One)*.

On the interior some of the same idiosyncrasies can be detected: relationships between vertical and horizontal elements appear disproportionate, the flattened-groin vaulting of the nave awkwardly meets the cross vaults of the barrel vaults. But the overall effect is of a remarkably crisp, clean space. Its focus is the riveting tripartite composition of clerk's desk, reader's desk, and wineglass pulpit with a bell-shaped sounding board to reflect the minister's words toward the congregation. The whole of this is unusually centered in the middle aisle and framed by the light-filled niche of the apse beyond. Completing the interior ornament are elaborate Union Jack panel work and what were originally balusters with a Baroque twist, now replaced by a more mundane nineteenth-century railing.

Finally, as if to herald the novelty of its architecture, the church possesses another rarity. Trinity, importantly, still contains one of the first church organs in New England.

In both character and volume, this meeting space seems wondrous. Unlike the more medieval feel of the earlier Friends Meeting House or the cramped spaces of smaller, residentially scaled meeting houses, this was a more billowing and airy interior than any previous Newport space. For his work on this distinguished building, either in partial payment or merely in honor of what he had achieved, Munday was granted pew 75. Along with the Friends Meeting House and the later Touro Synagogue, this stands as one of the masterworks of religious architecture in colonial Newport.

2

The building underwent extensive renovation and repair in the late twentieth century, including the drastic but necessary step of steel framing within its almost three-hundred-year-old walls. While this new frame is not visible, what may have caused the most concern was the very visible choice of which tone of white paint to use on its exterior. Some held out for the bright white of recent vintage, but it was finally determined that white paint in the eighteenth century was rarely without darkening impurities. After much debate and coverage of the controversy in the *New York Times*, the congregation finally settled on the current, off-white tone.

2   QUEEN ANNE SQUARE & SURROUNDING BUILDINGS

LANGLEY HOUSE (c. 1807)

28 Church Street

JOSEPH COTTON HOUSE (c. 1720)

32 Church Street

ERASTUS PEASE HOUSE (c. 1785)

36 Church Street

FIRE STATION NO. 1 (1885), RESTORED (1991)
LERNER/LADDS + BARTELS ARCHITECTS (EXTERIOR) AND NEWPORT COLLABORATIVE ARCHITECTS (INTERIOR)

25 Mill Street

BILLINGS-COGGESHALL HOUSE (c. 1784)

35-37 Mill Street

ALEXANDER JACK HOUSE (1811)

49 Mill Street

Fronting Trinity Church and surrounded by many eighteenth-century structures, Queen Anne Square represents the best and worst of Newport's built environment. To many visitors it seems

the quintessential colonial New England village common with its white-steepled church and park-like grounds. Nothing, however, could be further from the historical truth. For this townscape is not a colonial space but is instead a fantasy stemming from redevelopment efforts in the 1970s to create a coherent center where none has existed. This particular effort fabricates not just Newport's architectural history but concocts an architectural symbol contrary to the founding principles of the town itself.

From its earliest days and in contrast to most other English settlements in New England, Rhode Island was tolerant of many beliefs and thus had no single church dominating a common civic space the way, for example, many early Massachusetts Bay Colony towns had a congregational church on their central green. This pluralism is overturned here in Queen Anne Square by the imposition of a green space surrounding the glorious edifice of Trinity Church. When built, Trinity was almost surrounded by a dense plat of properties, so much so that enlarging Trinity or its church yard had grown difficult by the early eighteenth century. Many other sects were practicing in Newport by the time this Anglican church was built and some, such as the Quakers, had already erected visually grand houses for worship much earlier.

By the twentieth century, this area had become the center of Newport's waterfront — centered on the ferry terminal and possessing a stretch of stores, eateries, bars, and strip joints that *(as noted in the introduction to this tour)* catered to a clientele of locals and sailors who frequented its many harborside haunts. With the potential for tourism growing after the erection of the Newport Bridge, calls for redeveloping this zone between Trinity and the harbor gained momentum. Commercial buildings that did not fit in aesthetically were razed, colonial houses were moved, and streets closed until the simulation that is now Queen Anne Square was realized in 1976, just in time for the national bicentennial.

Such an effort could and should have provided historical insights into the particular sense of place that characterized the town.

Instead of evoking the true forms of colonial Newport in its urban density, its religious pluralism, and its working harborside, Queen Anne Square all but obliterates history. It works only if what you want is a comforting cliché of "ye olde New England." But if you are looking for colonial authenticity and individuality, it can be found almost everywhere else in Newport but in this Disneyland-ish mirage.

Apart from the church itself, the "Square" is ringed by houses, moved and much restored but still interesting in their variety of earlier American forms. Of the three along the north side of the green, the early-nineteenth-century John Langley House, with its gabled roof, was moved to this site and may be the most predictable in form. The gable-on-hipped-roof house owned by Dr Joseph Cotton, c. 1720, is an early variation in both framing, proportions, and detailing. But most notable is the late-eighteenth-century Erastus Pease House in which the lower plane of its gambrel roof is curved to flow over the eaves at both front and back. Although it may seem elaborately idiosyncratic, there is at least one other eighteenth-century house in Newport with a similar roofline configuration (at 2 Coddington Street).

Amid other early structures on Mill Street to the south, two other buildings, moved to this location, helped complete the early American gentrification of the Square. The Billings-Coggeshall House couples two separate buildings, each with its own simple, pedimented entryways, into a single lengthy block. The archway supporting a second-story extension and the cobbled courtyard beyond were imaginatively added during the "restoration." A little farther up the hill, the Alexander Jack House, moved in 1969, is an early-nineteenth-century structure whose form and trim suggest how building traditions in the first years of the new century had changed little from colonial antecedents. It is arranged in what is generally called a three-quarter-house form (in which the doorway divides the front elevation unequally), although it might more accurately be called a three-fifth form, since it has been distilled from the standard five-bay treatment.

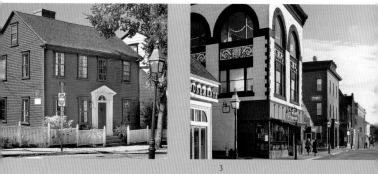

3

Finally, out of stylistic context is the later, ornately styled Fire Station No. 1. Its fancy wave pattern shingles, slightly projecting window bays, and tall tower (that functioned as a lookout and possibly a hose drying site as well), all atop a tall brick base, are one of the few extant examples of local civic architecture built in this style. It was the home of Old Torrent No. 1, one of the earliest fire companies organized in colonial America. Its impressive arched opening was of course functional, intended for the horse-drawn fire wagons that helped protect the surrounding neighborhood for many generations. However, it was the use of horses that eventually brought about the demise of this station, as the animals found it difficult to traverse the steep incline of Mill Street.

3   COMMERCIAL BUILDINGS ON THAMES

EDWARD D. NEWTON BLOCK (1889) J.D. JOHNSTON

270 Thames Street

KINSLEY BUILDING (1891-93) DUDLEY NEWTON

Thames Street at Green Street

MAIN POST OFFICE & CUSTOM HOUSE (1916)
JAMES A. WETMORE

Thames Street at Franklin Street

Even beyond Queen Anne Square, there is not much left to the architectural integrity of what used to be the commercial zone of Thames Street on either side of what was the old Market Square ferry landing about midway between Long Wharf and Memorial Boulevard. An early widening of Thames Street, along with later destructive urban redesign projects, has led to a mostly one-sided streetscape that is interrupted by parking lots and that holds little authentic sense of the old harborfront. A few large-scale structures remain scattered along the east side of Thames to suggest what was once a more architecturally cohesive commercial and civic zone.

The Edward Newton Block, designed and constructed by local architect-builder Johnston, is a tall masonry building that features arched windows stretching over two stories on its exposed street elevations. Their rough-cut trim and large size give the building a monumentality beyond its constricted, trapezoidal lot. Johnston also constructed a private residence, no longer extant, for the owner of this commercial block and worked, moreover, on a bank with which he was involved—something that hints at the network of contacts and commissions that were present among the year-round residents of late-nineteenth-century Newport.

A few years later, Dudley Newton treats his Kinsley Block quite differently as he emphasizes the angled site by placing his heavily rusticated entryway at the corner in a vaguely Romanesque Revival vocabulary that is a departure from most of his other work.

Finally, at the corner of Thames and Franklin Streets, the looming presence of the U.S. Post Office and Customs House was erected in a Georgian Revival style just then becoming popular for civic buildings. Set up on a story-high masonry podium, its upper stories feature arched windows, top fans, and grill work that suggest late-eighteenth-century Adamesque English sources. The block of this building is chamfered and allows for an early vest pocket park. Instead of an entryway, this green space features two magnificent grafted beech trees flanking a tall flagpole whose base sports shells, dolphins, and other marine motifs. Finally, the pole sits atop a large compass rose whose directional points remind us of a time when Newport's Customs House saw maritime traffic from all over the world.

4

4   SEAMAN'S CHURCH INSTITUTE (1929-30)
FREDERICK RHINELANDER KING, CHAPEL FRESCOES
(1930-33) DURR FREIDLY

18 Market Square

This institution, one of the few remaining architectural artifacts reflecting the life of the old central harbor and its ferry landing, was built before the area had become a tourist mecca. It houses a social organization for sailors that was founded with private monies. While in his choice of revival forms and materials the architect could easily have been influenced by colonial buildings from Boston to Philadelphia, the broken arched pediment and its gilded pineapple make a specific reference to Newport's own Colony House. More peculiar, perhaps, is its strangely shaped rear elevation, this due to the confines of the lot boundaries when an adjacent parcel of land could not be procured to fill out a rectangular shape.

Some of the interior furnishings are well preserved — an appropriately wood paneled library and a large painted map in the entryway — but the real treat here is on the second floor. A small chapel there is intensely decorated with metalwork fittings and stone trim that hint at Art Deco influences framing frescoes by the artist Durr Freidly. His hefty figures echo the mural style of the

5   6

decade while his multitude of saintly subjects all relate to maritime activities (did you know there is a patron saint of rope makers?).

5 HARBOR MASTERS OFFICE (2003) WILLIAM BURGIN

Perrotti Park

The shape of this small building suggests its maritime focus as does its orientation to the water. Facing the harbor is a layered set of spaces — an uppermost gable sheltering the top balcony, then more enclosed space with hipped roof over the curved canopy above the ground floor that projects farthest from the building. This is the most public space in the building, where ferry tickets can be purchased, so it is unfortunate that this is also where one has the greatest sense that the structure was shoehorned into its very limited site with an iron fence and the edge of the dock all but pressed up to the building itself.

There is a strong sense here of maritime culture. The overlooks and stepped arrangement of forms recall both the Shingle Style architecture for which Newport is justly famous but also play with the forms of nautical architecture — for example, a forecastle moved toward the prow of this landlocked structure. This naval imagery is underscored by a very nautical flagpole replete with yardarm jutting up from the top deck. On the interior, industrial style hardware, muscular steel plate fittings, and exposed beefy beams complete this particular architectural trope.

7 8

6   JOHN ODLIN-JONATHAN OTIS HOUSE (c. 1705)

109-111 Spring Street

This is a house, only one-room deep, whose lengthy gabled shape hugs the street and is more horizontally stretched than usual for such eighteenth-century structures. One of its early owners, Otis, was a goldsmith but the building was later used as a Quaker boys' school. Other notable features are its brick south elevation and the powerful projection of its overhanging eave, perhaps a vestige of medieval framing techniques seen on other Newport buildings of this early date.

7   JAMES BROWN-SAMUEL BARKER HOUSE (1714, MID-EIGHTEENTH CENTURY)

119 Spring Street

This house has a great presence, not least because of its two brick-end walls with paired chimneys. The tops of these broad, textural brick expanses are shaped by the angled ends of the gambrel roof. Although we can document that some form of this building existed by 1714, the size and detailing of what can still be seen here is more likely a renovation done during Newport's era of economic success in the mid-eighteenth century when numerous small houses were enlarged and aggrandized.

8   JOHN PRESTON MANN HOUSE (c. 1827, c. 1860)

129 Spring Street

Somewhat distinct from its colonial and later nineteenth-century neighbors, the Mann House has the Greek Revival trim of a triangular pediment window and big pilasters marking its corners. These features are only seen on a few other houses in Newport, notably in the Point neighborhood *(see Tour Two)*. The projecting entrance of the Mann House, with its Italianate arched windows over a granite foundation and the peculiarly large cross gable above both, appears to date from a later mid-nineteenth-century set of renovations.

9

9 VANDERBILT HALL (YOUNG MEN'S CHRISTIAN ASSOCIATION) (1908-10) ERVING & CHAPPELL, (1997-98, 2006-2007) NEWPORT COLLABORATIVE ARCHITECTS

Mary Street (at Clarke Street)

Erected by the Vanderbilt family as a memorial to Cornelius Vanderbilt, owner of the Breakers, this was initially intended to be an enlightened social club counteracting more unseemly entertainments for young men. The restraint and propriety of its Georgian Revival exterior augment its moralizing intent. As one of the earliest civic institutional buildings to employ Georgian and Federal Revival forms built during an era of massive European immigration, it provides us with a glimpse of the kind of nativist meaning (to counteract the unacceptable threat of newcomers) that such forms held at least in part for architectural clients with wealth and older family ties. Stylistically, its revivalism heralds what would become a dominant choice for Newport's institutional buildings in the first 40 years of the twentieth century.

In 1997-98, the Hall was attentively restored and expanded by Mohamad Farzan of the Newport Collaborative to serve as a modern hotel. An extension to the southwest edge and an additional level was added within the hotel to almost double the interior space while carefully retaining the same revival detailing. Finally, an elegant little conservatory was inserted onto a rear brick courtyard at the juncture of the two main wings.

10 VERNON HOUSE (WILLIAM GIBBS-METCALF BOWLER-WILLIAM VERNON HOUSE) (BEFORE 1708), RENOVATED (c. 1760) PETER HARRISON

46 Clarke Street

This is a distinguished example of mid-eighteenth-century American architecture and one of the most sophisticated residen-

*Metcalf Bowler
was an dilettante
who prized
this architectural
currency.*

10

tial designs in Newport. Like many of the other buildings whose histories reflect the economic boom of Newport in the two decades before the Revolutionary War, the current form of this house is the result of a substantial renovation and expansion, probably around 1760, when it was first owned by Metcalf Bowler. Framing features differ from one end of the house to the other, suggesting an original smaller house owned by Gibbs (set off the corner and facing Mary Street) that was updated after a subsequent owner, Charles Bowler, sold the house to his son, Metcalf, in 1759.

Documentation to back up the attribution to Peter Harrison is lacking but many of the stylistic elements of the house strongly suggest his authorship. Its hipped roof, modillion block cornice, wooden plank sheathing meant to emulate rusticated stone block, and its use of correctly proportioned classical elements such as the entry surround of attached Doric piers supporting an entablature of triglyphs and metopes all underscore this as a Harrison design. Moreover, the gentleman-architect would have had strong ties to the new owner who was a prominent mercantile and political leader in the town. Metcalf Bowler was just the kind of worldly amateur and dilettante, in the positive eighteenth-century uses of those terms, who would have prized the kind of architectural currency that only Harrison could offer. Not only was Bowler involved with the Redwood Library, through which he would have known Harrison's work firsthand, but he was well regarded in the broader social and political circles of his fractious era. He had a network of positions that eventually included a long tenure as a member of the colonial Assembly and as a Supreme Court Justice, even while serving for a time as a secret agent for Britain.

The enlargement he commissioned would have suited his elevated social status as he added a central hall, which shifted the entry to Clarke Street, and two additional rooms to create a balanced, generously proportioned interior. One need only compare this house to others along this block—big gambrel-roofed clapboarded structures

11 12

that retain the kind of small-scale details of window and molding trim used for decades — to see how distinctly elegant and stately was Harrison's vocabulary of historical forms. Instead of appending a classical entry onto an older set of forms, Harrison allows this newer classical spirit to inform every aspect of his design.

A remarkable set of interior paintings, probably created in the 1740s, was discovered under the parlor paneling during restoration in the twentieth century. These are walls covered in deep red tones and frescoed with arcane Chinese subjects probably prompted by the advent of the China trade. These are then framed in heavy bolection moldings as was the fashion in the early century.

With the coming of the Revolutionary War, both occupant and architect eventually retreated from Newport — Bowler to his country estate in Portsmouth, and Harrison, a few years later, to New Haven, where he found his professional reputation was overshadowed by his loyalist stance. The house on Clarke Street was purchased by the banker, merchant, and patriot, William Vernon, in 1773. It was later used by the Comte de Rochambeau, General of the French forces, as his headquarters. Here he met with Washington over dinner to plan strategy. For all its architectural and historical interest, this house is still in private hands and is not generally open to the public.

11 **ROBERT STEVENS HOUSE** (c. 1709, 1742-55)

31 Clarke Street

12 **CALEB HOLLINGSWORTH-JOSEPH BURRILL HOUSE** (EARLY EIGHTEENTH CENTURY, THIRD QUARTER OF EIGHTEENTH CENTURY)

28 Clarke Street

Two big houses that show variations on eighteenth-century forms. Both are two-and-a-half-story gambrel-roofed structures, and both are probably enlarged from earlier, smaller structures on

The pronounced random-course ashlar walls were the work of a Scot stone master.

13

these sites for which there is documentary evidence. The uneven floor levels on the interior of the Burrill House are also strong evidence of such a renovation. Their features are the same — doubled chimneys, roof line, elaborate framing elements around the main entry — but they differ in their proportions and siting. The Stevens House sits end to street, its entry opening onto the southern garden. The system of bays on this elevation is also eccentric, perhaps reflecting the later additions. The Hollingsworth-Burrill House is more symmetrically bayed, with a central entry door on the street. It is also a shallower building, and this, along with its taller foundation course, gives the entire building and its gambrel a more vertical set of proportions.

It is important to remember that these big houses were the residences of successful mid-eighteenth-century artisans in Newport. Burrill was a "Tinn plate worker" who probably expanded his residence after he purchased it in 1755; Robert Stevens was another artisan, an upholsterer, but his house had a number of well-known residents — including, during the Revolutionary War, Conte Axel de Fersen and the Marquis de Damas, two of Rochambeau's aides-de-camp. Later, at the beginning of the nineteenth century, the American painter Washington Allston boarded in the house while studying with Samuel King at a nearby academy.

13 NEWPORT ARTILLERY COMPANY (1835)
ALEXANDER McGREGOR

23 Clarke Street

The granite block walls, set off by the pronounced relief of quoining and door frame, were the work of a Scot stone master who had arrived in Newport a few years earlier to supervise construction at Fort Adams. Here he used the same random-course ashlar stonework that he employed on a number of other residential and commercial buildings in town. This shed was originally a thick-walled, single-storied armory for this, the oldest continuously active military company in the country (it was chartered in 1741).

14

15

Its current strange proportions are due to the addition of a second story added early in the twentieth century.

14 CONDOMINIUMS (SECOND CONGREGATIONAL CHURCH) (1735) COTTON PALMER (BUILDER), ALTERATIONS (1847, 1874-75, 1944), CONDOMINIUM CONVERSION (1983) NEWPORT COLLABORATIVE ARCHITECTS

15 Clarke Street

This is a much-altered structure whose origins date back to the early-eighteenth-century era when Massachusetts-based Congregationalists first established several churches in Newport. They enlisted one of their own, Cotton Palmer, to build this (and the nearby First Congregational Church, 83 Mill Street, in the same year but also much altered), and it was to this church that Ezra Stiles was called to preach in 1755. Palmer's forms are all but totally subsumed under the changes made when a Baptist congregation started worshiping there in the mid-nineteenth century. Beyond a drastic shift toward Greek Revival finishes on both interior and exterior, their renovations included absorbing Palmer's protruding tower into the body of the building and lengthening its shed. Some of this work still informs the image of this building, although the nineteenth-century bell tower and spire were removed in the late 1940s. Its conversion into condominiums has at least preserved its bulky presence along Clarke Street in close proximity to the Stiles House across the way.

15 EZRA STILES HOUSE (c. 1756, 1834, c. 1847)

14 Clarke Street

When its most famous resident was living here, this big gambrel-roofed house was turned end to street, with its main entry facing the garden to the south where Stiles experimented with silk worm culture. This was only one of many scientific and humanistic Enlightenment-era endeavors with which the young minister was involved during his Newport years, before assuming the presi-

16

dency of Yale University. One such notable experience among many in Newport was his viewing the transit of Venus on June 3, 1769 with his friend, Metcalf Bowler, a patron of the Redwood Library and Athenaeum, who lived just down the street. Not only had Stiles arrived in 1755 to become minister of the church across the way (and for whom this manse was built soon after), but he had spent a number of years as the librarian of the Redwood, the existence of which had attracted him to Newport in the first place and helped foster his expansive intellect.

Later owners turned the entrance to the street and altered the doorway into a more fashionable Greek Revival set of forms. By 1834, it was no longer a parsonage for the Congregationalists across the way, but some of the changes made in 1847 were probably still inspired by the Greek Revival alterations made that year to the earlier colonial structure.

16 WILLIAM REDWOOD HOUSE (MID-EIGHTEENTH CENTURY), ALTERED (c. 1800)

69 Spring Street

Both William Redwood and, later, his brother Abraham, benefactor of the Redwood Library, owned this house with its one brick wall. Except for that elevation, it was a typical gabled, five-bay house with central doorway until it was extended to the north, probably around 1800. While not the norm in Newport, a number of houses in this densely built neighborhood have such brick walls, perhaps as a precaution, for those who could afford it, against ruinous fires.

The elaborate classical entry and fanlight probably date from around the time of the addition. When looking at the doorway with its fluted pilasters, fine classical detailing, and rosettes, it is well to remember that such carpentered surrounds, although inspired by carved stone sources, had to be painstakingly constructed out of numerous, individually crafted wood parts that only gained visual coherency when assembled.

17   18

17 NEW JERSEY HOUSE (c. 1800)

72 Spring Street

If this house appears somewhat peculiar, it is because it is essentially a Dutch Colonial farmhouse, moved, as its name implies, from New Jersey by Doris Duke and the Newport Restoration Foundation. Its wide-planked sheathing, short second-story windows, and low-angled gable with almost flush eaves all reflect the rural architecture of the Netherlandish settlements around New Amsterdam (now better known as Manhattan). Although it has little to do with colonial Newport, its out-of-context preservation raises issues of what, where, and how to save old buildings that are a part of Newport's more recent architectural discourse.

18 TOURO SYNAGOGUE (1759-1763) PETER HARRISON

72 Touro Street

Built for a remarkable community that first came to Newport over a century before this house of worship was erected, this was originally called the Jew's Synagogue. As early as 1677 the Jewish community had purchased a lot farther up the hill to serve as their burying ground, but it wasn't until 1759 that this land was purchased as the site for their house of worship.

As with Peter Harrison's earlier Redwood Library, here on the Touro Synagogue he allows the functional program of the interior spaces to dictate the exterior massing of his building. The surprising element here is the reticence of Harrison's design, with two different-sized masonry blocks relieved only by the dark sandstone arched entry porch (based on earlier pattern book designs by English architect James Gibbs). The smaller wing originally held school rooms, and the larger sanctuary block was vertically divided with balconies and superimposed columns not unlike Harrison's church designs for Cambridge and Boston. The Synagogue is the only one of Harrison's buildings that has remained essentially unchanged by later renovations or additions.

This earliest surviving North American synagogue does, however, cloak such an elaborately appointed interior—replete with ornate metalwork, balustrades, English paneling, and Dutch-influenced furnishings—that it might best be appreciated as an architectural metaphor for the experience of Jewish life in eighteenth-century Newport: lives richly led within the community of their faith but presented with modest rectitude to the broader, albeit tolerant, citizenry. A similar symbolic approach might have led to other hidden meanings in the design. The twelve major columns on the interior probably symbolize the twelve tribes of Israel and the congregation installed a trap door at the center of the raised platform or Bimeh that has no utilitarian value, as it leads nowhere, but may serve as a powerful reminder of intolerance and exodus.

To the general public, though, it is only in the Synagogue's distinctive siting, which allows for the holy ark to face to the east and Jerusalem, that the building reveals its ancient, non-English roots. George Washington and many other notables have attended services here, a religious site which is now listed on the National Historic Register. Even more intriguing in architectural terms, Thomas Jefferson, while accompanying Washington on his trip to Newport in 1790, would have seen in this and Newport's other Harrison buildings an interest in Palladian classicism similar to his own, and one that would see its full expression at Monticello.

19

19 JEWISH COMMUNITY CENTER (LEVI GALE HOUSE) (c. 1835) RUSSELL WARREN, MOVED TO PRESENT SITE (1915)

85 Touro Street

Across the way from the Synagogue is this large residence created by the maverick Bristol, Rhode Island architect, Russell Warren, for a New Orleans merchant who moved to Newport. His own interpretation of a late Greek Revival idiom, this is a wood-framed, upright block with a projecting classical entry portico that is set beneath a heavy entablature. The most eye-catching parts of the design are the four deeply fluted monumental pilasters on the front that are capped with the most florid capitals imaginable. While the composition of these varied parts is not quite resolved, these four major elements are grouped toward the center. At the ends are the quirky hybrid forms for which Warren was known — corner piers whose rustication suggests quoining blocks. At the very top, stepped parapets once trimmed both the projecting attic story and the principal roof (these panels have long been lost).

The house sat on the eastern end of Washington Square but was split in two and moved up the hill to prepare that site for the new County Court House built in the 1920s. Today, the scale and sloping site of the Levi Gale House, not to mention its somewhat idiosyncratic forms and indecisive composition, make it appear ungainly in the context of the smaller, colonial buildings nearby. It is now used for offices and other social activities associated with the congregation.

20

20 NEWPORT HISTORICAL SOCIETY & SEVENTH DAY BAPTIST MEETING HOUSE

(1729) MEETING HOUSE ATTRIBUTED TO RICHARD MUNDAY, MEETING HOUSE RESTORED (1884) GEORGE CHAMPLIN MASON, JR, MEETING HOUSE MOVED TO PRESENT SITE (1887), ENTRY PORCH (1889), LIBRARY ADDITION (1902) G.H. RICHARDSON, (BUILDER?), CENTRAL WING (1915) JOSEPH G. STEVENS, FRONT ENTRY PORCH (1917) NORMAN ISHAM

82 Touro Street

The Newport Historical Society contains the most valuable collection of archives, artifacts, and sites for the study of Newport architecture. Its headquarters may have the lengthiest architectural pedigree in Newport. It is made up of buildings pieced together from historical, revival, and new components over the course of about 30 years, beginning in the 1880s. Founded in 1854, the Society was originally the southern cabinet of the older Rhode Island Historical Society and its myriad collections were housed in the originally separate seventeenth-century meeting house, all hung floor to ceiling in a nineteenth-century-style arrangement that comes across now more as attic storage than museum display. Today the early meeting house is the most important component of the complex, situated at the rear of the lot and accessible only through other rooms and galleries. In religiously tolerant Newport, this was the place of worship for the denomination founded by Stephen Mumford. The meeting house was only a short distance away from the home on Broadway he built some years earlier that is now known as the Wanton-Lyman Hazard House *(see Tour One).*

21

Although its original wooden exterior is now encased in a brick veneer, most of the meeting house interior remain — including window openings, paneling taken from earlier pews that filled the floor space, balcony, and the stunning elevated pulpit. This last is in a wine-glass configuration with side extensions that sport eighteenth-century tombstone-shaped paneling and a sounding board above. While its placement centered on a long wall opposite the entry is in keeping with conventions of meeting house form, its details of panel work, such as the Union Jack cross motif under the sounding board, and its decorative elements, such as the amazingly double-twisted balusters, are similar to elements found on Richard Munday's Trinity Church designed a few years earlier *(see Entry 1 of this Tour)*.

After being moved to Touro Street, the meeting house was joined on the site by a hipped-roof library wing probably configured to echo the forms of the Touro Synagogue next door. This was in turn enlarged for additional storage and gallery space about a decade later via the banality of the bricked central wing. The final piece of this complex was added in 1917, when an elevated entry porch in a fitting Colonial Revival style was designed by the early preservationist architect Norman M. Isham, who later worked with the Society restoring the Wanton-Lyman-Hazard House *(see Tour One)*, which they acquired in the 1920s.

22

There have long been calls for a new, updated facility to more properly display and store the Society's unique collections. Some of these plans include the notion of moving the meeting house out from behind its utilitarian wings, revealing its original clapboards and creating a small "campus" for the study of Newport history.

21 BENJAMIN MARSH HOUSE (c. 1845)

20 School Street

Try to imagine the visual surprise of such a delightfully decorated cottage in the midst of the unrelenting sameness of its colonial neighbors. Here, the cruciform-plan, high-pitch cross gables and ornamental pendants and droplets evoke medieval forms, at least as conceived of and romanticized by a designer in the early nineteenth century. While some of the sawn cutouts do derive from medieval sources, the whole ensemble is more closely linked to the kind of cottage orné once popularized nationally by the designs and publications of Andrew Jackson Downing and Alexander Jackson Davis.

22 AUGUSTUS LUCAS HOUSE (1721), ENLARGED (c. 1745-50)

40 Division Street

There are numerous anomalies on both the exterior and interior of this house that betray its mid-eighteenth-century alteration. Doubled stairwells on the interior, each with a different stylistic finish, and the off-centered chimneys, one behind the other, are clear evidence of these changes. The gablet on the hipped roof might here be another indication that a smaller house was made grander around the mid-eighteenth century by Lucas, who was known locally as one of the biggest slave traders at a time when such trade helped fuel Newport's economy. This was no clandestine operation, however, as he may have housed his slaves in this building, even advertising his human consignments in *The Newport Mercury*. His more benign experiments in fruit grafts

It is ironic that Hopkins, a clergyman and early abolitionist, lived so close to Lucas, a slavetrader.

23

conducted in the orchard on his property remind us that even in this densely built district many colonial houses still had sizeable gardens close by.

23 DR SAMUEL HOPKINS HOUSE (c. 1751)

46 Division Street

This gambrel-roofed house, set end to street, has an off-center, inset doorway. In the eighteenth century, with so little space between front elevations and streets, builders found numerous ways to compose entry stairs, running them at right angles to the entrance or, as in this case, setting them within the plane of the building. The overall typical shape of this house is made even more picturesque today by the irregularities of the north wall caused by structural deflections.

Given its proximity to the Lucas residence two doors away, which housed a slave trader and probably some of his slaves, it is ironic that Hopkins (who lived here from 1770 to 1805) was a clergy-man, author, and theologian known for being a follower of Jonathan Edwards but remembered more today for being an early abolitionist. His progressive beliefs made him the model for "Dr H," the moral compass and hero of Harriet Beecher Stowe's novel *The Minister's Wooing*, serialized in 1858-59. The novel is set in eighteenth-century Newport and Hopkins' "old manse" must have attracted the novelist in her search for a romanticized American past.

24

25

24 UNION CONGREGATIONAL CHURCH (1834)

49 Division Street

The verticality of this building, a former African-American church—accented by its high-pitched gable, ornate finial, and tall board-and-batten sheathing—is doubly emphasized in its context of earlier colonial structures. Its exposed beams and curved trusses under roof eaves and around the entry porch trim are an early expression of stickwork in a Carpenter Gothic style. This was an idiom used locally for other wood-frame chapels, but most of these have long since disappeared.

25 MARY B. NEWTON HOUSE (c. 1883) DUDLEY NEWTON

52 Division Street

Another delightfully different house amid the earlier, more regimented look of its colonial neighbors, this presents a potpourri of ornamental effects with intersecting gables, coves, bay windows, multiple shingle patterns, lathed posts, and cut-out panel work. It also differs from earlier houses by sitting back from the street and adjacent lots, set off with more surrounding space. There are strong overtones in some of these elements of the Colonial Revival but, in Newton's hands, these forms are more decorative than historical. Although listed under the name of the architect's mother, this was also Newton's home. He likely considered such a tour de force of ornament to be a convincing advertisement for his skills and sensibility.

26

26 JOHN VARS-BENJAMIN TISDALE HOUSE (c. 1833)

70 Church Street

THOMAS GODDARD HOUSE (c. 1800)

78 Church Street

WILLIAM CARD HOUSE (1811)

73 Division Street

CHRISTOPHER ELLERY HOUSE (c. 1750-60), ALTERED (NINETEENTH CENTURY), RESTORED (LATE TWENTIETH CENTURY) RICHARD LONG

80 Division Street

The house, at 80 Division Street, is an ample, gable-on-hip-roofed edifice raised above street level in compensation for its sloping site. In its handsome proportions and reserved classical detailing, it is very much part of the mid-eighteenth century decade when the design sensibility of Peter Harrison held sway over Newport architecture. Much of its early interior woodwork survived later alterations and, most recently, the house has undergone restoration by its owner, Richard Long, a Newport architect known for his work in historical contexts.

The remaining three houses show different early-nineteenth-century approaches to exterior design while still adhering closely to the plan and general form of earlier buildings. Of the three, the Goddard House is the earliest and closest to colonial precedents—except for the strange, rusticated window caps, crudely reminiscent of Peter Harrison's work, that were evidently added to make the house more fashionable at the turn of the nineteenth century. As the residence for a member of the famed Goddard furniture-making family, the house also has exceptional interior woodwork.

The Card House is another early-nineteenth-century, three-quarter house set amid a fine block of similarly designed buildings. Still retaining the gabled shape, windows pushed up under the

eaves, and clapboards from the earlier colonial period, there are newer exterior details here as well. Its entryway surround is topped by a glazed fan that projects up into the triangular pediment, condensing two elemental geometric shapes. More subtly, window trim is set flush with the clapboarding, so that the older carpentered reveals of sills and caps are lessened, creating a greater sense of unity on the elevation.

The Vars-Tisdale House from the 1830s shows how different elements began to influence architectural design in the second quarter of the nineteenth century so that the design can be seen to edge toward a fuller classical revival. A porch, with Doric columns and a wreath relief entablature, now boldly projects from the front elevation (the story above the porch is a later enclosure). Flat, paneled end boards intended to be read as attached pilasters define the corners, while a monitor attic story projects above the main roof. Vars is probably responsible for the look of the house, built soon after he purchased the property in 1833. Tisdale was a silversmith who bought it in 1846.

27 ST JOHN'S LODGE MASONIC TEMPLE (1803, 1830, 1846, 1860, 1876, c. 1880)

50 School Street

No less an architectural figure than Peter Harrison is associated with the origins of this Masonic Temple constructed for a lodge that was founded in 1749. Harrison may have drawn up plans for such a Masonic building in 1760, but little if anything was constructed above foundation level until later. One recently identified early watercolor shows a modest gabled structure on the site that was possibly constructed by a local contractor, J. Cahoone and Sons, by 1803. What we see today is the result of a long series of expansions and alterations throughout the nineteenth century that created what may be the largest non-religious wood-frame structure still standing from that period in Newport.

27

28

The current configuration, reached by 1887, appears as two Federal-style gabled buildings running parallel to each other and joined by a flat-topped entry tower that extends to the rear as a monitor-roofed projection. From the front, this tower motif, decorated with carpentered crenellations and set atop a triumphal arched entryway of Doric columns, might be an interpretive allusion to Solomon's Temple, the ancient building at the core of Masonic belief and ritual. The circular panels within each flanking gable held wooden reliefs of Masonic symbols. Although derelict today, the somewhat surprising scale of this structure reminds us how widespread and important a role this organization once played in Newport.

28 SPRING STREET COMMERCIAL BUILDINGS

DOUBLE STORE BUILDING (c. 1830)

105-107 Spring Street

STORE BLOCK (EARLY NINETEENTH CENTURY) (c. 1895) DUDLEY NEWTON

135-137 Spring Street

THEODORE R. HELME BLOCK (1860s) DUDLEY NEWTON

148-160 Spring Street

Much of the hill above Thames Street is residential, but by the nineteenth century business buildings began cropping up among the private homes on the busy thoroughfare of Spring Street. Several notable examples still survive along this stretch of the narrow street — some with Colonial Revival accents, others retaining much-earlier design elements.

105-107 Spring Street is a relatively rare, well-restored example of an early-nineteenth-century brick store block with hipped-roof and granite trim. The stone wheat sheaf relief, set high on the street elevation, identified the building as a bakery. Nearby, at 135-137 Spring Street, the odd proportions and decorative details of another

hipped-roof double storefront, this one in wood, is the result of a late-19-century Queen Anne renovation by Newporter Dudley Newton, which he layered onto an earlier Federal period structure.

Across the way is perhaps an earlier work by the same architect. The copious glazing of the Helme block, stretching as it does across multiple storefronts, must have persuaded promenading strollers to stop and shop. It has been sensitively restored to its original Second Empire design, down to the detail of polychrome paint, decorative moldings, and ornate metal roofline rails. If it is by Newton, it would be a work from very early in his career, perhaps during or just after his apprenticeship in the office of another prominent local architect, George C. Mason, Sr.

29 SAMUEL BOURS HOUSE (1777)

175 Spring Street

JONATHAN GIBBS HOUSE (BEFORE 1777)

181 Spring Street

JONATHAN GIBBS HOUSE (1784)

185 Spring Street

Here is an unself-consciously vernacular grouping of late-eighteenth-century houses: one with entry set along the street, another set close to it, and the last with its gambrel end facing the street — adjacencies that were typical of colonial Newport. The varied shapes — one and two stories, gambrel and gable — reflect architecturally the social mix of their residents. Bours was a merchant whose son Jonathan took possession of the house in 1805. An important merchant in his own right, Jonathan had his portrait painted by John Singleton Copley (his wife's was done by Joseph Blackburn). Gibbs was a housewright who built both the other structures and sold them in the 1780s. The house at 185 Spring Street has an irregularly shaped ell at the rear and was given some Greek Revival detailing, perhaps after it was sold to a new owner in 1836.

29   30

30 NEWPORT CONGREGATIONAL CHURCH (UNITED CONGREGATIONAL CHURCH) (1857)
JOSEPH WELLS, MURALS (1880-81) JOHN LA FARGE

Spring Street at Pelham Street

As designed by New York architect Wells, this sandstone edifice is specifically inspired by Lombard Romanesque precedents. But it more generally conforms to the style deemed appropriate in a Congregational Church publication of 1853 — round-arched forms thought simpler than the Gothic imagery favored by other denominations. Its dour blockiness was originally lightened by the more elegant forms of tapering roofs that once capped each tower.

While it has a commodious interior with a big medieval arcade and flat ceiling, it is the ornament, not the space, that is most compelling here. A generation after it was erected, John La Farge was commissioned to decorate this vast space and he took his cues from exotic sources — intricate color patterns inspired by Oriental carpets and the marble work of southern Italian churches. La Farge had just finished his decorative work on Boston's Trinity Church under the direction of H. H. Richardson. Add to his rug-patterned panels the beautiful opalescent stained glass in geometric patterns, the painted tabernacle to the east, and a Tiffany lamp hanging above and the result is a highly elaborate ensemble of color and light, perhaps not what the previous generation of church leaders had in mind with the original sandstone building and its minimal interior décor. This contrast creates a kind of separation between the vitality of La Farge's surface ornament and the simplicity of its raw space, which creates a more disjunctive effect than that of his Boston work where more intricate architectural detail helps complement and anchor La Farge's efforts.

Ironically, a well-known leader of Newport's African American community lived here under his slave name.

31

There is an interesting historical note on the architect Wells. He went on to become a major figure in the office of McKim, Mead & White and there, in the 1880s, advocated the use of Renaissance Revival forms for which the firm became so well known.

31 CAPTAIN JOHN MAWDSLEY HOUSE (c. 1680, c. 1750)

228 Spring Street

The gable on hip-roofed house set back from the busy street seems at first glance a typically formed eighteenth-century house in the grand manner—with elegant proportions and ornate details of pedimented doorway, modillion cornice, and a central-segmented scroll dormer. While the front block of this house dates from that era, the rear section was originally the small two-room Jireh Bull House from about 1680. Although covered over in an eighteenth-century skin, that seventeenth-century house structure remains all but intact and is today most visible in the brawny chamfered summer beams still evident on the interior (the division between the seventeenth- and eighteenth-century sections is visible on the outside in the slight offset about halfway back along the John Street elevation, and in the different cadence of the windows toward the rear). Soon after he married, Captain John Mawdsley, a wealthy ship owner and privateer, acquired the smaller house, probably enlarging and updating it to confirm his social standing in a community of other wealthy maritime merchants. The correct Georgian classicism of its composition and details is clearly informed by the then-current sensibility of Peter Harrison.

Like the owner of the Augustus Lucas House a few blocks away, Mawdsley possessed a large number of slaves, many of whom may also have lived here in the Revolutionary War era. Ironically, some years later the house was purchased by another merchant, Caleb Gardner, and during that time a well-known leader of Newport's African American community lived here under his slave name of

All steps projecting from doorways were removed so that his officers would not trip over them.

32

Newport Gardner. He helped found the African Humane Society, and often went by his African name, Occramar Marycoo. After manumission, he eventually purchased his own small house south of here on Pope Street *(see Tour Nine)*.

32 JOHN BANISTER TOWN HOUSE (1751-64), DOORWAY (EARLY-NINETEENTH-CENTURY)

56 Pelham Street

The first owner of this fine in-town residence is thoroughly documented in detailed account books, letters, and other sources in the collection of the Newport Historical Society. He records the date that this house was begun in one of his ledgers. As a wealthy merchant and the brother-in-law of architect Peter Harrison, Banister was a man of substance in pre-Revolutionary Newport. As with many mid-eighteenth-century merchants, his town house was sited just up the hill from his warehouses and other properties on Thames Street. Some of his income came from smuggling, not that uncommon an activity in the age of tariffs and tax stamps.

This is an impressive, spacious residence with a central staircase hall, two chimneys, and a generous gambrel roof and Harrison-like pediments on its dormers. Harrison had been employed by Banister in his maritime business before marrying Elisabeth Pelham, the sister of Banister's wife, Hermione Pelham, through whom this lot had been inherited. There are visual relationships here to other prominent houses of the era, most notably to the Hunter House on Washington Street *(see Tour Two)*. On the interior, however, only the hearth walls of the Banister House are fully paneled and this woodwork is beveled and flat, unlike the more common, earlier use of heavy bolection moldings.

The house had another, more infamous resident. During the British occupation of Newport, from 1776 to 1779, the British commander, General Richard Prescott, unpopular with much of the town's citizenry, was billeted here and used this house as the

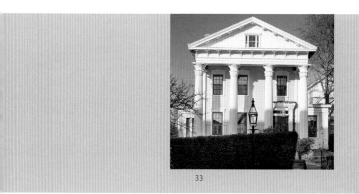

33

headquarters of his occupying force. One probably apocryphal architectural tale related to Prescott is that he ordered all steps projecting from Newport doorways to be removed so that his officers would not trip over them after a night of drinking. Folklore has it that residents then had to enter their houses by means of short ladders that could then be taken in at night until the occupation ended. This is sometimes used to explain the preponderance of recessed doorways in Newport, but the truth is that the inset doorway here, with its classical details and low-arched opening, was added later, perhaps around the time that the house was sold out of the Banister family in 1821. It was probably a fashionable update attempting to offer entry protection against the weather.

33 CAPTAIN AUGUSTUS LITTLEFIELD HOUSE
(1836) JOHN LADD (BUILDER)

70 Pelham Street

Seldom do we see such an exuberant use of the Greek Revival in Newport. The relatively fanciful combination of Greek and Egyptianate motifs on the colonnade probably reflect a provincial practitioner and a late revival phase, though surely the Italianate pediment brackets are there to satisfy the owner's desire for "an authentic copy of an Italian Villa" requested after a trip to southern Italy. Two later inhabitants confirm the impressive, status-bearing effect this house must have had in mid-nineteenth-century Newport: Governor Charles Van Zandt, and then architect J.D. Johnston, who used it as a studio/office and whose large construction business and mill were located just to the rear on Mill Street.

34

35

34 BUTLER HOUSE (c. 1860)

92-94 Pelham Street

One of the few large Italianate villas in Newport, the Butler House makes effective use of its bold three-story tower to assert its corner site. The imposing proportions of the tower are made still more so by the addition of tall thin windows set with different shapes and trim rising at its center. The middle block is organized into bays by the monumental pilasters and capped by a peculiarly doubled round-arch dormer. On the right, the smallest wing is an attached office whose entry is recessed behind a set of Ionic columns. The whole is an admixture of historical elements, loosely based on classical antecedents but combined more freely than on earlier Greek Revival designs. In both composition and details, the Butler House makes for an interesting comparison to two other notable Italianate villas: the more resolved design of the Edward King House, and the more rambling forms of the Joseph Hart House *(see Tour Eight)*.

35 MICHEL FELICE CORNÉ HOUSE (BEFORE 1822)

2 Corne Street

The eccentric composition of front windows and doorway may be the only hint on the present exterior that part of this building was originally a barn converted to residential use in 1822 by the Neapolitan painter Corné. Before coming to Newport, Corné had gained an elite clientele, having decorated major Federal style houses in Salem, Boston, and Providence. Besides the typicality of its early-nineteenth-century entryway, this house is as famous for what its owner painted on the interior (murals on canvas of seascapes and other scenes since removed) and for what he planted in its garden (purported to be the first cultivation of the tomato in America).

Across Corne Street is a row of attached townhouse-type residences that, despite their overall eighteenth-century appearance, were

36   37

built only recently. Like a number of other faux-historic structures in Newport (e.g., those on Bridge and Thames Streets), these are a caution to anyone trying to date buildings in Newport based solely on visual information.

Just up the street, the petite Gothic cottage at 82 Mill Street was the home and studio in the mid-nineteenth century of another artist, Jane Stuart, daughter of Gilbert Stuart and a noted painter in her own right.

36 ROBERT LAWTON HOUSE (1809)
118 Mill Street

The Lawton House is a striking example of a large Federal house, a few of which were built in Newport despite the early-nineteenth-century downturn in Newport's economy. Its severe block is capped with a monitor roof, brick walls with crisp corners, and inset windows cleanly cut into the flat wall. This reductivist geometry is used to define the central bay, as arched and circle openings sit above the straightforward Doric columns of the classical porch. These all reaffirm the erect sensibility of this impressive house whose Federal style is somewhat compromised by later additions of decorative ironwork that recall southern sources.

37 JOHN TILLINGHAST HOUSE (1760)
142 Mill Street

This is a handsome gable-on-hipped-roof house whose size and fashionable Georgian details are in keeping with the then-current taste of the Peter Harrison era in Newport. Tillinghast had been a member of the small building committee that had commissioned Harrison to design the Redwood Library in the late 1740s, so he would have been familiar with both Harrison and his pattern book-inspired designs. One of the most appealing flourishes here, individualizing this design, is the replacement of rectilinear modillion blocks with more ornamental floral scroll brackets.

38

Some details in the railings and wings to the west and on the rear are later additions.

This house was for a short time the residence of a famous Rhode Islander—Revolutionary War general Nathaniel Greene. Given his rural upbringing, Greene must have felt he had achieved a measure of success by residing in such a sophisticated Newport house. It clearly afforded an august setting within which he could consult with other prominent military figures of the era, such as Baron von Steuben and General Kosciusko.

38 CHANNING MEMORIAL CHURCH (1880-81)
ELBRIDGE BOYDEN & SON

135 Pelham Street

Designed by a Worcester, Massachusetts architect in rough-cut, random course granite blocks, the most prominent forms here evoke late-nineteenth-century variations of the Gothic Revival. The main elevation is organized around a single dominant gable over a large, triple-bayed stained glass window and an independently positioned entry tower on the downhill side. A spindle turret, high-pitched dormers, pointed arch windows, and a tall tapering spire complete the effect originally referred to as English Gothic.

This Unitarian church is an architectural memorial, funded by international donations to honor the denomination founder, William Ellery Channing, who was born on nearby Division Street a century earlier. In keeping with such a significant site, great effort was lavished on its interior decoration. As the art historian James Yarnall has written, the Channing Memorial interior "exemplifies the English Arts and Crafts Movement, combining intricately carved woodwork and painted stucco" as well as the most important array of stained glass in Newport. Innovative techniques are used by John LaFarge on two works here as well as others by the Belcher Glass Company, Donald MacDonald, and Samuel West. Complementing these colorful works is another notable fixture: the bronze memorial relief of the congregation's first minister by Augustus Saint Gaudens.

The notion persists that this is still an artifact of an early Viking settlement.

39

Facing the church in Touro Park is a second memorial to Channing, completed a few years later. This full-length standing bronze figure of the minister in a rather imperial pose was designed in 1892 by William Clarke Noble, another Newport native, but was commissioned by William G. Weld of Massachusetts, where Channing spent so much of his career.

39 STONE MILL (c. 1673)

Touro Park

MATTHEW CALBRAITH PERRY MONUMENT
(1868) JOHN QUINCY ADAMS WARD, SCULPTOR, AND RICHARD MORRIS HUNT, ARCHITECT

Touro Park

The memorable stone cylinder atop a high circular arcade has long inspired myth and controversy about its origins and its function. One of Newport's most notable architectural treasures, it is no longer strictly speaking a building at all but rather the ruin of a seventeenth-century windmill. Despite documentary, historical, and scientific evidence all confirming its date and English colonial form, the notion persists that this is somehow an artifact of an early Viking settlement whose existence is lost in the coastal mists of time. The myth is a popular one that has prompted the adoption of "Vikings" as the high school mascots and provided the name of an early-twentieth-century hotel and dozens of other businesses, as well as the call letters of the old "VI" telephone exchange. But the truth is Vikings had nothing to do with this field stone structure.

From a conclusive array of evidence — including archaeological artifacts, carbon dating of the mortar, written documents, and architectural comparison with other known Anglo-American mill structures—we know that this is the windmill referred to by a wealthy seventeenth-century Newporter, Benedict Arnold (ancestor of the revolutionary spy), as his "stone built milne." Its

wooden parts, which would have included heavy beams supporting an interior floor at the arch level, wind vanes, and a rotating cap, were at least partially derelict by the 1740s. Look inside the cylinder and, amazingly, you will see traces of niches, openings, and other features corresponding to windows, a hearth, a staircase, and joists where these now-absent fixtures were set into the stone wall.

While its original use may have been quickly forgotten by most of the town's residents, the ancient agrarian structure was put to use in the eighteenth century as a hay loft and powder magazine before its Norse mythology began developing in the early nineteenth century. The tall tales may have at least partly served an effort to attract curiosity seekers to Newport as part of a proto-marketing tourism campaign. Perhaps just as tellingly, both its status as a ruin and its potential as a lookout point set high on the hill overlooking the Bay encouraged James Fenimore Cooper to use it in the opening and closing pages of his romantic pirate tale, *The Red Rover* (1828). The author, however, makes it clear in an introductory note that the Viking stories are flights of fantasy and that this wonderful stone construction is from Newport's nascent days. Cooper realized early on that the fanciful stories about its creation had already become folkloric in their retelling, yet those fictions are beside the point because the skeleton of Mr Arnold's stone mill remains a very real and visually compelling reminder of the earliest English town.

One of the other fixtures in the park is the larger-than-life figure of a favorite son, Matthew Calbraith Perry. His naval exploits, particularly his expedition of 1854-55 which "opened Japan" and

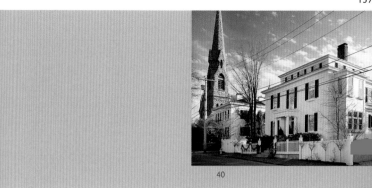

40

ended that country's two centuries of self-isolation, are commemorated here in a public monument resulting from an early collaboration between Ward and Hunt. The bronze shows Perry in a diplomatic pose and conveys dignity and rank; the realistic face may have been derived from an 1859 bust of Perry by the sculptor Erastus Dow Palmer.

The stepped and cylindrical shaft of granite was designed by Hunt and influenced by the faceted forms of the French-derived Second Empire style. Its shaft is encircled with a belt of bronze relief plaques also by Ward, which represent in great narrative detail various vignettes from Perry's career—not just those in Japan but others from his earlier successes in Africa and Mexico as well. The sculptor and architect were each at the beginning of long, illustrious professional lives and would go on to become preeminent leaders in their respective fields. Newport has many other works by Hunt but is also lucky to have a second, later bronze by Ward of another Newporter, August Belmont, now sited at the corner of Narragansett and Bellevue Avenues *(see Tour Seven)*. The Belmont and Perry families were related through marriage and they commissioned a number of monuments and memorials in Newport that combined private and public commemoration.

40 GREEK REVIVAL HOUSES (BEFORE 1850)

115 and 123 Pelham Street and vicinity

The south side of Pelham Street, close to Touro Park, has a subtly varied array of Greek Revival houses. Each has a hipped-roof main block set on a high foundation and an entry porch composed of cut-granite blocks, but each also has variations in composition or detailing. Although of wood construction, they attempt to emulate broader stone surfaces—as can be seen on the Swinburne House, at 115 Pelham, with its horizontal-board sheathing and flat-quioned corners. Projecting porches with classical columns, ornate door and light treatments, and bold cornices, all reflect the fashionable style of the 1840s and '50s, paralleling the

The Redwood Library is the perfect symbol of the town's mid-eighteenth-century intellectual sophistication and vitality.

41

design work of Alexander McGregor, the Scot stonemason active in Newport during those decades. Similar features can also be seen on his own house built about 1835 just two blocks away at 63 John Street.

41 REDWOOD LIBRARY & ATHENAEUM

(1748-1750) PETER HARRISON, GARDEN HOUSE FROM REDWOOD'S COUNTRY ESTATE IN MIDDLETOWN (LATE 1740s) PETER HARRISON, READING ROOM (1858) GEORGE SNELL, REAR ADDITION (NOW CALLED DELIVERY ROOM) (1875) GEORGE CHAMPLIN MASON, SR, FIREPROOF STACKROOM (1912-13), RESTORED (1915) NORMAN ISHAM, GARDEN HOUSE ALLÉE (1935) JOHN RUSSELL POPE, ENLARGED STACKS (1978-79) IRVING HAYNES, RESTORED HARRISON EXTERIOR (1998), ADDITIONS AND RENOVATIONS (1997-2006) SHEPLEY, BULFINCH, RICHARDSON AND ABBOTT

Bellevue Avenue between Redwood Street and Old Beach Road

Just as the Stone Mill across the way is emblematic of Newport's distant seventeenth-century agrarian past, the Redwood Library is the perfect symbol of the town's mid-eighteenth-century intellectual sophistication and economic vitality. Its site abuts the core of the old town down the hill, elevated above the crowded seaport with its din of daily life and bustling fray of mercantilism. Even more so than today, this center of intellectual life must have seemed like a temple to the secular ideal of learning, set up on an American acropolis. This singular building is the result of an earlier organization in Newport, the Philosophical Club, whose gentleman members met to read and discuss matters of the day. They gathered around Bishop Berkeley, the noted philosopher, poet, and churchman who for a time lived a few miles away at Whitehall (now in nearby Middletown). Even when he returned to England in 1732, the desire to perpetuate such an organization that encouraged intellectually free discourse was fostered by others,

notably with gifts from two successful merchants that helped erect the library building and amass its early collection of books (about the size of a wealthy gentleman's library); it was Abraham Redwood, Jr, who contributed 500 pounds for the purchase of books, and Henry Collins, who offered the lot of land on the perimeter of the built-up townscape.

Commissioned as it was by the leading businessmen of the era, it might be no surprise that we have a detailed contract outlining what the library was to look like upon completion. The contract, signed by Peter Harrison's brother Joseph, who was also a drafts-man, suggests that Joseph might be at least partially responsible for the finished design. Whoever initiated the contract, we know that Peter Harrison clearly directed the later stages of its con-struction after he had returned from an extended trip to London. Moreover, we know that much of his design sense was derived from an extensive library of pattern books, examples of which still exist in the Redwood Collections. Details taken from Edward Hoppus's *Palladio* (1735) and William Kent's *Designs of Inigo Jones and Others* (1727) were adopted for elements of the Redwood. Harrison's fundamental composition is drawn from a plate in Hoppus that shows a fully developed Roman temple front with projecting wings to either side and one bay-wide window. As built, the small office wings — with their sloping roofs — under-score the central pedimented portico that is supported by a monumental Doric colonnade more classically correct and grander in its ancient form than anything previously built in Newport. From the contract we know that the building was always intended to be a wooden structure "in Imitation of Rustick," perhaps the first such use of this sheathing in the

American colonies. The Harrison building had one large room, with proportions nearly that of a "double cube" (considered an ideal interior space in mid-nineteenth-century England). On the original rear wall were a set of Palladian windows so popular at the time that all the pattern books used by Harrison include this motif. They are now on the south side of the Snell Reading Room, having been moved there when that addition was constructed in 1858. The change in order from the Doric on the front to the more delicate Ionic on these windows suggests the way in which designs drawn from pattern books might result in less unified compositions in which each elevation is considered somewhat separately.

He may have received remuneration for his architectural work, but Harrison was an amateur in the eighteenth-century sense of the word and he approached his design work like the worldly, educated gentleman that he was, designing with one eye on the socially fashionable forms of Lord Burlington and his circle in London. Because of his reliance on graphic sources and his need to be current and correct in his classicism, there may be minor flaws here such as the way in which the wings are awkwardly joined to the main block or the fact that the scale of the portico and the sandstone platform, with its full-width flight of steps, are too majestic for the mullioned windows and minor trim of the library itself. Nevertheless, Harrison here creates the first public building in the colonies so thoroughly invested in Palladian classical forms. It is tempting to think that when Thomas Jefferson visited Newport some years later, Harrison's Redwood helped inspire Jefferson's ongoing work on that other famous Palladian structure, Monticello.

Luckily for Harrison's design, later additions have all respected his temple form (although one aborted idea in the nineteenth century did call for raising the Harrison building and setting it atop a new

*He designed with one eye
on the socially fashionable
forms of Lord Burlington and
his circle in London.*

addition!). Snell, Mason, and all the other architects who have worked here since then have distinguished their work from the original library by discreetly adding to the rear of the building, and through their different handling of surface treatment and reduced detail.

Behind the library is the bell-capped summer house that was originally part of Abraham Redwood's country house, several miles north of town. The small hexagonal structure, with its planking rusticated in similar fashion to the library, was probably used as an idyllic retreat or teahouse. Despite the fact that the Newport area was known for its elaborate colonial gardens, this little folly is one of the only such eighteenth-century garden structures to survive. It is set amid the mature arboreal specimens of the Redwood grounds and at the end of a long allée designed in the mid-twentieth century by John Russell Pope, another Newport resident.

Also on the grounds is the handsome sculpture of George Washington, a twentieth-century Gorham cast after the 1788-91 original by the French neoclassical sculptor, Jean Antoine Houdon, who was commissioned to produce this likeness by Thomas Jefferson. The General's very realistic face was created from a life cast made by Houdon on a trip to America. Its siting, unfortunately, obstructs a clear view to what is one of the most important elevations in America, although its subject is particularly fitting for the classically fronted library. Washington is depicted in the guise of the Roman hero Cincinnatus who left the comfort of his family farm to fight for his country. Even the symbolic Roman axe handle, or *fasces*, on which he leans constitutes the visual symbolic equivalent of the Federalist motto, "*e pluribus unum*." It is just this kind of symbolic language and classical idealism, so potent in the eighteenth century, that are evoked in the architectural forms of Harrison's knowledgeable design.

6. KAY-CATHERINE-OLD BEACH

Situated at the top of the hill leading up from the harbor, this neighborhood is dominated by late-nineteenth-century architecture. Once the back end of colonial properties that stretched up from Thames Street, the area encompassed today by Bellevue Avenue, Kay Street, Easton Pond, and Memorial Boulevard was developed in the 1840s and '50s from only a few gentleman's farms. Soon after the Civil War, however, it became the site of a great building boom. The roughly parallel roadways of Kay-Catherine-Old Beach are the major thoroughfares leading through the area from the old town, over the hilltop, and eastward to the pond and beach.

Local professionals and business leaders were clustered along Kay Street but much of this neighborhood reflects the influx of non-Newporters into the city, as it was fast becoming an important resort of the Gilded Age. Artists such as John La Farge (whose summer home was at 10 Sunnyside Place) and the writer Clement Moore of "Twas the night before Christmas" fame (he lived at 25 Catherine Street) joined other literary and scientific luminaries in residence along these streets. Moreover, this neighborhood was the center of architectural practice during those boom years—not just in the number of buildings erected but as the locale of most major architectural offices in town—Richard Morris Hunt, the Mason firm, Dudley Newton, Clarence Luce, J. D. Johnston, and local contractor James Fludder all had their practices along a stretch of Bellevue and nearby streets between Kay Street and Pelham.

Many of these local architects designed residences here, as did such renowned figures as Richard Morris Hunt (who lived nearby), McKim, Mead & White, Peabody & Stearns and other nationally known practitioners. This dense area is one of the best places in the country to perceive the development of the Colonial Revival and Shingle styles between the 1870s and the 1890s and remains as a testament to the great florescence of American architectural experimentation and creativity during those years.

◀ NEWPORT ART MUSEUM (GRISWOLD HOUSE)

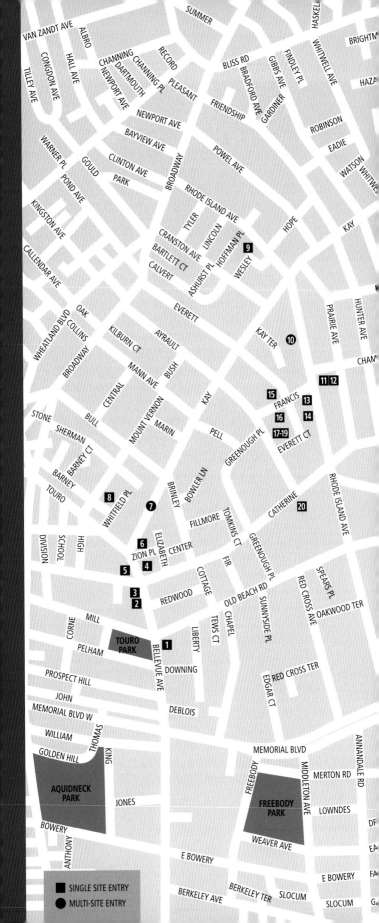

1

1 NEWPORT ART MUSEUM (J.N.A. GRISWOLD HOUSE) (1861-1864) RICHARD MORRIS HUNT, CUSHING MEMORIAL GALLERY (1919) DELANO AND ALDRICH, ADDITION TO CUSHING (1990) PETER ROUDEBUSH AND ASSOCIATES

76 Bellevue Avenue

This is the first major Newport project of Richard Morris Hunt (there were eventually over 30 for Newport!) and one of his earliest extant buildings. It was designed and built as a summer residence for a wealthy New York businessman whom Hunt had encountered in Europe. In many regards it announced a new era for Newport and American architecture.

Much of what went into the design here is taken from the experiences that Hunt had on the continent. He wraps the house in a surface of clapboards and half timbering, with deep shading porches on the west and south sides that are supported by simple posts and braces. What Hunt might have referred to as "Modern Gothic" for his externally expressed structure was later categorized by architectural historian Vincent Scully as the "stick style," a nickname by which this style is still known. Hunt is combining several tendencies here: the rationalist approach of his recent Parisian training; a romantic reaction to the vernacular structures such as Alpine lodges, farmhouses, and rustic pavilions; and his desire to echo American building traditions in clapboard and brick. Little of this is, however, real structure because Hunt has cleverly created the image of a wood-frame skeleton, droplets, and brackets as a kind of applied ornament. While he never achieves a Colonial Revival idiom, several distinctive elements such as the arched chimney and the clapboard surfaces presage the revival architecture of the 1880s. Most dramatically, perhaps, the exterior is no longer a conventional composition of four flat walls but is instead inventively sculptural, with interior spaces pushing and pulling at the elevations, creating deep recesses, engaged towers, bays, dormers, and offset wall planes.

It was a gentleman's diversion, a country house for an urban sophisticate.

The house, as originally conceived, appeared more vertical: the horizontal mass to the left—a carriage house—was moved from another corner of the property and attached as a gallery to the original residence after it was taken over by the Art Association of Newport in 1916. Other alterations were made after this time, including the large studio window to the right of the main entrance.

Several interior spaces are worth noting, including the entry path under the heavy overhanging porte-cochère, which leads through a small hall (with original English tilework) and up to a polygonal landing. Looming above is a light-filled space that rises three stories. Glancing back, a second major landing juts out over the entryway and creates the sheltering block suspended over the main door. This central space is filled with light traceries of railings and powerful plastic projections and doorways to other rooms. Straight ahead (beyond the recent museum entry desk) is an attractive, light-filled conservatory, to either side of which are two well-preserved spaces: a dining room whose paint and wood surfaces were restored based on modern paint analysis, and the darker-toned library whose foliate screens and floor-length windows open out onto the shaded porch. Surprisingly, some of this original sequence—the compressed entryway opening into the vertical space of a multi-level hall and lit on the first floor by a broadly glazed rear wall—is retained by Hunt and more fully developed in his later designs for some of Newport's grandest "cottages," including Ochre Court and the Breakers.

The delightful decorative schemes of these rooms (note the hunting dogs carved into the dining room fireplace) tell us something about the way in which Griswold and Hunt must have envisioned this project. It was a kind of gentleman's diversion, a lodge on the outskirts of an old colonial town, a country house for an urban sophisticate meant to please the eye with its patterns and references and provide a convenient spot from which to enjoy the natural beauty of Newport Neck and the coastline nearby.

2   3

On the grounds of the Griswold House we also find the classically severe Cushing Gallery dedicated to the memory of a local society portraitist and conceived as the formal entryway to a complex of other museum spaces. These were only partially realized more than 70 years later when the Cambridge, Massachusetts firm of Peter Roudebush and Associates extended the planar block of the Cushing eastward, replicating its classical trim and providing the museum with much-needed work spaces and climate-controlled exhibition galleries.

2   SAMUEL PRATT HOUSE (BIRD'S NEST COTTAGE) (1872)

49 Bellevue Avenue

Among the most idiosyncratic of Newport's many architectural diversions, this diminutive cottage is a lively experiment in colors, textures, and shapes. Note such visual delights as the carved dragon heads on the stickwork, the way the polychromed roof tiles slide down onto the vertical walls, and the unpredictable asymmetry of the porch, dormers, and tiny turret on the right. Although its architect is unknown, its date and the relative simplicity of its carpentered details suggest a vernacular version of Richard Morris Hunt's nearby experiments in defining a novel architectural language for a summer cottage.

3   NEWPORT READING ROOM (c. 1835), RENOVATIONS AND ADDITION (1850s) GEORGE CHAMPLIN MASON, SR

29 Bellevue Avenue

This, one of the oldest private men's clubs in the country, is interesting for its early readaptive use of a small Federal-style hotel; for its wonderful billiard room addition to the rear; and for what may be its role in the later establishment of the Newport Casino a few blocks south on Bellevue Avenue. The main entrance was embellished with a front porch and other functional additions after it was turned into a clubhouse for Newport's elite in 1853. More than two decades

A typical Newton design, which creates a wonderful unrestrained, quixotic building.

4

later, it was through that front door that James Gordon Bennett, a member (and the irascible publisher of the *New York Herald*) dared one of his guests to ride a horse up to the bar. He took the dare and when his host was chastised by the club, Bennett responded by setting up what he considered to be a different type of club, giving Newport a casino designed to attract a broader public with more varied recreational opportunities *(see Entry 2 in Tour Seven)*.

The senior George Mason designed the wonderfully airy monitor-roofed billiard room at the rear. As a scion of one of Newport's older families, he was one of only two nineteenth-century architects to be a member (the other was Richard Morris Hunt).

Although it is not open to the public, much of the nineteenth-century interior fabric, including the bar with spittoon trough, mercury pendulum clock, arcane memorabilia, and framed caricatures of many past members, remains intact.

4 DUDLEY NEWTON OFFICE & STUDIO (1872)
DUDLEY NEWTON

20 Bellevue Avenue

This diminutive building is little more than a single bay fronting a very narrow structure that housed local architect Newton's own office and drawing studio.

Its compressed arrangement of elements —bay, diamond-paned window, double-glazed door, wide dormer, and patterned poly-chromed roof slates—visually bursts over the small elevation and is typical of Newton's unrestrained design sense that employs scale and ornament to create wonderfully quixotic buildings. Notably, this was one of several architects' offices that were located within a few blocks of here—perhaps gathered around the studio of Richard Morris Hunt (now the site of the Hotel Viking) or because this was the neighborhood with the most clients in the two decades after the Civil War.

5   6

5   HOTEL VIKING (1924-26) THOMAS, MARTIN & KIRKPATRICK, ADDITIONS (1972 AND LATER)

1 Bellevue Avenue

Since the end of the nineteenth century, civic leaders had been calling for an updated hotel facility that would attract new visitors and bolster Newport's economy. The result of that campaign, the Hotel Viking, was designed in the Georgian Revival style employed on other public buildings in Newport during the early years of the twentieth century. Here the idiom is expanded to a grandiose size (even before later unfortunate motel-like additions to the rear and north sides)—so much so that its oversized openings and wall surfaces no longer coincide with its historical precedents. Of more professional interest might be that this was the site of the "Hill Top" property owned by Richard Morris Hunt and his family (and the locale of his studio) until it was sold by his widow about a decade after his death.

6   JEWISH CEMETERY LAND PURCHASED (1677), FIRST BURIAL (1715), ENLARGED (1768), GATE AND FENCE (1841) ISAIAH ROGERS

Corner Bellevue Avenue and Kay Street

This small field of colonial gravestones and cenotaphs is the earliest extant Jewish cemetery in North America. So picturesque and thought-provoking was its imagery that it prompted Henry Wadsworth Longfellow to compose "The Jewish Cemetery in Newport" after a visit in 1852. What he saw was much more derelict than the well-kept graveyard we see now (he'd written of "these sepulchral stones, so old and brown"). Most notable today, besides the graduated array of obelisks, is the eighteenth-century gravestone with both Hebrew and English text chiseled by the local John Stevens shop of stonecutters. The surrounding granite-posted fence with corner obelisk and towering pylon-shaped gate date from the mid-nineteenth century when architects equated all things Egyptian with cemeteries and funerary rites.

7

7   KAY STREET HOUSES

ANTHONY SHERMAN HOUSE (c. 1892)

10 Kay Street

11 Kay Street (c. 1835), 20 Kay Street (c. 1860)

21 Kay Street (c. 1865)

JOHN & FANNY IRISH HOUSE (c. 1855)

26 Kay Street

JOSEPH BAILEY HOUSE (c. 1855)

30 Kay Street

JOB PECKHAM HOUSE (c. 1855)

33 Kay Street

54 Kay Street (c. 1865) GEORGE CHAMPLIN MASON, SR

SUSAN WEAVER HOUSE (1897) DUDLEY NEWTON

59 Kay Street

CAROLYN SEYMOUR HOUSE (HAWKHURST OR HAWXHURST) (1882) DUDLEY NEWTON

66-66 1/2 Kay Street

LETITIA B. SARGENT HOUSE (AUFENTHALT) (1881) CLARENCE S. LUCE

80 Kay Street

Many houses on Kay Street represent the nineteenth-century middle-class values of their owners, most of whom were successful business owners and professionals in the local community rather than the population of summer residents found nearby. While some houses close to Bellevue Avenue, such as 11 Kay Street with its neoclassical colonnade, are from the first half of the century, most were developed after 1850. These announce their owners' status through their grand size and elaborate ornamenta-

tion such as the peculiar arcaded porch brackets of 20 Kay Street, the flamboyant scroll sawn arabesques under the cross gable at 21 Kay Street, or the eyelet trim on George Mason's design at 54 Kay Street that with its bonnet-shaped gable seems most to mirror quaint American millinery.

A little farther along Kay is a trio of houses built by Job Peckham, the owner of the largest lumberyard in Newport during the mid-nineteenth century. These are forthright blocks, set on large lots (originally equipped with carriage houses) and distinguished from one another and their neighbors by the relatively exotic trim of the projecting porches and eaves. Bulbous columns with a seemingly Eastern influence mark central entryways. Doubled brackets under the deep projecting eaves add visual appeal, and what were originally ornate cupolas (only retained on the Irish House) made these among the most substantial middle-class houses of their era.

On these first few blocks of Kay Street, later architects experiment with the Shingle and Queen Anne vocabularies. The Sherman House at 10 Kay Street, by J.D. Johnston, with its big rotund corner tower (now unfortunately covered with vertical aluminum siding), is accented with the kind of popular carved panels of foliate and shell forms that Johnston could produce in his own mill in an effort to individualize his designs.

The Seymour House, split since the 1930s into several separate structures, must have originally been an enormous mass centered on the almost baroque flaring curve of the two-story porch-tower. Off-centered projections, carved seaweed panels, and a medley of shingle patterns show the mercurial Newton adopting and adapting the Queen Anne to his own idiosyncratic impulses.

From the same period, the Sargent House at the corner of Rhode Island Avenue is a crescendo of gables, turrets, and finials rising toward the corner. Unlike the unified effect on some of his other contemporary work (see Entry 13 of this Tour), Clarence Luce here never brings these separate forms together. Instead they are

arrayed in a cacophonous rhythm above a flared shingle skirt demarcating the second story from its stuccoed first-story base. Luce may have derived his ideas from European sources but they were not, as its charmingly homey nickname implies, from Germany. Rather, they derive from illustrations seen in popular English publications like *Studio* that helped disseminate both the kind of window details and asymmetry seen here.

Finally, along this end of Kay Street stands the 1897 Susan Weaver House, one of Dudley Newton's last works. Its colonial motifs around doors and windows have lost their sculptural value and have become strangely diluted into a thin appliqué of oversize accents crowded onto a rather mundane clapboarded block. It is not clear whether Newton had no sense of scale or merely an idiosyncratic one, but the kind of disjunctively sized elements used here are typical of his career.

8 MARGARET C. & HENRY F. ROONEY HOUSE
(1895) J.D. JOHNSTON

7 Mt. Vernon Street

Most of the houses built in the last quarter of the nineteenth century between Kay Street and Broadway were designed by local architects, perhaps because its proximity to the business district made it somewhat less appealing as a residential zone. Some of these are distinguished by their owners (such as the home of Bellevue Avenue developer Alfred Smith at 12 Mt. Vernon) but others are notable for their visual appeal, such as the Rooney House.

With everything you could want in a Queen Anne design but the suburbanized lot, Newport architect J.D. Johnston has on the Rooney House successfully compressed voids of sleeping porches, swelling glazed bays, furniture-like moldings, and ornamental window shapes into a tightly compressed block and then capped them all with broad crossed gables. This is Johnston at his best, employing a fashionable style while incorporating local influ-

8   9

ences like the inset entryway found on many old Newport town houses. His design is here doubly confined—a tidy cubic block squeezed onto its restricted urban site—but he makes it work visually despite such limitations.

9 MRS H.W. BRIGGS HOUSE (1887) J.D. JOHNSTON

31 Rhode Island Avenue

Unlike his successful work on the Rooney House, Johnston here seems tentative as he mixes a number of forms typical of the '70s and '80s—the wraparound porch abruptly projecting from the main block, minor revival details such as dentil window caps and doubled arched windows, and incongruous, arabesque brackets—that never cohere into the kind of compact, resolved composition he is capable of achieving. One interesting note here is that Johnston was part of a generation of architects open to new building technologies in heating, plumbing, electricity and materials—the Briggs House may have been one of the first Newport residences heated by a hot water system.

J.D JOHNSTON ADVERTISEMENT from 1886 City Directory
SOURCE: *Collection of the Newport Historical Society*

10

10 RHODE ISLAND AVENUE HOUSES

MATILDA LIEBER HOUSE (c. 1882) DUDLEY NEWTON
69 Rhode Island Avenue

MARY & ANNE STEVENS HOUSE (1881-82)
CLARENCE LUCE
73 Rhode Island Avenue

THOMAS R. HUNTER HOUSE (1881-82)
CLARENCE LUCE
77 Rhode Island Avenue

RAY SPINK HOUSE (c. 1864) GEORGE C. MASON, SR
83 Rhode Island Avenue

Another sequence of impressive houses dating from the two decades after the Civil War that document a range of architectural ornament. While 83 Rhode Island Avenue displays the rather pedestrian bracketed porch and heavy timbering typical of the 1860s, the other houses along this stretch of what was once a country road called Lover's Lane with bowered trees and old stone walls are very much in keeping with the more effusive decorative energy of the 1880s.

Newport-born, Boston-based architect Luce incorporates historical references in each of his efforts here. For the Hunter residence he employs a wooden frieze with shell and rippling ribbon motifs to evoke Renaissance sources, while the bays and molding work of the Stevens House suggest Anglo-American colonial sources. Luce was so successful gathering commissions for these and other projects in the early 1880s that he decided to move to Newport for a short time.

Only the Lieber House by Dudley Newton defies easy categorization. Newton is so offbeat that he merges elements of Queen Anne and Colonial Revival (cut shingle patterns, random course stonework, etc.) in combination with more personalized touches such as the swooping entry canopy with its exotic overtones.

11

11

11 FRANCIS MORRIS HOUSE (1882-83) GEORGE CHAMPLIN MASON AND SON

86 Rhode Island Avenue

12 GEORGE CHAMPLIN MASON, JR HOUSE (CA1885) GEORGE CHAMPLIN MASON AND SON

5 Champlin Street

The corner-sited Morris House reads like an oversized piece of late-nineteenth-century furniture with its gigantic stained glass screen by John La Farge suspended between a wonderful bombe-curved base below and a horizontally stretched carved-shell hood above. This combination of forms, derived from a taste for domestic trappings, serves a specific aesthetic purpose: it not only frames the window that lights the main interior staircase, it also clearly directs visual attention to the elevation along the main thoroughfare of Rhode Island Avenue even though the primary entryway faces the smaller Champlin Street.

But the references here are even more complex. This architectural firm, which helped instigate the Colonial Revival movement, alludes in its design to other local forms such as the swelling eaves under the cross gable that echo the peculiar cove molding of the noted seventeenth-century Wanton Lyman Hazard House on Broadway. This should be no surprise since Mason had long been interested in the history of Newport, having been a founder of the Newport Historical Society and a published author on its colonial heritage. His son, George Jr, later went on to become one of the first preservation-conscious architects in Philadelphia.

Add to this antiquarian interest a medley of eclectic ornamental incidents apparent on the Morris House—bull's-eye glazing, spindle screens, acanthus brackets, and carved panel work—and it becomes clear that Mason and his son were part of the architectural vanguard exploring a range of decorative impulses around 1880 that eventually came to be called the Queen Anne and Colonial Revival styles.

12

13

A little later, George Mason, Jr designed his own house just behind the Morris property using similar elements—such as the stack of tripled windows, half timbering, and undercut porches offering glancing views toward Easton's Bay to the southeast. Here the asymmetrical whole is organized under the extended roofline that may itself be an echo of earlier colonial forms (not unlike the memorable shingled incline of Bishop Berkeley's colonial homestead in nearby Middletown, whose photograph was famously published by Charles Follen McKim in 1874).

13 NOYES-LUCE HOUSE (1883) CLARENCE LUCE
15 Francis Street

14 JANE YARDLEY HOUSE (1882) J.D. JOHNSTON
91 Rhode Island Avenue

If the Queen Anne, Colonial Revival and Shingle styles of the 1880s are variants along a range of design options, then this house built for Stephen Luce, head of the Naval War College, helps define one end of that spectrum. Bostonian architect Clarence Luce (probably a relative of the owner) gives us a broad barn-like shape covered with plain rows of shingles, irregular window patterns, a Dutch front door, and even the little conical roof over the entryway alluding to a thatched hood. While these all emphasize the organic-American, rural-vernacular qualities of the Shingle Style, more sophisticated decorative forms are in fact employed here but confined to secondary elevations: a keyhole-shaped side porch door and a rear-facing Palladian window.

Next door, the Jane Yardley House mixes this same set of impulses with the elaborated elements of Colonial Revival and Queen Anne. Here half timbering and pebble-and-dash panels are set against more ornate scroll brackets and panels reminiscent of colonial furniture. Decorative latticework merges with half timbering, while flaring skirts and moldings are used to organize a varied composition of window voids and projecting shapes.

14

15

The surprising proximity of these two houses, built with little space between them and within a year of each other, suggests just how rapidly this popular neighborhood was being developed. Such a dense building pattern almost undermines the picturesque allusions and rural imagery of such houses and clearly sets this neighborhood apart from areas to the south along the cliffs and Bellevue Avenue, which were developed only a few years later by a different economic strata of patronage.

15 SAMUEL HONEY HOUSE (1873)

12 Francis Street

At an intersection crowded with homes built between 1870 and the early 1880s, this house, sitting diagonally on its corner site, stands apart from its neighbors largely because the wood detailing that frames its central door employs the uniquely Moorish flair of rounded arches. The boxy projection over the entry even echoes a kind of Americanized version of a Mashraybeyya—the luxurious grilled bays of wooden latticework projecting from Egyptian homes—but here its skeletal trim is extended downward to create a shallow inset porch.

16   17   18

16 MRS ARCHIE D. PELL HOUSE (1881) CLARENCE LUCE

11 Francis Street

Luce brings a variety of typical Queen Anne forms together here
—from large gestures such as the porch undercutting the main
mass of the house, to smaller details such as carved panels and
moldings—resolving them into a pleasant, if not particularly daring, unified composition. The small gable on the Everett Street
side is an early example of the use of stucco-embedded glass, a
technique soon to be employed by McKim, Mead & White and
others. On the interior, not open to the public, is a strikingly
sculptural brick fireplace that nearly overpowers the main parlor.

17 CHURCHILL-YARNELL HOUSE (1872, 1879) DUDLEY NEWTON

62 Ayrault Street

18 ISAAC P. WHITE HOUSE (1872) GEORGE CHAMPLIN MASON AND SON

66 Ayrault Street

Built at the same time, these are variations on Hunt's local experiments with chalet-style houses by the two leading architects in
the city. Mason's big upright block was designed for the rector of
Trinity Church and features exposed cross-bracing exposed timbers and decoratively sawn brackets under the eaves.

Newton's more delicately scaled design, on the other hand,
reimagines the chalet as a one-and-a-half-story mansard-roofed
cottage for his client, a naval officer. By employing elaborated
eaves, dropped skirt of boards, half-round battens, and sawtooth
bottom edge, he typically emphasizes a decorative rather than a
structural sensibility. There are several similar houses by Newton
nearby and he came back a few years later to add the matching
rear addition here.

19 20

19 REAR ADMIRAL REED WARDEN HOUSE (1881)
CLARENCE LUCE

68 Ayrault Street

In the last quarter of the nineteenth century, a number of naval officers lived in this newly developed neighborhood. For this officer, architect Luce created his own eccentric version of the Queen Anne style with a front porch roofed with doubled gables that are supported by asymmetrical posts and diagonally offset by the bay window on the second story. Only the sunburst pattern radiating down on this varied composition adds a more predictable touch. The quirky originality of this house is a prime example of Luce's most creative phase as well as being a good representative of the visually appealing formal diversity found in Newport's decorated cottages.

20 VIRGINIA SCOTT HOYT HOUSE (AYRAULT HOUSE) (1916) CROSS AND CROSS

45 Catherine Street

This formal summer residence in brick shows how revival styles remained viable well into the early twentieth century. Here a New York firm adopts, rather literally, a Neo-Georgian vocabulary, even re-using a staircase removed from an eighteenth-century New York townhouse. Until the 1940s, this kind of colonial imagery laden with early Americana undertones was more frequently used in Newport for civic buildings, such as the Main Post Office or Central Fire Station, than for private resort cottages.

21

22

21 RICHARDSON-BLATCHFORD HOUSE (1870, 1883)
PROBABLY WILLIAM RALPH EMERSON

37 Catherine Street

What started out earlier as a gabled cottage was transformed, little more than a decade later, by New Yorker Sophia Blatchford into the more updated Shingle Style. Everything here is covered in what appears to be a stretched skin of shingles—the umbrella cones of the dormers, the upper sleeping porch, the flared skirt between floors, and even the porch posts. The cleanly cut dovecote grid and the creative design of the entrance are tell-tale signs that this is likely the work of Boston's William Ralph Emerson, a noted Shingle Style innovator.

22 COLONEL GEORGE WARING HOUSE (THE HYPOTENUSE) (1870-71) RICHARD MORRIS HUNT

33 Catherine Street

This house is the result of an early Hunt project—the making over of an existing Greek Revival structure originally located on his family property nearby. The quartet of fluted Doric columns supporting an overhang at the entry alcove area are all that is left of its earlier configuration, as the young architect cloaked the building in the kind of decorative vernacular forms that he was exploring in the 1860s and '70s. The bonnet gable caps numerous ornamental elements on the facade—the jigsaw patterns of the eave skirts, bracing struts, and half-timber effects (not unlike those on the earlier Griswold House) all made popular by Hunt's efforts to establish new architectural forms.

Waring was a prominent member of Newport's intellectual community, a member of the famed Town and Country Club and a published author of civil engineering manuals who helped institute Newport's sewage system. The hybrid house was moved to its present site and given by Hunt—sometime after 1876—to Waring, who probably gave it its mathematical nickname.

23   24

23 MRS JAMES C. PORTER HOUSE (PORTER VILLA, OLD CASTLE) (1855-56) SETH BRADFORD

25 Greenough Place

Bradford was one of the few professionals working in Newport in the 1850s and most of his houses make use of this rough block stonework. This one was designed for a Louisiana woman who retreated to Newport for its pleasant climate as part of an antebellum southern summer contingent. When built, the Porter Villa sat amid open fields as there were few houses nearby. It has its Fall River granite walls trimmed in flat-cut windows surrounds, and entryway with bracketed eaves hinting at Italianate sources, another contemporary architectural vogue.

24 JOSEPH TOMPKINS HOUSE (1853) THOMAS A. TEFFT

38 Catherine Street

This rather staid, atypical composition in wood is from a Providence architect better known for more dynamic Romanesque revival designs in stone. The simple block of the house is punctuated by ornament around the projecting entry porch with its Doric columns, the wide eave skirting the hipped roof, the cupola, and chimneys. There are subtler touches here as well—for example, the way in which Tefft masks the top of each window with a flat arched board—but they mostly serve to remind us that these are all surface applications onto a basic rectilinear mass.

25 KING-BIRKHEAD HOUSE (1872) DUDLEY NEWTON

20 Catherine Street

This is Newton near his best, working toward the "Modern Gothic" idiom he helped to popularize (today it's better known as the "stick style"). This delightful small cottage is all mansard roof and thick-set corner tower—both older forms but here used as occasions for ornamentation—multicolored slate patterns, jigsaw trim, carpentered brackets and moldings. Newton employed the

25   26

mansard roof form so frequently that he even invented and patented a "Newton Roof," which allowed for better gutter construction beneath the junction of wall and roof planes and that he uses here on the King-Birkhead House.

26 COMMODORE WILLIAM EDGAR HOUSE (1886)
McKIM, MEAD & WHITE

25 Old Beach Road

This house is best considered as a transitional one for the famous New York firm—done at a time when they began to shift stylistically from the gifted massing of their shingled houses to more formal compositions in both wood and masonry. Close in date and location to earlier projects (such as the Skinner, Tilton, and Colman houses of 1880-82), the Edgar House adopts a distinctly different architectural language based on symmetry, sharp linear brick and masonry details, arched openings, and Palladian motifs.

As different as it is from the earlier projects, the Edgar House still reveals a solid grasp of historical American sources—here not the weathered organic shapes of New England wood-frame structures but the elegant eighteenth-century brick mansions of the Tidewater in Virginia. This broadened revival vocabulary now includes the horizontal massing, brick surfaces, high-pitched hipped roofs, and open-arched, pilastered chimneys of the middle Atlantic coast.

Along with this historicism, McKim, Mead & White's masterful compositional skills are apparent as they successfully balance the open porch on the right side with the opacity of the service wing to the left. Similarly, the cylindrical bay to one side of the entrance is opposed by the polygonal bay on the other. Their deft sense of complexity is evident in the asymmetrical placement of an elegant "oval debut" window in one upper corner of an otherwise blank front brick wall. This brave gesture is all but obscured today by the later and thoughtless insertion of power lines through the taut plane of brick.

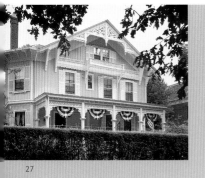

27

While the interior has been changed into a multiple family dwelling, much still remains of the fireplaced entrance hall, dining room, music room (beneath the open loggia) and library, all with their woodwork largely intact.

27 GEORGE CHAMPLIN MASON, SR HOUSE (SUNNYSIDE) (1873-74) GEORGE CHAMPLIN MASON SR

31 Old Beach Road

George Champlin Mason was one of the leading intellectual lights of nineteenth-century Newport—not just in his role as an architect who helped pave the way toward the Colonial Revival, but as a journalist, author, historian and landscape painter as well. He also mentored the next generation of local architects in Newport —working with his own son, George, Jr as well as Dudley Newton, J.D. Johnston, and James Fludder. Mason was known statewide as well; he was one of the founders of the Rhode Island chapter of the American Institute of Architects.

The immediate inspiration for his own chalet-styled house may well be Richard Morris Hunt, but Mason is more conservative in the symmetry of his main façade, relying more heavily on ornament to evoke Alpine folk traditions.

Although the address and main entrance are on Old Beach Road, the most visually arresting elevation faces west along the eponymous Sunnyside Place. When built, the house would have inevitably been approached from the town side (the west) and Mason expends the most effort at decorating every element there —brackets are drilled, railings are cutout, eaves are trimmed with intricately sawn filigrees. All of this is grouped under a deep overhanging gable supported by exposed struts and clearly informed by notions of Swiss architecture. The very best time to see this house is late on a sunny afternoon when all his intended effects of natural light and shadow are cast across the western elevation, creating yet another level of ever-changing ornament.

28

Around this time, Mason wrote a fictionalized account of the relationship between an architect and his clients in *The Old House Altered* and it is this, his own house, to which he refers in the text and illustration.

28 SAMUEL TILTON HOUSE (1881-82) McKIM, MEAD & WHITE

12 Sunnyside Place

The rich variety of surface ornament and texture makes this house stand out, even from adjacent projects by the same firm. Their attention is divided, however, between the elaborate treatment on the street side and the more restrained woodwork of the garden elevation. Approaching the house, one can see two sides literally encrusted with rough-cut granite, painted half timbers, a spectrum of shingle patterns (wave, saw tooth, and various notches), and exuberant stucco panels with colored inclusions. A huge sun ray pattern and a shield are the most prominent of these latter designs created from bits of colored glass, shells, beach stone and even coal that are embedded into the plaster. McKim saw such panel work on a seventeenth-century house in Salem; even Nathaniel Hawthorne, the literary progenitor of the era's interest in colonial Americana, had described the glistening effect of just such a surface treatment in his earlier novel, *The Scarlet Letter*.

From the street side, the Tilton House seems small, set with its end to the street. Its broad main gable runs deep across the north end of the lot, leaving a wide three-story wall facing the true sunny side of the house, which is opened up with bands of asymmetrical window patterns and porches. The entry porch, which

This was constructed just as the hilltop was being divided into sizable gentleman's farms.

29

today seems like an abrupt projection, was once a two-story, gable-topped pavilion with fancy turned spindles along a second-level balustrade. Unlike the contemporary Skinner House nearby *(see Entry 31 of this Tour)*, which is distinguished by its inventive collision of shaped masses, the simple mass of the Tilton House is reticently organized under one sheltering gable.

While the interior is not open to the public, it is equally rich in its materials and references. Its textured ceilings, leaded-glass windows, spindle screens, metal fixtures, and wood trim are informed by Anglo-American, Bretonese, Japanese, and even Indian sources. Just as important, perhaps, it and the nearby Skinner House show that the firm is working in a novel, progressive way to organize interior spaces that flow into each other and around central cores, not unlike the open plans associated with the onset of Modernism.

29 H. ALLEN WRIGHT HOUSE (BELAIR) (1850)
SETH BRADFORD, (1870, 1875 STABLE AND GATEHOUSE)
DUDLEY NEWTON

50 Old Beach Road

This large mid-block mansion of rustic stone, built for New Yorker Wright, was constructed just as this hilltop was being divided into sizable gentleman's farms. Although it is related to Bradford's original work on Chateau Sur Mer *(see Tour Eight)*, built about a year later, it is now much altered from its original form and has been turned into condominiums.

Better preserved are the two auxiliary stone structures on the grounds designed by Dudley Newton (they can best be viewed at a rear drive off Old Beach Road). The type of weighty materials and thick opacity found on the main house give Newton his starting point. He goes on, however, to compromise the no-nonsense style of the earlier architect by embellishing the gatehouse with charmingly fussy wood trim and perversely enlarging the forms on the stable so that its polygonal turret, trefoil gable, and crenellated tower completely overpower the building itself.

30

30 KATHRINE PRESCOTT WORMELEY HOUSE
(c. 1876) CHARLES FOLLEN McKIM, (1882 AND LATER) McKIM, MEAD & WHITE

2 Red Cross Avenue

There is so much to look at on this early work by Charles Follen McKim that it is hard to know where to start. One can almost imagine the young architect sifting though an array of international sources before selecting his eclectic mix of forms for the summer home of his patron, a Boston-based translator and author. He somewhat brashly included a panoply of visual delights—an onion-shaped dome (originally gilded) capping a cylindrical tower, a medieval oriel window lighting the main interior staircase, an Anglophilic overhang (influenced by both Norman Shaw and McKim's mentor H.H. Richardson), and even colonial American overtones in the seventeenth-century-inspired cove molding tucked under the second story, or the eighteenth-century turned balusters on his impossibly small balcony.

This was designed as a two-family house, with the two wings intersecting at a right angle and joined by the hinge pin tower, but its disparate elements never coalesce into a unified composition as they do on slightly later works by McKim after he entered into his famed partnership with William Rutherford Mead and Stanford White. One need only consider the same decorative impulses ordered into an organic unity on the nearby Skinner or Tilton houses to see what a difference a few years makes in an architectural career. Yet despite such shortcomings, McKim's youthful litany of eye-catching decorative and historical references on the Wormley House sets the tone for the next generation of architectural design.

31

31 FRANCES L. SKINNER HOUSE (VILLINO)
(1881-82) McKIM, MEAD & WHITE, (c. 1950) LIBRARY
ADDITION

6 Red Cross Avenue

This tiny house is one of Newport's architectural gems. It is also
one of McKim, Mead & White's earliest and most successful residential designs (they formed their partnership in the September
of 1879), although it is also among the smallest in size. The exterior forms, whether large volumetric shapes or more intimate
decorative details, are organized around the attenuated chimney
at its core: the veritable image of a house around its hearth. Many
of these elements are based, as Leland Roth has pointed out, on
McKim's continuing study of colonial geometries—but other
ideas and images abound here as well. Some of these inspirations
may have been collected when McKim and White were working
for H.H. Richardson, or sketched on their individual trips to
Europe, or seen during a famous trip taken by all three to view
American colonial architecture from Newport to the North Shore
in the late 1870s. For the Skinner design, they seem to come spill-
ing off their drawing board with a kind of youthful exuberance.

This small but dignified house was built for a Bostonian and cost less than $8000 when completed.

Like other projects of this time in Short Hills, New Jersey, Montauk Point, New York, and elsewhere, the Skinner House features a tower pulled into one corner of the building. Yet here on the southern elevation the embrace of the shingled skin is seamless, so that the bloated conical form blends organically into the rest of the block. White had recently drawn similar towers in Normandy, yet here the particular way in which the cylinder of the upper story sits on the polygonal base simultaneously suggests the agrarian utility of a windmill. A long-shingled roof reaches from above the chimney down to the entry porch and it too references colonial antecedents even as it is supported by slender sets of free-standing classical piers. For such a small house, there are lots of other occasions here for experimentation—pebble-and-dash work appears as a small horizontal panel under the entry overhang, shingles are cut into decorative patterns — some of which swell over window tops — and a strip of windows tucked under the second-story eave are folded like a Japanese screen even as they presage the way early modernists dissolve a corner with glazing. By juxtaposing the broad forms of the tower and other simple planes against tighter grouping of decorative elements around the entryway, the architects avoid any sense of overstuffing their design.

The geometries of the exterior strongly suggest the kind of spatial variety and open plan of the first-floor rooms. Entering on the north side, there is a continuous flow of space around a chimney core as differently shaped rooms open onto each other in another proto-modern aspect of this fertile design.

This small but dignified house was built for another Bostonian (one of many who resided in the neighborhood) and cost less than $8,000 when completed! Although it is well preserved, some changes have occurred, including a boxy 1950s library wing on the southeast, the loss of original porchwork on the south elevation, and the truncation of more extensive gardens. Again, belying its size, or perhaps because it is so domestically scaled, the house has had a long roster of prominent residents. For many

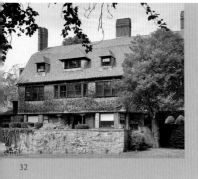

32

years in the twentieth century it was owned by a prominent local doctor, John E. Carey, who established the modern practice of obstetrics and gynecology at the Newport Hospital. Later, in the early 1990s, a small decoratively shingled cottage designed to conform with its older, shingled neighbors was tucked within the stone-walled garden to the south when the main house was owned by John Grosvenor, one of the founding partners of Newport Collaborative Architects.

32 SAMUEL COLMAN HOUSE (WHILEAWAY, BOXCROFT) (1882-83) McKIM, MEAD & WHITE

7 Red Cross Avenue

This commodious summer house and studio for the noted American watercolorist Samuel Colman finds McKim, Mead & White transforming the compact picturesque imagery of their Skinner House across the street into a more orderly yet complex Colonial Revival design.

The big barn-like bulk of the gambrel main block sits end to the street, its broad southern face looking out over the gardens and elevated grassed terrace, interrupted by overhangs and scooped-out porches. This site plan is typical for the firm—they invariably set their buildings from the 1880s at the northern end of the lot, with an entry (public) on the north or western side and the elevation opened with porches (private), loggias, and extended windows always facing gardens to the south.

The spread of this large roofline is reminiscent of the big colonial houses along Washington Street but the firm combines it here with the equally potent colonial reference of a steeply pitched salt box roof for the service wing. Under the eaves, another decorative cove again recalls seventeenth-century Newport sources, just as McKim does earlier on the nearby Wormeley House. The entire composition may be more straightforward and balanced than other designs from this phase of the firm's work, but they complicate their more obvious references by hanging their upper

33

34

shingled stories over a base of stone-trimmed Roman-style bricks and inserting ornate panel work around windows and doorways on the entry façade. This eclecticism was in keeping with Colman's own hybrid taste, as he was a well-known collector of Asian art, some of which was housed in this Newport house.

33 GRACE W. RIVES HOUSE (1879) PEABODY & STEARNS, (1881, NORTHWEST WING) GEORGE CHAMPLIN MASON AND SON

30 Red Cross Avenue

A rare expression of Victorian Gothic in Newport, this house flanked by two differently shaped towers presents a very different architectural image from that of neighboring residences. Its pointed arch windows and polychromed patterned-brick-and-stone moldings suggest a dour religious or academic structure, for which this style was often employed.

34 GEORGE GORDON KING HOUSE (OAKWOOD) (1902) McKIM, MEAD & WHITE

1-3 Oakwood Terrace

Two decades after working on nearly a half-dozen houses in this part of the neighborhood, the firm of McKim, Mead & White return to create this elongated, gambrel-roofed, Georgian Revival house for a local philanthropist, quite different from their shingled efforts of the early 1880s. Its most notable feature may be its peculiarly extensive use of pebble and dash for its outer wall covering. This and other features make the house seem formal yet quirky, with monumental Corinthian columns defining a pedimented entry bay and, on the south elevation, a second-story porch ornamented with Palladian motifs.

35   36

35 SARAH T. ZABRISKIE HOUSE (1889) GEORGE CHAMPLIN MASON AND SON

100 Rhode Island Avenue

Created in an architectural language unique for both its designers and for Newport, this elaborate stone house has stepped gables, decorated chimney pots, a rotund tower/porch at the rear, and myriad flourishes of gargoyles, stone plaques, and copper finials that—despite a rather unruly composition—allude to sources in late-medieval Flemish architecture. Much of this imagery might come from the client who was also a patron of the slightly later St John the Evangelist Church on the Point, which employed another medieval idiom emulating 13th-century English forms.

36 HENRY SWINBURNE HOUSE (1875-76) DUDLEY NEWTON

97 Rhode Island Avenue

This is a quintessential summer cottage image for the 1870s— "Modern Gothic" in its vernacular stick work, ornamented with flourishes such as sawn-trim boards, and textured in a variety of materials, all of which explore the expressive and structural use of materials and forms. Newton pushes this design beyond his earlier formula of mansarded roofs and bulky towers *(see Entry 25 of this Tour)* by incorporating chalet influences such as the steeply pitched roof for the rear section, the polygonal tower to one side, and a front gable tilting its jerkin head roof over the sleeping porch. The wonderful tracery of the sawn boards around the upper porch is set over the thin timber framing of the main porch, giving the entire façade the sense of floating in front of the half-timbered brick core. Built for a client who helped engineer Newport's water system, the Swinburne House suggests earthy rusticity in a playful, sophisticated way.

37   38

37 **LANSING ZABRISKIE HOUSE** (1889-1890) J.D. JOHNSTON

90 Rhode Island Avenue

Revivalist mostly in its projecting portico, this house is notable for its early use of extruded concrete blocks molded to resemble rough stone. This is an example of a novel mass-produced building material that was marketed as both economical and fire proof. Johnston, an architect-builder and a supplier of construction materials, was one of the first to employ it in Newport.

38 **ARMISTEAD HOUSE** (1882) BRUCE PRICE, (c. 1980s ALTERED SOUTH SIDE)

55 Hunter Avenue

A little-known early work by Bruce Price reveals him, in the early 1880s, to be among the group of young architects working with historical references. Here, early in his career, Price experiments with such picturesque, Anglo-colonial revival elements as multiple gables, mullioned windows, and the idiosyncratically rotund porch posts (inspired by seventeenth-century colonial furniture). In this exploratory design they remain separate elements, never quite resolved into the kind of organic compositions for which he later achieved notoriety at Tuxedo Park, New York.

39   40

39 CHARLES D. FICKE HOUSE (1984) CHARLES D. FICKE

130 Eustis Avenue

This small house nearly hidden behind a thick screen of planting has a high-pitched gable set end to street. With simple forms and exposed interior structure inspired by timber-framing traditions, it was designed by the architect as his family residence. Just as notably, it employs an organic system of heating and cooling features. On the exterior these include extensive arbors, verdant plant screens, and a site oriented for optimum sun and shade. On the interior, open planning and conductive airflow between floors help achieve a model of passive energy efficiency.

40 ARTHUR EMMONS HOUSE (1882-83) PEABODY & STEARNS

300 Gibbs Avenue

This is Peabody & Stearns's most thorough exploration of the shingled Queen Anne style in a neighborhood known for its many early projects in this new idiom. They employ a novel set of forms seemingly unique to their office: the pronounced sweep of the porte-cochère roof as it flows over the main entry, the brick wall rising to a stepped gable, and an elongated chimney. Like many of the houses along this stretch of Gibbs, its rear elevation reaches up from the eastward-facing slope and features balconies and porches designed to afford views of the pond and Bay beyond.

41   42

41 LINDEN GATE PORTER'S LODGE (1872) RICHARD MORRIS HUNT

333 Gibbs Avenue

Sadly, this small outbuilding and a few stone walls are all that remain of the estate, Linden Gate, designed by Hunt for Henry G. Marquand, who is best remembered today as the one-time president of the Metropolitan Museum of Art. Linden Gate was built in the early 1870s and destroyed a century later. Just as the main house employed stickwork trusses, high-pitched gables, and woven-brick patterns that recalled Hunt's European sources, this small structure features a deep balcony, exposed timbers, and decorative brick work evocative of similar continental sources.

42 MRS FREDERICK EUSTIS HOUSE (ELM TREE COTTAGE) (1882) WILLIAM RALPH EMERSON

336 Gibbs Avenue

Emerson has sheathed this summer house, which sits with its end to the street, in what was typical of his work in the 1880s: a stretched skin of (originally) unpainted shingles. Wrapped around curving corners and conical elements, this skin emphasizes spatial volume over structural rectilinearity (like that found in such 1870s designs as Emerson's M.H. Sanford House in the Point neighborhood) *(see Tour Two)*. These forms are augmented by other ornamental moments, such as the gigantic carved bracket on the street elevation and the decorative grid of a dovecote over the entryway. More than most architects of the 1880s, Emerson has a way of using a particular type of volumetric shingling that serves to unify all these separate forms into a more organically sculptural whole.

43

43 T.K. GIBBS HOUSE (BETHSHAN) (c. 1883) DUDLEY NEWTON

396 Gibbs Avenue

As idiosyncratic as ever, Newton here mixes his architectural metaphors with random coursed-stone walls and a peculiar palette of bricks, pink granite, ruddy slates, and rust-colored pointing. There is a great stone arch reminiscent of H.H. Richardson on the service wing and an oversized gambrel roof that provides at least a nod to the Colonial Revival then gaining currency in Newport.

44 ST MICHAEL'S COUNTRY DAY SCHOOL (MISS ELLEN MASON HOUSE) (1902) IRVING GILL, HILL HOUSE (1995) ROBERT LUCHETTI, RENOVATED VAN BEUREN BUILDING (2006) OLSON, LEWIS, DIOLI AND DOKTOR

180 Rhode Island Avenue

Although it has now been turned into a private primary school, the masonry structure that was once the residence of Miss Ellen Mason makes a fitting finale to the generation of eclectic, revivalist architecture represented in this hilltop neighborhood. If the tile roof and stucco walls seem out of place in New England, it is because the architect here is Irving Gill, an easterner trained in Louis Sullivan's Chicago office who had moved to Southern California about a decade earlier to become one of the first registered architects in that state.

Through a connection with the Olmsted firm in California, Gill made a number of contacts back east, including Miss Mason, who had used the Olmsted firm for her extensive gardens (they also designed the fabulous high stone wall along what is now Memorial Boulevard). After meeting his client in San Diego, the architect traveled to Rhode Island in the first years of the twentieth century in part to replace her earlier (H.H. Richardson-designed) house that had been destroyed by a disastrous fire. Gill

44

decided to experiment with forms and materials derived from his experience with vernacular Hispanic architecture. The unadorned planes and arched openings that would eventually give Gill his reputation as a proto-modernist are, ironically, used here for the first time in his career since most of his prior work in California was based on wooden, shingled, and Colonial Revival forms (which must have seemed equally novel in Southern California).

Although Gill uses smooth stick balusters, reduced molding, and machined hardware on the interior, some of which still survives, don't mistake this for the pared-down international style. Instead, he finds myriad ways to accent the building's exterior—fanciful chimney pots, curved mullions, sinuously swelling iron work, arts-and-craft lanterns, diamond-paned windows, and even Churiggurresque columns flanking an upstairs balcony.

The school's more recent additions of buildings attempt to fit in with Gill's design—with rather awkward results in the utilitarian 1995 Hill House gymnasium and more precise results in the 2006 renovation of the middle school classroom building. There, the Manchester, Massachusetts firm of Olson, Lewis, Dioli and Doktor has carefully mimed both the composition and stucco detailing of the early-twentieth-century building for their updated extension of an earlier classroom building.

7. BELLEVUE AVENUE & THE CLIFFS

Bellevue Avenue is the most recognized street name in Newport, and the ornate summer mansions that line its route and are somewhat oddly called "cottages" have long stood for a bygone opulence that, since the 1960s, has helped to attract thousands of visitors to the city. Traversing an axis south of the town toward the rocky coast of Newport Neck, Bellevue Avenue is, like Broadway to the North, a spine off which other side streets also developed. Unlike its more workaday sister street, however, Bellevue does not trace its roots to Newport's founding years and is of much more recent, nineteenth-century vintage. Under a land development partnership led by transplanted New Yorker Alfred Smith, Bellevue Avenue was imposed on a largely rural, undeveloped part of the island in order to entice new residents. The few families who owned or farmed land in this quarter of the island, such as the Hazards, realized that this would bring dramatic changes to their way of life and moved west to Jamestown and South County.

First beginning in the early 1850s, development here occurred in several phases over the next fifty years or so. In the first years after Bellevue Avenue was laid out, a few stone walled houses were built on large lots (such as the first phase of Chateau-sur-Mer or the Hedges discussed in Entries 29 and 26 of this Tour). Slightly later, more picturesque and largely wood-frame homes were erected on increasingly smaller lots (such as the clump of 1870s buildings at the southern end of Bellevue also discussed in Entry 40). It was only in the 1880s that a majority of the largest and most ornate houses for which Bellevue is best known began to supercede these earlier structures, in some cases replacing an earlier and more modest building on the same site (as in the case of Marble House).

Where Bellevue starts to leave the confines of the old town grid (at the intersection of what is now Memorial Boulevard), a commercial district sprang up in the 1870s with a novel building, the Travers Block. This features long, horizontal street front and shop windows made for genteel promenading and shopping. By the beginning of

continued on page 299

◀ MARBLE HOUSE

SINGLE SITE ENTRY

MULTI-SITE ENTRY

1

1   TRAVERS BLOCK (1870-1871) RICHARD MORRIS HUNT

162 Bellevue Avenue

Hunt's early works were mostly residential designs, including one for William R. Travers. His patron must have been pleased since the commission for this commercial block quickly followed.

On the first level, large plate-glass windows encourage pedestrians to stroll by the displays and window shop. Above, Hunt uses the same ornamental grid of bracework that he developed for his residential work of the 1860s. In its varied roof line of different-sized dormers, projecting bays, and cross gables — as well as its horizontality and the height of its floor levels — Hunt's design is drawn from both historical English and vernacular agrarian buildings, many of which he recorded while studying abroad. Hunt's picturesque surface treatment of the European-derived half timbering resulted in a novel-looking building whose newness served a commercial purpose: it announces the beginning of a new type of upscale shopping district, clearly different from the smaller and plainer shops that existed to the north. With this new architectural language and its great size (it was the largest retail structure of its day in Newport), it not only stood out from the buildings around it but also visually symbolized the population of sophisticated wealth and status that the land development on either side of Bellevue Avenue was just beginning to attract.

2   THE CASINO (1879-1881) McKIM, MEAD & WHITE

186-202 Bellevue Avenue

Commissioned by James Gordon Bennett, the New York newspaper publisher whose house, Stone Villa, sat just across Bellevue where there is now a shopping plaza and parking lot, the Casino was intended to be a new type of social club. Its genesis may have been a social gaffe set in motion by Bennett who was a member of The Newport Reading Room, a gentlemen's club a few blocks away. Daring (successfully) a friend to ride his horse into the old

The recently formed firm of McKim, Mead & White envisioned a new type of entertainment complex.

club, Bennett was later chastised by some of its membership, which prompted him to set up this social center. Bennett's facility would be open to a broader public and feature more wide-ranging forms of recreation: not just a bar, billiards, and cards but also lawn tennis and croquet, as well as theater, court tennis, and —perhaps most important—a restaurant and retail stores where one could window shop while promenading along the Avenue. Propitiously, he turned to the young trio of architects who had the right social and professional credentials and whose earliest work suggested a novel, eye-catching, less-conventional approach to architecture.

At the end of the 1870s, the recently formed firm of McKim, Mead & White envisioned a new form of entertainment complex. Although not the first such American structure, the Newport Casino is often credited with popularizing and establishing the standard by which other such "country clubhouses" were judged. Laid out on a rhomboid-shaped property, it takes full advantage of its site, stretching its façade horizontally along Bellevue Avenue and using an Anglo-American or "Modernized Colonial" idiom that marked other McKim, Mead & White projects: broad gables, tall prominent chimneys, textural mixtures of brick, shingle, and stonework, second-story overhangs, gridded decorative panels, and small-paned windows.

A few years earlier, on the eve of the American Centennial, McKim helped initiate the revival of such forms with a set of photographs he commissioned that recorded picturesque early-American houses and antique furniture in and around Newport. These were intended for purchase through subscription but were also published in the early professional journal, *The New York Sketchbook of Architecture*. In addition, McKim and White worked in the office of H.H. Richardson, whose work evoked a parallel set of historic forms based on English antecedents. In its composition and effect, one can even see close echoes of the British architect Norman Shaw, such as the "old English" imagery of his Hostelry and Stores designed for the town of Bedford in

*The prosaic world
of the Avenue and the
town drop away.*

1878, but these are more vertical, wrapped around an extant private house, and less symmetrically disposed. Where their predecessors used bolder, beefier forms and elements, McKim, Mead & White contrast the glazed windows, principal archway, brick piers, and heavy stone brackets of their first story with a lighter treatment above. The wall is sculpturally pushed and pulled across the second story and the gables above, covered in bands of shingle patterns (waved and scalloped) and lightened with spindle screens and colonialized railings above the eaves (which are now lost). This degree of ornament and surface articulation creates a lighter, airier effect despite the considerable dimensions of the structure.

Some of the Casino composition is derived from the cues set up by Hunt on his adjacent Travers Block. McKim, the principal designer on the Casino, extends the commercial front, story heights, and horizontality of Hunt's work as well as Hunt's periodic spacing of cross gables. But, under the single sheltering roof plane on the Casino, the effect is different. This is due in part to what Richard Guy Wilson has defined as a tendency toward order and consolidation in the firm's designs. Here this order is manifested in separate elements contained in the simpler overall geometry of the front elevation. Today the front slope of the roof has lost its original turned balusters and railings that connected the cross gables, making it appear even more monolithic than intended.

The Bellevue Avenue façade originally contained six stores and a broad archway flanked by ornate ironwork lanterns (long gone) that marked the principal entrance to the complex. This leads to an outdoor space behind the front block where long side ells embrace a central greensward used for croquet. At its rear is a curving piazza whose sweeping roof and screens allowed for sheltered walks around the outdoor court. When you walk under the entry arch, through the stair hall with its Colonial and Renaissance Revival details and into the court area, the prosaic world of the Avenue and the town drop away, the strong summer

2

sun filtering through lattice and woven grilles. You are enclosed by a kind of fantasy architecture alluding to other times and places. Look, for instance, at the entry bay and its accompanying tall bell-capped clock tower. Here, a rich palette of sculptural walls, shadowy overhangs, random stonework, shingles, and window patterns are detailed with intricately carved wood trim and Renaissance-style ribbon-work reliefs. Scrutinize the details over the flat arch of the big entry doors to see the kind of witty humor that the young architects were willing to bring to their design work. Over the arch, two carved dragons bare teeth that then become the small dentil-like serration of a classical border. This decorative flourish can be read as a kind of architectural footnote and personal paean to a professional mentor, since these playful snouts may be intended as diminutive versions of the bolder dragon heads found on the well-known railroad station designed by H H. Richardson in North Easton, Massachusetts, not very far away.

It was probably McKim, with his strong sense of site planning, who adjusted the building to the odd shape of the property, which has side boundaries set at an angle to Bellevue. This adjustment is most evident in the parallelogram shape of the entryway arch mosaic pavement—and in the way that the inner wall of the upper balcony recedes at an angle while the rest of the front elevation matches the street line. McKim's partner White certainly contributed in other ways. Beyond the horseshoe court are two additional buildings that added to the diversions available at the Casino. One of the few court tennis facilities in the United States was built in the large shingled building to the south, its interior playing space defined by the arcane intricacies of this game based

3

on medieval sources. To the north, a companion building housed a theater that, along with the decorative ensemble of the clock tower, suggests the extravagantly ornamental eye of Stanford White. For the theater a dazzling skin of plaster roundels, scallop shells, and basket-weave surfaces cover the balcony arcade. Smaller mullioned windows, Renaissance geometries, and tightly clustered turned balusters are an adaptation of similar motifs found on the exterior.

While some of its original form and function have been lost or altered over the years, most recently it has been restored through the knowledgeable efforts of Newport architect Richard Long and the Providence architectural firm of Durkee, Brown, Viveiros and Werenfels Architects. Today it houses the Tennis Hall of Fame, but soon after its completion, in 1881, it was the site of the first National Lawn Tennis Tournament, a sport just then gaining in popularity. Ironically in that same year, its patron James Gordon Bennett sold his shares at a profit, having successfully made his point to the old guard of Newport society. Even today, the Casino remains one of Newport's most significant and architecturally original historic structures.

3   **KING BLOCK** (1892-1893) PERKINS AND BETTON

204-214 Bellevue Avenue

AUDRAIN BUILDING (1902-03) BRUCE PRICE

220-230 Bellevue Avenue

While the terse brick surfaces and modest gable work of the King Block serve, rather timidly, to extend the orchestration of textures and shapes of McKim, Mead & White's earlier Casino, the fantastically elaborate glazed tile work and the monumentality of the Audrain Block's arched windows boldly separate it from the rest of this distinguished commercial row. By the end of the century, the Audrain's designer, Bruce Price, had moved away from the wood-framed shingled structures on which his reputation was

based and had begun working in masonry, on a grander scale and with a renewed sense of classical imagery. On the Audrain Building (one of Price's last works before he died in 1903) the self-conscious, colorful ornamentality of its Renaissance Revival vocabulary might have served, in advance of neon signage, to visually attract customers to its retail shops and services.

4 GEORGE NOBLE JONES HOUSE (KINGSCOTE)
(1839-1841) RICHARD UPJOHN, ALTERED (1876) GEORGE CHAMPLIN MASON, JR, ADDITION OF DINING ROOM AND ALTERED INTERIOR (1880) STANFORD WHITE, CARRIAGE HOUSE (1893) DUDLEY NEWTON

Bowery Street at corner of Bellevue Avenue

This is one of the first houses constructed as an ornate summer retreat in Newport — as such, it was sited on what was then the edge of the town, looking south toward the undisturbed natural beauty of Newport Neck. When this was built, Bellevue Avenue didn't yet exist, so dirt roads led to this rural retreat. Jones, a southerner, probably chose Richard Upjohn as his architect because Upjohn had been the architect for an earlier house owned by Jones's in-laws in Maine. Since colonial times numerous southerners had been visiting Newport during the summer months, and Jones's house was sited not only to catch the salubrious breezes and water views toward the west and east, but also so that it was close by the properties of other summer colonists from the South. Equally of importance for Jones, his house stood near ponds and fields, long since filled in, where he could enjoy his favorite pastime, bird hunting.

Upjohn gives Jones a cottage orné, a small, intensely decorated house intended to sit comfortably in its natural environment. For his ornamental vocabulary he employs motifs inspired by medieval fact and fantasy — the high-pitched gables, polygonal towers, and diamond-paned windows all allude to a place long ago and far away. The Gothic Revival icing of carpentered details

4

— such as sawn, serpentine barge boards, crenellated balcony rail, and the striped awning-like porch roof with its trefoil droplets — all evoke the pageantry of castles, keeps, and country faires. Much of this exterior is intact, although there have been alterations and losses — including a paint scheme darker than the original sand-textured buff color, and the replacement of wood roof shingles with red slate. An eye-catching cloth awning over the second-story pointed arch window is now gone, as are the colorful birds that filled the aviary room above the entry and that might have been visible from below.

Many of these changes occurred after the house was purchased in 1863 by the King family (hence Kingscote or "King's cottage"). When David King, Jr took over the house in the mid-1870s he had George Champlin Mason, Jr update and enlarge the house with a dining room and service addition. Only a few years later, in 1880, this was separated from the house and moved so that a newer two-story addition of the dining room (with bedrooms above) could be inserted between the two by Stanford White. Although White attempted to blend his work into the earlier Upjohn vocabulary, with a picturesque roofline and textured shingles, by stretching the mass horizontally, this addition alters the original cottage effect sought by Upjohn and Jones. To view the house as it was originally intended, it is best to stand off the southeast corner of the building where the bulk of the projecting polygonal tower hides the later wings.

The interiors of Kingscote are well preserved. Much of this was commissioned by King, including the dark paneled woodwork and heavy-coved moldings that complement Upjohn's medieval-ism. It is only the remarkable 1880 Stanford White addition that

5

departs from this revival idiom. White creates a light-filled space, with low, horizontal proportions, an orderly gridded geometry, and a dazzling array of materials and textures. Perhaps nowhere else in Newport has such a visually innovative interior been inserted into an older house, with the Tiffany glass, glazed tiles, brass, marble, cork, and stained woodwork a prime example of the look McKim, Mead & White achieved in many of their earliest residential commissions. Dining here by candlelight as it flickered off sumptuous, polished surfaces would have made for a memorable visual experience.

Also on the grounds, Dudley Newton's redesign of an earlier stable was in keeping with the style of the main house, now owned by the Preservation Society of Newport County.

5 EDWARD KING HOUSE (1845-47) RICHARD UPJOHN

Aquidneck Park (east of Bowery and Spring Streets)

This was Upjohn's second commission in Newport, done soon after the completion of the adjacent Jones residence. Responding to both its different site on the west-facing slope of a hill, as well as the increasing taste for myriad revival styles, Upjohn creates a tall Italianate villa whose bold, three-story tower is able to better capture the view toward the Bay. Executed in brick, with round arches, scalloped canopies, and projecting balconies, its broader rectangular forms are clearly distinguished from those of neighboring Kingscote — but are equally fanciful. This house was illustrated by Andrew Jackson Downing in his influential volume, *The Architecture of Country Houses* (1850) — thus it would have had a wider, more immediate impact on other designers than Kingscote. The house was originally painted so as to lighten and unify its brick surface, but today the best time to view it is in the late afternoon, when the ruddy brick is gilded by the rays of the setting sun.

*The new design theories of Codman and co-author Edith Wharton were espoused in **The Decoration of Houses**.*

6

6   MARTHA CODMAN HOUSE (BERKELEY VILLA, BERKELEY HOUSE) (1910) OGDEN CODMAN, JR

304 Bellevue Avenue

Ogden Codman's interest in Federal-style architecture led him to design this handsome residence for his cousin, Martha, with an exterior that echoed earlier American houses. The paired columns of a monumental entry porch are reiterated by the two-story fluted pilasters at either end of the front elevation. The front plane of its hipped, balustraded roof has dormers whose compass-topped windows are inset with the arced mullions of colonial entryways. As the architectural historian Pauline Metcalf notes, many of these elements are drawn from several grand-style early-American buildings, including the famous Shirley Eustis House (from about 1746) in Roxbury that is often attributed to Newporter Peter Harrison, and the Perez Morton House, built by Charles Bulfinch in 1796. The architect knew his client well (she was both his relative and the owner of a house he had just built for her in Washington, D.C.), so his historicism was not simply academic but also prompted by Martha Codman's traditional tastes and the numerous pieces of eighteenth-century American furniture she possessed.

Even more impressive is the interior hall with its multi-storied cylindrical volume holding a spiral staircase and topped with an elegant dome. Here Codman's inspiration seems more English than American, with shallow inset arches and a canopy of appliqué reliefs informed by the designs of Robert Adams. Codman updated all of this with his own sense of interior design, meant to clarify and lighten the kind of dark, claustrophobic interiors of the late-nineteenth-century "Brown decades." The intended interior here has a sequence of spaces opening onto each other—the public space of the library, drawing room, and dining hall arranged *en filade* along the garden side of the house—with the effect of more space and light within each room. This was complemented with delicate, classically inspired furniture, a

7

reduction in hanging and draped fabric, and a paler color scheme. These interiors are based on the new design theories Codman and his co-author Edith Wharton espoused in their book, *The Decoration of Houses*. This same house later made a fitting setting for some of the important collection of American art amassed by Martha Codman and her husband, Maxim Karolik, much of which is today in the Boston Museum of Fine Arts.

On the north side of the rear garden is a two-story pavilion designed a little later by Fiske Kimball; it was directly inspired by a Samuel McIntire Federal-styled summer house in Salem, Massachusetts. The original was built for Elias Derby, one of Martha Codman's ancestors. The classical forms of Kimball's version have recently been joined by the addition of another garden house to the south, with both complementing the original sensibility of Codman's main house.

7 SEARS ROEBUCK HOUSES (c. 1924)

Berkeley Terrace

In the early 1920s this row of similar hipped-roofed houses with front entry porches was a small cluster development for middle-class Newporters. Although individually altered, they were all based on plans sold by Sears and Roebuck, the mail order company, which extended the concept of pattern books into the modern era. These are not the summer cottages, nor the social stage sets, of the better-known Bellevue Avenue district. They were the quotidian homes of clerks, factory superintendents, and other workers. While their modesty may contradict the ostentatious reputation of the mansions, they represent the more typical scale of twentieth-century houses, dozens of which are scattered along the streets east of Bellevue and north of Narragansett behind the scrim of grand edifices lining those avenues.

8

8 LEROY KING HOUSE (1884-86) McKIM, MEAD & WHITE, ADDITIONS (1911) FREDERICK R. KING

324 Bellevue Avenue

Having completed a substantial renovation for David King on Kingscote *(see Entry 4 of this Tour)*, the firm of McKim, Mead & White designed this new house for his brother LeRoy a block away. This is an elaboration on the firm's Queen Anne-style houses from the early 1880s. Their orchestration of varied materials and textures—predominantly natural stone work and brick, offset with smaller panels of peculiarly stripped pebble and dash—is clearly related to the kinds of vibrant experiments in surface decoration the firm explored in smaller commissions such as the Skinner and Tilton Houses two or three years earlier *(see Tour Six)*. Also related to the Skinner commission is the inclusion of rather delicate Ionic columns at the entryway.

For King, however, the New York firm arranged these surfaces in a more balanced composition than found on those more delight-fully eccentric early projects. Despite the sculptural modulation of the front elevation, the two wings flanking the central entry porch have a roughly symmetrical organization that ultimately leads to the kind of formality found on the firm's Edgar House designed a little later *(see Tour Six)*.

Like many early McKim, Mead & White houses in Newport, the LeRoy King House (sometimes called Berkeley Villa, like one of its later neighbors) sits on the northern edge of its lot, with a north-facing entrance and a private garden extending from the porches and terraces on its southern side. In this case, due to its busier Bellevue Avenue site, the garden space, intended for family use, is now enclosed by a high brick wall. LeRoy King responded in another way to the busy traffic of Bellevue Avenue when he developed, in partnership with his brother, the commercial King Block a short distance north of his residence in the early 1890s.

9

9 ISAAC BELL, JR HOUSE (EDNA VILLA) (1882-83)
McKIM, MEAD & WHITE

Bellevue Avenue and Perry Street

Isaac Bell was a prominent cotton broker from New York who married the sister of James Gordon Bennett. Shortly after Bennett's nearby Casino was completed, Bell turned to the same firm to design this house (which he paid for himself, despite a longstanding rumor that it was financed by Bennett). Bell himself was a man of substance who, a few years later in 1885, would become the United States ambassador to the Netherlands.

This is the culmination of the firm's work in the Queen Anne and Colonial Revival idioms that they began to develop on earlier Newport houses at the beginning of the decade. Moreover, as Richard Guy Wilson has stated, the Bell House "represents the creative interplay of the talents of the three partners in the early 1880's," with no one partner dominating the design. The house sits far back, its entrance on the side street, but its primary elevation clearly faces the more public Bellevue Avenue. The main vantage point is from the corner of the lot where both elevations bend around the "hinge" of a multi-paned window bay. The facades are unified by the shingled skin, sometimes with bands of cut patterns, the wraparound porches, and the tall tower volumes at either end. These last elements are distinguished by different proportions and shapes: the tall, tapering, and enclosed bell-capped tower at the entrance (perhaps a pun on the owner's name?), and the more skeletal and broadly proportioned polygon bay with its stacked porches that terminates the Bellevue Avenue elevation with its open voids.

The firm has made use of every opportunity to delight and surprise a visitor. At the entrance, they have quixotically centered a porch support on the entry axis between porch steps and front door. Other unexpected details include the reedy porch columns turned to look like tall shoots of bamboo — a clear allusion to fashionable Orientalism. From Bellevue, the primary elevation

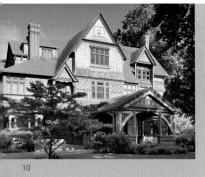

The broad low arch is a porte-cochère that reaches out towards Bellevue Avenue.

10

appears flat, its doubled gables each featuring different window displays — a classical arched trio on the left juxtaposed with the asymmetrical duet of the square window and eccentric shape of a flat oval on the right. These decorative motifs are accentuated by the big copper gutter box sitting between the two gables like a big verdigris brooch on a lowcut gown by Worth, the famous couturier favored by Bellevue Avenue hostesses.

Just as architecturally significant here are the interiors. The main entry hall has an inglenook fireplace, located just beyond the entrance, surrounded with ornate wooden panel work and spindle screens. These were adapted from an actual piece of Breton furniture (White was already doubling as a dealer in European antiques), although they might also appear to evoke a *Japonisme* filtered through the design work of the Aesthetic movement. Other rooms were paneled in oak, swathed in silk, and lit with windows of colored and bottle glass. Whatever the sources of its ornament, this interior is also spatially inventive: the main spaces on the first floor — including dining and drawing rooms and the paneled stairwell — all flow into one another and through the hub of this hearthed hall.

The house was purchased by Samuel Barger, the Vanderbilt family lawyer, in 1891, who gave it the name Edna Villa. Although it had fallen into disrepair by the late twentieth century, the house was recently restored by its current owner, the Preservation Society of Newport County. Now open to the public, it is a prime example of the tastes and sensibilities that were so popular in the early 1880s, embodying a residential architecture whose more intimate scale and organic decoration stands in contrast to the grandiose monumental houses that began to appear only a few years later.

11

10 C.H. BALDWIN HOUSE (1877-78) POTTER & ROBERTSON

328 Bellevue Avenue

Distinctly Queen Anne in the newly restored exuberance of its varied shapes, projections, shadowy voids, and colorful trim, the C.H. Baldwin House continues the stylistic approach initiated, a few years earlier, in Newport by H.H. Richardson on the Watts Sherman House. While Richardson's work is comparable in its decorative surface effects (which paralleled that of English architect Norman Shaw) the massing of the Baldwin House is arranged differently from these precedents. For unlike the sometimes weighty overhanging upper stories and jets found in the work of Richardson and Shaw, the New York firm of Potter and Robertson anchor their design on a wide base whose proportions seem to lighten as it rises, with roof slopes and somewhat smaller projecting elements grouped toward the top. The broad low arch beginning at the entryway is a porte-cochère that reaches out toward the avenue, its scale and form helping to visually tie the first story to the vibrant tapestry of striated patterns on the upper walls. There the architects orchestrate a panoply of surface effects: brick courses, shingled walls, and painted half timbers between which patches of clapboard appear.

11 WILLIAM WELD HOUSE (DE LA SALLE) (1882-84) DUDLEY NEWTON

364 Bellevue Avenue

Newton's experiments with historical forms freely reinterpreted in scale or shape are apparent here. Medieval turrets, steep pitched roofs, and Jacobean-inspired gables do not seem as idiosyncratically outsized when arranged here on these three-story elevations as they do on a smaller set of stone buildings designed by Newton about a decade earlier *(see Belair, Tour Six)*.

12

12 EDWARD JULIUS BERWIND HOUSE (THE ELMS) (1899-1902) HORACE TRUMBAUER

367 Bellevue Avenue

The architect for The Elms, Horace Trumbauer, once told a client, "Madame, if money bothers you, then I'm not your architect." The patrons for this summer house, Pennsylvania coal magnate Edward Berwind and his wife Herminie Strawbridge Torrie, clearly had no such problems with financing fellow Philadelphian Trumbauer's architectural choices. As he did with many of his grand style houses, he turned to a French antecedent—in this case the Chateau D'Argenson at Asnieres. The entire garden elevation on the west is an enlarged version of that chateau's garden elevation, which the Berwinds themselves had seen at Asnieres. The two sculptures installed as an integral part of their garden wall in Newport were purchased at that time. The Apollo and Aphrodite are by the noted sculptor, Guillaume Coustou, and date from about 1750.

Blending the authenticity of such artifacts with a kind of restrained classicism, Trumbauer gives the Berwinds a building that in some respects addresses its private garden more than it does Bellevue Avenue. The main entryway is solemnly flanked by monumental columns and piers set in a projecting bay centered on a façade faced in smooth limestone. There is a third story here but it is hidden from view behind the blind stone balustrade that caps the entire cornice. The geometric rigidity of this arrangement is loosened on the garden façade, where a central bay swells from the main block in a graceful volume, echoing the sinuous curves of the surrounding windows, moldings, and decorative grillwork.

13

The interior of The Elms is intact from the period of Berwind's ownership. An arcaded wall set on Ionic columns of variegated marble frames the major entry passage. The interior scheme of furniture, draperies, and hardwood, orchestrated by the Parisian firm used in many of Newport's major Bellevue Avenue residences, Allard *et fils*, conjures sumptuous eighteenth-century French interiors. But in keeping with the eclectic taste so much a part of the Gilded Age, other styles are blended in the décor—from sixteenth-century Venice to nineteenth-century Vienna.

The eleven-acre property has elaborate gardens that are largely intact. Among the most developed of Newport's formal gardens from this period, these are replete with fountains, geometrically planted parterres, and statuary—much of which was also purchased in Europe. The Elms is now owned by the Preservation Society of Newport County.

13 CHRISTOPHER COLUMBUS BALDWIN HOUSE (CHATEAU-NOOGA, CHATTERBOX)
(1870s), FAÇADE AND ADDITIONS (1881) GEORGE B. POST, RENOVATED (2002) NEWPORT COLLABORATIVE ARCHITECTS

420 Bellevue Avenue

Post's effort to create a memorable street elevation on an extant building is particularly striking now that Baldwin House's original color scheme and detailing have been resurrected by the recent work done by the Newport Collaborative Architects firm. For years the multi-colored treatment of half-timbering, brick work, and carved-wood trim was obscured by a later all-white painting, but now Post's intentions have finally been clarified. In its picturesque variety and dependence on a single large gable to establish an organizing focus, Post updated Baldwin's property by relating it to that of H.H. Richardson's Watts Sherman House (just to its south on Shepherd Avenue) completed in 1875.

Fittingly, this sculpture may be one of the most peripatetic of American monuments.

14

Baldwin was the newly appointed president of a southern railroad company, hence the punning nickname of Chateau-Nooga. Notably, Mariana Griswold Van Rensselaer was moved to designate it Newport's "most unique" house, hyperbole prompted perhaps by the artisanry of the graceful fern reliefs on the bargeboards and by its bold orchestration of colors.

14 AUGUSTUS BELMONT (1910) JOHN QUINCY ADAMS WARD AND F. HERMAN PARKER

Corner of Bellevue and Narragansett Avenue

This realistic, larger-than-life bronze monument depicts the relaxed seated figure of Augustus Belmont, financier to the Rothschild family, dressed in overcoat, gloves, and spats as if ready to travel. Fittingly, this sculpture may be one of the most peripatetic of American monuments, having been moved many times since it was cast at the nationally renowned Gorham Foundry in Providence. The noted American critic Montgomery Schuyler suggested in a letter to Richard Morris Hunt's firm that it be placed in the central space of the Belmont tomb (which the firm had designed some years earlier), but the idea was rejected. It was originally on view at Belcourt, the house that Hunt had designed for the Belmont family, but was then given to the city in 1941 and installed on Washington Square. By the 1960s, still owned by the city, it was transferred to a site in front of the Belmont Chapel in Island Cemetery that pensively looked out toward the same Belmont tomb suggested by Schuyler many years earlier. After spending more than a decade on loan to New York's Metropolitan Museum of Art, it was brought back to Newport through a grass roots effort and sited on the grounds of the Pell House, the headquarters of the Preservation Society of Newport County.

Newport seems to be the most appropriate site, despite all its travels, for one of the last sculptures by Ward (it was finished by his studio assistant, Parker), since Newport is also the home of one of his earliest works, the 1868 Matthew Calbraith Perry Monument *(see Tour Five)*. Both works document the Belmont family's interest in

15

public monuments, the long-standing ties between Richard Morris Hunt and Ward, and two subjects whose lives are entwined with the history of nineteenth-century Newport.

15 ALBERT SUMNER HOUSE (ROCKRY HALL) (1848)
SETH C. BRADFORD, ADDITIONS (1880s), RESTORED (1997)
NEWPORT COLLABORATIVE ARCHITECTS

425 Bellevue Avenue

When this house was built, it consisted of only the small, random-course stone gabled structure that is now the wing sitting closest to Bellevue Avenue. It was built by Seth Bradford for Bostonian Albert Sumner (brother of famed abolitionist Charles Sumner) when one of the closest neighboring houses would have been Kingscote. This pair of rustic retreats shows two different versions of the same stylistic impulse of the Gothic Revival: the stone walls of the Sumner House seem more sober and staid than the fanciful painted wood forms employed by Upjohn on his earlier ornamented cottage. Sumner's architect, Bradford, known for his work in heavy stone, might also have drawn his inspiration for this house from published sources such as those of A.J. Downing.

Rockry Hall, with its trefoil windows and high-pitched roof lines, was enlarged in an unlikely way in the 1890s by the long, angled, shingle-covered wing to the west. This extension was actually a nearby house built in 1889, moved and attached to the old stone structure after a serious fire damaged the mid-century building. This "new addition" plays off the medieval imagery of the stone wing (note the crenellated tower at the western end) while adding the kinds of textural patterns and variety more in keeping with the Queen Anne idiom of the 1880s, Most recently, the entire house was researched and restored through the efforts of John Grosvenor from the Newport Collaborative Architects, who also added the porch with low pointed arch openings in keeping with the original sensibility of the house.

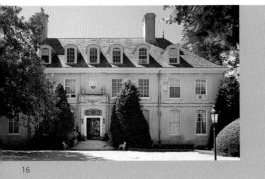

16

16 WILLIAM FAHNESTOCK HOUSE (BOIS DORÉ)
(1928) CHARLES ADAMS PLATT

115 Narragansett Avenue

This is a late house by the well-known New York architect, Charles Adams Platt, who years earlier had helped establish the famed Cornish Colony in New Hampshire. It was designed for yet another wealthy Pennsylvanian who summered in Newport. Despite echoes of the Gilded Age in its name, and unlike more grandiose houses from an earlier period (such as The Elms or Ochre Court), Bois Doré's simple lines of composition and muted walls of limestone suggest this slightly later generation's desire for a more reserved ambience. Only its central entry is more elaborately decorated with classical relief. Discussing this phase of early-twentieth-century mansion design, an article in the 1915 *Architectural Record* pointed out that houses like Bois Doré were "none of them palatial in dimension, ostentatious in material, or lavish in ornament." Such modesty is relative, however, as the house is filled with fine classicizing woodwork in the French manner, an elegant ballroom, more than a dozen bedrooms, and eight marble fireplaces. On the south side, the gentle arc of the rear terrace steps down to what was originally an almost four-acre site. Today the most visually memorable aspect of Bois Doré is perhaps not the building itself but the grotesque pair of eighteenth-century French-style sphinxes guarding the entryway that clearly proclaim its cultural ancestry.

17 EDWARD H. SCHERMERHORN HOUSE (CHEPSTOW) (1860) GEORGE CHAMPLIN MASON, SR

120 Narragansett Avenue

This is typical of Mason's work before the advent of the showier decorative styles advanced by "outsiders" such as Richard Morris Hunt and McKim, Mead & White. Now a property of the Preservation Society of Newport County, Chepstow is a more typical mid-nineteenth-century summer cottage, with its arch-windowed,

17   18

Italianate bottom and French mansard roof. A self-contained block lacking much sculptural play, its elements of entry tower and bays are distinguished by their modest projections from the core block even while sheltered by the extended flare of the correctly proportioned mansard. Adding to its modesty is the exterior surface, covered in flush, horizontal boards and meant to read as dressed masonry walls, particularly when viewed from the street across its broad lawn.

18 JOSEPH HART HOUSE (BIENVENUE) (c. 1854)
ATTRIBUTED TO JOSEPH WELLS, ALTERATIONS (1984)
NEWPORT COLLABORATIVE ARCHITECTS

97 Narragansett Avenue

Narragansett Avenue is a broad street giving access across the Bellevue district to a gathering place on the cliffs called the Forty Steps that has long had access to the water below. Several of its most prominent homes feature styles that reflect the eclectic tastes of the mid-nineteenth century rather than the more extravagant modes of the later and better-known big mansions farther south (the construction of which necessitated the razing of several mid-century houses). Bienvenue is composed as an Italianate villa with its tallest, three story tower denoting the main entrance. On either side, somewhat shorter gabled projections flank the entry but never quite break into defined tower forms. The architect used carpentered quoining blocks on the entry porch and specified horizontal planking (a variant of the sheathing on nearby Chepstow) to further mime masonry construction. Unfortunately, any effect of lithic monumentality is compromised by the clutter of double- and triple-arched windows, key stones, triangular pediments, and the busy doubling of eave brackets above. Even the fancy scalloped roof of the eastern porch (now enclosed) mimes lighter materials, as if it were the windblown edge of a tent canopy, and ultimately competes with the implication of masonry elsewhere on the design.

19

20

By 1876, this house was owned by Edwin D. Morgan, the New York governor whose grandson, Edwin D. Morgan III, would spend summers here. The younger Morgan would go on to commission McKim, Mead & White to design his own grand estate house, Beacon Rock, overlooking the inner harbor in 1891.

19 PINARD COTTAGES (1882) JOHN DIXON JOHNSTON, (1982) NEWPORT COLLABORATIVE ARCHITECTS

Corner of Annadale Road and Narragansett Avenue

Much of the housing in the Cliffs area, such as the Pinard Cottages, was originally built as individual rental units, as opposed to the kind of large hotel facilities that were the norm earlier in the century. This set of structures was designed by local architect-builder J.D. Johnston in the fashionable idiom of the Queen Anne style. The original plan called for six such units, but only four were actually constructed in 1882, although Johnston later built another in 1891. Their cross gables and dormers, undercut shadowed porches, and Anglo-colonial details were composed on a relatively simple block, typical for Johnston. A century later, in 1982, John Grosvenor of Newport Collaborative Architects converted these to condominium units, simplifying wall openings and altering surface treatments to emphasize their decorative shingled volumes.

20 65 MERTON ROAD (c. 1870) GEORGE CHAMPLIN MASON, SR

This Upper Cliffs neighborhood north of Narragansett Avenue stretches along the northern end of Cliff Walk, a picturesque path running several miles along the coastline that affords some of the best views of the later nineteenth-century mansions. Overlooking the rocky cliffs that line the eastern coastline, this house was part of the earliest summer development of this area in the third quarter of the nineteenth century—its main attraction being its cool breezes and proximity to Easton's Beach. While many nearby buildings, such as the Pinard Cottages (*see Entry 19 of this Tour*),

21

were intended as modest summer cottages, and later as housing for middle-class Newport residents, 65 Merton Road is larger and more elaborate in design.

It sits today as if ignoring the later buildings around it, turning its back on the town. Rising over three stories high, with stepped porches and windows facing the water, it is wrapped by large open porches. A mid-block structure whose shingled mass looms over lesser houses nearby, its towering size is relieved by the fancy carved braces and crossed stick work under the upper gable, and by the small detail of rather frilly window caps that read as eye-catching exterior valences. These are allusions to the kind of vernacular and even rustic sources that influenced the design of seaside villas and whose use on residential projects was popularized by Richard Morris Hunt in the 1860s. For this cliffside retreat, however, Mason conservatively retained the mansard found on many of his projects into the 1870s.

21 EASTON'S BEACH PAVILION (c. 1939), (1993)
WILLIAM BURGIN

Easton's Beach

Local residents often refer to the three largest beaches in the area as First, Second, and Third Beach, as if all were located in the town of Newport. In fact, only First, or Easton's Beach as it is more officially known, lies primarily within the town's jurisdiction. This beach was Newport's most accessible beach, lying at the bottom of the hill sloping downward from the Upper Cliffs and reachable by the old Bath Road that more or less followed the path of what is now Memorial Boulevard. By the late 1880s this beach had been privately developed and possessed a set of bathhouses and a conically topped central pavilion built by Peabody & Stearns. These, and facilities added later such as a boardwalk and the hot salt water (or Roman) baths, were completely demolished by the tidal wave unleashed by the disastrous 1938 Hurricane. What had originally been a place for the social elite

22

has become, over the years, a place for everyone to enjoy the coastline. When it was eventually cleared of the hurricane debris, the beach became a municipal beach as over the following year more pedestrian brick structures were erected. The newest version of the beach's facilities, designed by William Burgin, incorporates some of the older elements (such as the carousel pavilion) but extends them with a series of gabled changing rooms, arranged like rows of small individual houses, whose shingles, trellises, and wood trim reflect old-fashioned bathing shelters with a scale that is intimate and inviting. These are cleverly raised on piers over a mostly empty first story to help them better survive any future hurricanes.

22 DRESSER STREET HOUSES (c. 1891) ATTRIBUTED TO JAMES SMITH

9, 11, and 15 Dresser Street

These three Queen Anne houses, built for middle-class Newporters, are little known but delightfully detailed. Drawings by local architect James Smith exist at the Newport Historical Society for a house similar to numbers 11 and 15 with comparable massing, fancy window trim, and carved panel work; Smith may have worked on these with the prolific architect/builder/mill owner, J.D. Johnston. The third house, at 9 Dresser, differs from the other two and in its decorative scheme is by far the most idiosyncratic — suggesting this is perhaps the work of another architect. Here the geometry is more inventive, with engaged bays erupting into bulbous turrets at the eave line and peculiar details such as the window bay on the third story of the entry tower tucked under the truncated jerkin-head roof line. These forms — and the particularly elaborate exterior skin of clapboards topped with bands of cut and notched shingles and serpentine trim boards — make it one of the most fanciful ornamented cottages of its day for a middle-class client.

23

23 COLONEL GEORGE R. FEARING HOUSE (THE ORCHARD) (1873-1874) GEORGE CHAMPLIN MASON AND SON

180 Narragansett Avenue

Sited on a near axis where Ochre Point Avenue intersects with Narragansett Avenue, this summer house was built for New Yorker and Civil War veteran, Colonel George R. Fearing, in a decidedly earlier French manner. Constructed of yellow brick, and with sandstone trim, it is balanced and symmetrical with the high-pitched roof lines, classical entry surround, and low crescent dormers of French tradition. Set behind enormous iron gates, it is approached down an allée of trees that echoes the geometry of seventeenth- and eighteenth-century French landscaping.

The architect of record, George Mason, Sr, admitted to relying on a European source when he identified a French-style house near Geneva, Switzerland as his inspiration; we know plans were procured directly from Europe. The house also bears a close resemblance to suburban villa designs published in 1872 by French architect Cesar Daly in *L'Architecture Prive*. Given that the Orchard is unlike any of the Mason firm's other work, in either its style or materials, it seems likely that the firm acted primarily as project managers overseeing site construction, rather than as independent designers.

24 OGDEN GOELET HOUSE (OCHRE COURT) (1888-1892) RICHARD MORRIS HUNT

100 Ochre Point Avenue

Currently the main Administration Building of Salve Regina University, this house was built by Richard Morris Hunt as one of the first grand-style summer mansions at a time (the close of the nineteenth-century) when clients and architects worked feverishly to outdo one another in grandiose scale, grandiloquent decoration, and social ambition. That said, Hunt proved himself a master of such monumental architectural symbols, often employing the

24

highest levels of craftsmanship and new building technologies to achieve seemingly traditional forms based on historical models.

This house is still startling in scale, its three and a half stories thrusting up from rather spare grounds. This effect is emphasized by this being one of those Newport mansions that, while very large, is squeezed onto a relatively small — and in this case, narrow — parcel of land. The site choice is no accident, however, as it is just across the street from the house built by Ogden's brother, Robert, who commissioned McKim, Mead & White to build him a monumental shingled house in 1882 (it is still privately held by the original family heirs and only partially visible through its hedge border across Webster Avenue).

What Hunt imagines here is a pastiche of French styles that mix the Renaissance style of François Premier (note his royal symbol of a flaming salamander in carved details) with an older set of medieval forms that can be seen in the window configurations, crockets, and Gothic-style ornament. This mélange of historical forms is most likely a kind of architectural reflection on another Francophile Hunt building, the William Kissam Vanderbilt House on Fifth Avenue in New York City, no longer extant.

Like many of its neighbors along the Cliffs, Ochre Court has two main elevations. Its seaside façade has an open arcade forming a loggia, atop which is an inset balcony. If the entry elevation seems opaque and closed (particularly on the north service wing), the central block on the water side — with the big glazed panes of its many arched windows — is far more transparent.

*The house is still startling
in scale as squeezed
onto a small parcel of land.*

Beyond the porte-cochère and entry doors the space expands both outward and upward in an elaborate carved stone stairwell that immediately opens onto the three-story hall that is the core of Hunt's design. At the opposite end of this hall, light floods in through the ample arched windows illuminating the vast space on the first level. Both Hunt and his client were surely aware that there is a similar feature next door in the Robert Goelet House that had been recently designed by McKim, Mead & White (although that shingled residence uses different materials and a somewhat more intimate scale). This sequence of a compressed entryway opening onto a stairwell and the accompanying thrust of vertical space in a core hall also figures in earlier Hunt projects such as the Griswold House. But where the Griswold House points up earlier American architecture and vernacular sources, Hunt is clearly asserting a different set of references here in one of the earliest grandiose houses of the Gilded Age. And in case the overall imagery on Ochre Court does not make it clear enough that Hunt was informed by late medieval forms, he added one more clue. To the right of the main entry is an ornate garden screen of carved stone, fashioned rather like an ecclesiastical rood screen. Just below the central pedestal (which only later was supplied with a religious sculpture by the college) is a portrait of Hunt. Here Hunt is depicted (most likely by his stonecutters with whom he often had a collegial relationship) as if pondering his own work, hand to chin and not unlike the portraits of great master architects, builders, and masons found in the cathedrals of the Middle Ages.

While the house still evokes the courtly stage set intended by Hunt, some of its interior decoration and most of its original art work have been altered or lost as it was transformed from a private residence to an institutional building under earlier college administrations. Today the school is a more sensitive steward of its unique architectural environment and has gone to great lengths to restore and maintain Ochre Court and many of its other significant structures.

25

25 SALVE REGINA UNIVERSITY CAMPUS

VINLAND FARM HENNERY (1884-85) PEABODY & STEARNS

RODGERS RECREATIONAL CENTER (2002) ROBERT A.M. STERN

MILEY HALL (1964) MAGINNIS, WALSH AND KENNEDY, ADDITION (2003) NEWPORT COLLABORATIVE ARCHITECTS

J.J. VAN ALEN HOUSE (WAKEHURST) (1884-1888) DUDLEY NEWTON FROM PLANS BY C.E. KEMPE

McKILLOP LIBRARY (1989-1994) ROBINSON GREEN BERETTA

CATHERINE LORILLARD WOLFE HOUSE & GATE HOUSE (VINLAND) (1883) PEABODY & STEARNS, ENLARGED (1907-1908)

MRS JULIA H. ELDRIDGE HOUSE (OCHRE LODGE) (1882-1883) DUDLEY NEWTON

JOHN THOMPSON SPENSER HOUSE (ALTHORPE, NOW FOUNDERS HALL) (1889-1890) PEABODY & STEARNS

EDSON BRADLEY HOUSE (SEA VIEW OR SEA VIEW TERRACE, NOW CAREY MANSION) (c. 1870) GEORGE CHAMPLIN MASON, SR, REMODELED (1887-88) J.D. JOHNSTON, (1923-25) HOWARD GREENLEY

MRS ANDREW RITCHIE HOUSE (FAIRLAWN, NOW YOUNG BUILDING) (1852-1853) SETH BRADFORD, EXPANDED (1869) RICHARD MORRIS HUNT, ALTERED AND ADDITION (1880) McKIM , MEAD & WHITE, PORTE-COCHÈRE AND OTHER ALTERATIONS (1891) PEABODY & STEARNS, RENOVATED AND RESTORED (1998) NEWPORT COLLABORATIVE ARCHITECTS

In the closing decades of the nineteenth century, the campus of what is now Salve Regina University was a district of large houses, many with extensive grounds, situated to the south of Narragansett Avenue between Bellevue Avenue and the Cliffs. While many buildings have been readapted to the functions of the educational institution, with some loss to their original character, and others have been erected in styles not always in keeping with the residential feel of the neighborhood, this small school operates and maintains a truly unparalleled collection of historically significant buildings. A short walk around the tree-lined streets and expansive lawns of its campus reveals much that is still intact in these mostly Gilded Age cottages. Surprisingly, there are also a few newer structures that also hold architectural interest.

The two most historically significant buildings on campus — the Ogden Goelet House (Ochre Court) and the Watts Sherman House — are treated in separate Entries 24 and 30 in this Tour. The tour of the other buildings begins at Ochre Court.

Predating the chateau-esque Ochre Court, and facing its grand entry gates across Ochre Point Avenue, is the strangely composed North and South Hall. The low horizontal lines of the building emphasize the planes of its gabled roof that stretch downward toward the ground. The two wings (north and south) are bridged by a bold stepped arch that, despite its fabrication in wood, recalls the kind of rustic archways used to such dramatic effect by H.H. Richardson a few years earlier on his famous Ames Gate Lodge in North Easton, Massachusetts. This feature is accented by the scale of the wrought iron brace and the top-heavy finial of a big birdhouse that graces the central cross gable. Peabody & Stearns seem to be in a playful mood here as there are no fewer than six different roof and dormer shapes (including a salt box profile and a hipped roof whose ridges swoop upward toward a central pinnacle). Heavy random-block walls are interlocked with organic, swelling, shingled walls. Most are hemmed by a sawtooth edge; some are even replete with wave patterns. The contrast between the formal and severe verticality of Ochre Court and the low

textural decoration of this building could not be greater—particularly when one realizes that it was originally a utility outbuilding on the chicken farm run by Vinland owner Catherine Lorillard. Called the Hennery, it had a chicken coop on one side and the Hen Keeper's cottage on the other—which served to screen the property from Ochre Point Avenue and created the focal point of an arched entryway to the farm gardens beyond, again somewhat akin to Richardson's earlier Gate Lodge.

Peeking through the archway, one catches a glimpse of another shingled structure, this one also intended for a specific prosaic function but designed much more recently by Robert A.M. Stern. For the Rogers Recreational Center, it was Stern's challenge to contextualize the requisite bulk of a gymnasium (some 60,000 square feet) so as to make it appear less institutional and thereby complement the private tone of the surrounding residential neighborhood and smaller buildings nearby. He employs a wide range of shingled elements—grouped gables, engaged towers, polygonal bays, big stubby columns, undercut porches, and the eccentric rhythms of these features across his asymmetrical design—to make the mass of his building seem more intimate and human scaled. Stern has long understood the visual language of the historic shingle style of the 1880s (of which Newport has many prime examples) and is sensitive to the history of American campus planning as well. In addition to his Post-Modern virtuosity with these historic elements, Stern cleverly depressed the massive volume of the gymnasium itself so that it sits a full story below grade to lessen the profile of the building.

To the north, across Webster Avenue, is Miley Hall—another structure commissioned by the college (for use as a dining hall

and other services). Built in 1964, its reductivist composition of interlocking blocks and gridded surface composition reflects the International Style—albeit here in a very late, somewhat derivative version. The use of industrial materials such as plate glass, stainless steel, and concrete, so much a part of the early modern vocabulary, is softened on Miley Hall by the expanses of textured-brick walls. Might there even be contextual references here, which were held to be an anathema in the abstractions of the pure International Style, with echoes of ships railings and porthole windows hinting at the college's seaside environment?

Walking back along Ochre Point Avenue, past the Hennery, we come across Wakehurst—set far back on its site for its owner, J.J. Van Alen. The design for Wakehurst, one of the earliest of the grand style monumental mansions influenced by historical European forms, was based on plans purchased by Van Alen, a lover of all things English, from the British architect C.E. Kempe. Approached down a corner lane between a row of trees, it must have been even more reminiscent then than it is today of Wakehurst Place, a so-called "prodigy house" in England (1590), which it carefully

ARCHITECT RICHARD MORRIS HUNT adorns an Ochre Court garden screen.

replicates in both its massing and details. Kempe's expertise as a stained glass artist, and his knowledge of Tudor architecture, would have recommended him to his friend Van Alen, particularly after the Newporter had visited the English manor house in 1883.

Except for the entry surround, its flush-laid walls show remarkably restrained decoration — although each elevation does manage to display a lively sense of modeling, from the gridded window frames to the thicket of finials gracing its zigzag roofline. Much of the interior, such as the large entry hall that sits across the entry axis and opens onto the ornately paneled staircase beyond, was imported directly from Europe—with period rooms having been saved from recently demolished houses there. Hung with tapestries and chandeliers, lit through large stained glass windows, and decorated with the intricate geometric plaster moldings on the ceiling, the effect — even though diminished today—is still redolent of Renaissance England. Today it is used for offices, a student café, and other student services.

It is fairly easy to see how the adjacent McKillop Library, built a century after the completion of Wakehurst, mimes that building's forms. Its institutional scale and plan differ greatly from those of its neighbor, although it plays with the multiplicity of gabled bays and projections found on Wakehurst. These echoes are timid, however, for it is the tall grids of glass and the peculiar machined rustication of the stonework that dominate the design. Subtle details — such as the window reveals whose shadow lines add substance and variety to the planarity of the Wakehurst design — are abandoned here. The flattening effect results in a contemporary building with only the most obvious hints at Post-Modern contextualism.

Across Ochre Point Avenue, on land extending to the Cliffs, is the large house, Vinland, that was designed as a summer residence for Miss Catherine Lorillard Wolfe. A contemporary of Wakehurst, and pre-dating other large "cottages" nearby, Vinland differs greatly in almost every aspect from the historicism of these neighbors. Vinland, vaguely Nordic and Richardsonian Romanesque in

its references, is a low, dark, rusticated brownstone house stretching along a rise overlooking the ocean. Its linear composition was further lengthened in 1907 by Hamilton and Florence Twombly (she was the youngest grandchild of Commodore Vanderbilt), who had purchased it about a decade earlier. Despite its brooding color and hulking mass, delightful visual flourishes are provided by stone-carved reliefs, which echo Celtic ornament, and the extravagant copper flashing—particular the representations of icicles and rivulets of water—that grace its ridgeline.

Such chilly references, along with its stout stonework and even its name, evoke Nordic Europe via the popular nineteenth-century myth of an early Viking colony on Aquidneck Island. The dining room at Vinland once contained a marvelous group of paintings by Walter Crane, showing various scenes from such an imaginary Viking past, that echo Longfellow's "The Skeleton in Armor" with its references to the Stone Mill (which has long been wrongly identified by some as a Viking-built church). Although Crane's cycle was removed and sold several decades ago, it was originally part of elaborate interiors that notably included stained glass by Edward Burne-Jones depicting Odin, Thor, and Frey, three Norse gods. Today the much-altered interior is used for academic purposes.

Almost as interesting on the Lorillard property is the small Vinland gatehouse whose lantern, with its serpentine ironwork arm, reaches out toward the street as if beckoning to visitors while a plaque simultaneously announces the name of the grand house beyond. Like the design of the Vinland stable just to the north, the arched windows, carved stone trim, and engaged turret of the gatehouse all match the detailing of the main house.

On the southern edge of the campus along Ruggles Avenue are three large houses of interest. The Eldridge House, by Dudley Newton, gathers much Queen Anne detail under its big gambrel. In it overall shape, undercut balconies, and the covered porch on the eastern side, it clearly recalls the Samuel Colman House designed at the same time by McKim, Mead & White. Only Newton's strange, short, twisted porch posts remind us how quixotic an architect he could be. It is now called Ochre Lodge and is used as a dormitory. A block away, Founders Hall was originally the John Thompson Spencer House (completed in 1889). The symmetrical volumes and revival details of this ample wood-frame structure could not be further removed from Peabody & Stearns' earlier Vinland nearby, demonstrating the firm's eclectic range of stylistic options. The basic composition focus here is provided by a central entry that is enhanced by a Palladian window, ornate dormers, and a Chippendale railing on the upper stories. This is all flanked by rotund towers and unified by the skirt of a porch stretching across the entire front. Such a handsome arrangement was used again by the same firm—but this time reinterpreted in brick and cast iron—on the Fanny Foster House (Ridgemere) from 1897-98, located a short distance away on Leroy Avenue but not part of the Salve Regina campus.

Finally, the Edson Bradley House or Sea View Terrace—now known as the Carey Mansion after later owners—is the third Salve Regina University building along Ruggles Avenue. One of Newport's largest mansions, this is a massive, rambling hodge-podge with elements dating from 1870 to 1925; unfortunately, it never visually coheres into a unified whole. No wonder, since the building we now see masks the earlier wings via the imposition of a crowded array of turrets, half-timbered gables, and tall chimneys in which no single element acts as an organizing focus. Bradley, the president of a distillery, had removed the interior finishes and contents of his primary residence in Washington, D.C. in order to fill this vaguely Tudoresque summer house. With its

mixed bag of historical furnishings, and a pastiche of architectural tropes on the exterior, this was clearly architecture as stage set — perhaps more blatantly so than in the more resolved designs of others such as Hunt and McKim, Mead & White. As if to underscore this quality, the house is best remembered today for serving as the eerie backdrop to the Gothic-camp soap opera, *Dark Shadows*, broadcast on national television in the 1960s.

One last University building, Young Hall, brings us back to Bellevue Avenue. This was an early house in this area, built in 1852-53 as Fairlawn for Mrs Andrew Ritchie by Seth Bradford — who was among the most productive architects in Newport during that decade. Much changed by several major campaigns involving additions, renovations, and restorations, the triple gables of the house today still echo the double, high-pitched gables originally derived from English Tudor architecture but somewhat out of keeping with Bradford's other work. Its grouped chimney pots, masonry-trimmed brick walls, and original slate-patterned roof still show their English roots. Helping to unify the cross block at the rear with the front elevation is the curved porch (originally added by Peabody & Stearns), which was most recently rebuilt during an extensive restoration — guided by John Grosvenor of Newport Collaborative Architects — so that Fairlawn could be used for academic conferences.

26

26 MARY BRUEN HOUSE (THE HEDGES)
(c. 1853) SETH BRADFORD, RENOVATED (1872) RICHARD
MORRIS HUNT

6 Howe Avenue

MARY BRUEN HOUSE (1882-83) WILLIAM RALPH
EMERSON

453 Bellevue Avenue

These two houses built for the same client reflect changing architectural tastes in the third quarter of the nineteenth century. Early
in the 1870s, Richard Morris Hunt was brought in by Mary
Bruen, a Bostonian who summered in Newport, to renovate an
already existing stone house. Playing off the rusticity of the rub-
blestone structure, Hunt added a picturesque cap of gables,
balconies, and stickwork bracing. A number of his most important Newport buildings from this period no longer exist (such as
the Appleton and Marquand Houses), but the Bruen House gives
us a good indication of how he continued his exploration of the
motifs he had begun to work with almost a decade earlier, when
he designed the J.N.A. Griswold House *(see Tour Six).*

The Howe Avenue House, which seems to have little relationship
to Bellevue Avenue today, was originally approached from that
side, since it was at that time set far back on the property that
reached to the main street. About a decade later, however, Bruen
asked Boston architect William Ralph Emerson to create a newer
house at the front of her lot, directly on Bellevue. This shingled
structure, in which the front porch and entry back swell out from
the long gabled mass behind, exhibits Emerson's inventiveness
with soft organic building forms. Where Hunt's work is all rectilinear and intricate, Emerson simplifies his surfaces and
emphasizes volume as much as line. Both compositions are sculptural, but Emerson's stresses the tonal contrasts between his
broad, bulging wall planes and the deep shadowy voids of balconies, windows, and porches.

27

In the early twentieth century the deep lot was finally split up and the earlier house acquired its name, the Hedges, some time after the Bruen family sold the property.

27 JOHN M. HODGSON COTTAGE (THE FLOWER COTTAGE) (1882) CLARENCE LUCE, ALTERED (1920) SCHUYLER L. PARSONS

2 Leroy Avenue

WASHINGTON IRVING RESIDENCE (QUHOLME) (2005) NEWPORT COLLABORATIVE ARCHITECTS

14 Leroy Avenue

Although much altered, the small Flower Cottage was once both a residence and a retail shop, with greenhouses and garden plots to its rear. Built for Hodgson, a New Yorker who had earlier established a florist business serving the summer colony, this was originally a more delicate, shapely structure—the second story extended over the first and perched over broad-coved supports, the flare of which can still be partially discerned today on the north elevation of the cottage. This form—along with the deeply undercut porch (now replaced by a Palladian window), the shingled exterior, and its diminutive size—strongly evoked the kind of vernacular structures (rustic farm sheds and corn cribs, boat houses, and life saving stations) that were in vogue as architectural source materials in the 1880s.

Less than a block away, at 14 Leroy Avenue, stands another small house that is picturesque in a more imagistic way. It is also one of only a handful of such twenty-first-century houses in this largely built-out neighborhood (another, in a more predictable coastal New England shingle style, is right next door at 20 Leroy Avenue; yet another, by architect Jim Estes, is all but hidden behind the high wall at the end of Yznaga Avenue, a few blocks away). On the Irving residence, instead of suggesting a utilitarian function, the stepped gables, flared porch, and coupled, high-pitched roofs (by

28

Mohamad Farzan of NCA) make direct reference to traits of Hudson River Valley Dutch architecture and simultaneously honor a noted literary ancestor of the owner. In fact, much of the house's composition and details (such as what appear to be cut-stone blocks along the lower part of the wall) are directly inspired by Sunnyside, the famous home of author Washington Irving in Tarrytown, New York. There the writer took an eighteenth-century house and romanticized it into what he called his "little nookery" of a Dutch fantasy. Although Newport's Irving site is no sleepy hollow, and the residence is modest in size, the Leroy Avenue house creates visual surprise even in a neighborhood of opulent architectural effects. Just as the famous author said about his own house, this Newport cottage evokes "illusions which fancy has cast over commonplace realities."

28　JOHN CARTER BROWN HOUSE (BEFORE 1866), RENOVATED (1866) CARPENTER AND CHILDS

Bellevue Avenue and Hazard Avenue

HAROLD CARTER BROWN HOUSE (1893) DUDLEY NEWTON, OGDEN CODMAN, JR (INTERIORS), FREDERICK LAW OLMSTED (LANDSCAPING)

459 Bellevue Avenue

The pleasing ensemble of curved forms on which the John Carter Brown House is centered were the result of a renovation undertaken by the owner on his summer residence. The planarity of the (possibly earlier) quoined and clapboarded main block is softened by the novelty of rounded porch roof, windows, and roofline —although the numerous repetitious forms such as brackets, blocks, and balusters admittedly make for a somewhat cluttered overall effect. The Browns may be associated more with Providence but have long summered in Newport. John Carter Brown was the astute rare book collector whose philanthropy created the eponymous library at Brown University famous for its unparalleled collection of books on the Americas.

The Browns, with obvious ancient Rhode Island roots desired a house more fully screened from public view.

A generation later, another member of this venerable Rhode Island family, Harold Carter Brown, commissioned the house at 459 Bellevue Avenue for his new bride, Georgette Wetmore Sherman. Here he opted for balancing architect Newton's heavy stonework with the most current interior designs by Ogden Codman, Jr. For this, his first major project, Codman drew inspiration from lighter classical French sources. Since Brown collected French furniture, the young designer's novel Francophile approach would have appealed to him as well.

There was no need here for the type of ostentatious display that marked other Bellevue Avenue mansions at the end of the century. The Browns, with obvious ancient Rhode Island roots, probably desired a house more fully screened from public view than most of their neighbors' and the now mature Olmsted planned grounds are still effective at maintaining its discreet privacy.

29 WILLIAM SHEPARD WETMORE HOUSE (CHATEAU-SUR-MER) (1854) SETH BRADFORD, RENOVATED (1870-1880) RICHARD MORRIS HUNT, EDITH WETMORE GARDEN HOUSE (c. 1920) FREDERIC RHINELANDER KING, ALTERED, ADDED TOWER WINDOW BAY (1915) JOHN RUSSELL POPE

474 Bellevue Avenue

Chateau-sur-Mer was indeed a grand house on the sea; it originally stood alone off the newly developed Bellevue Avenue with water views mostly unimpeded to the east and south. The use of Fall River granite and the asymmetrical placement of the entry tower were typical of Seth Bradford's other work in Newport, including "Belair" and the first Mary Bruen House *(see Tour Six and Entry 26 of this Tour)*.

Almost a decade after inheriting the property from his father, and while still in his teens and recently married, George Peabody Wetmore turned to Richard Morris Hunt to augment the house with additions and updates. Hunt had designed the monument at

29

Island Cemetery for the elder Wetmore in 1863 and it might have been this personal connection that caused the younger Wetmore to enlist Hunt's services in two campaigns of work (1870-73 and 1874-1880). Hunt took the Bradford building, with its overtones of Italianate composition, and reworked its interior decoration and plan. The results made it more Neo-Grec, the fashionable Second Empire style that Hunt had known from his studies at the Ecole des Beaux Arts in Paris. Hunt corrected the form of the mansard by raising its profile and altering its copper detailing. He formalized the entryway with a projecting porch whose stone piers were carved in the stylized classical forms of recent Parisian architecture. Additional faceted stonework was done in the current French mode.

The house, now owned by the Preservation Society of Newport County, lays claim to a distinguished roster of architects who worked on it in later years. After George Peabody Wetmore's death, Ogden Codman, Jr did the interior design for the Green Salon (1903); Frederick Rhinelander King built the small garden house at the northern edge of the property (c. 1920); and John Russell Pope added a bay around 1915 and other alterations to the house.

A nearby garden folly, the stone Moongate, stands along Shepard Avenue. Although now on the edge of the property, it once stood surrounded by Wetmore land, its little stone seat elevated to get a better view of the Atlantic Ocean a short distance away. An intriguing later addition to the grounds is the *Sod Maze* by site artist Richard Fleischner, installed in 1974 near the northwest corner of the property, the only remaining work from Newport's international "Monumenta/74" exhibition of outdoor sculpture.

30

30 WATTS SHERMAN HOUSE (1874-1875) HENRY HOBSON RICHARDSON, INTERIOR REDECORATION, LIBRARY AND DINING ROOM FIREPLACE (1880-81) STANFORD WHITE, LATER WING ADDITION (c. 1890) DUDLEY NEWTON, ALTERATIONS (c. 1960).

15-17 Shepard Avenue

This is the only surviving example of several buildings designed by Henry Hobson Richardson for Newport clients. Its grounds are a six-acre lot that was once part of the Chateau-sur-Mer property across the way, split off when George Peabody Wetmore gave the land as a gift to his sister Annie on the occasion of her marriage to New York banker William Watts Sherman. While it is frequently referred to as the William Watts Sherman House, landowner evidence and contemporary newspaper accounts strongly suggest it would be more appropriately named the Anne Wetmore Watts Sherman House, as she alone funded the project.

Vintage photographs show the house in its original state, standing—like so many others of the time—in a more open landscape with clear water views. Richardson's design was more emphatically vertical but this has been compromised by the later additions to the left of the main entrance that complement the original materials and textures but stretch the composition horizontally. Despite these changes, the principle organizing form is still Richardson's all-encompassing entry gable. This, crossed with the main gabled block to its south, forms two monumental intersecting masses whose size is moderated by the pattern and texture bands of his surface effects. Rustic stone, set randomly, jig-sawn shingle patterns, small insets of half timbering, strips of multi-paned windows, and carving work added great visual variety to

The Watts Sherman House is the only surviving house designed by H.H. Richardson for Newport clients.

the broad underlying forms. In its original top-heavy verticality, with upper elements projected over the lower stories, its tactile materials and its historical references (such as the attenuated chimneys and half timbering), this parallels the strong revival idiom of a Richardson contemporary, English architect Norman Shaw. Richardson, however, blended this Shavian historicism with Americanized elements such as the sheltering gable sloping down toward the ground and undercut porches with balconies on the secondary elevations. This expressed an original sensibility that resembled neither Shaw's nor that of Richard Morris Hunt, another architect working with historical-vernacular sources in the 1870s *(see, for example, his work on the first Mary Bruen House and the J.T. Gibert House nearby, Entries 26 and 40 in this Tour).*

There are impressive interior features here as well—many of which were designed by Stanford White when he was still a young designer in Richardson's office. Slightly later, in 1880, White was brought back to redecorate the library and dining room. The delicate carved paneling of the library with wooded grills over reflective surfaces parallels White's experimentation with a novel interior vocabulary seen on other houses of the period, such as the Isaac Bell House *(see Entry 9 in this Tour).*

The lower roofline behind and to the left of the entry gable is an addition by Newport architect, Dudley Newton, who maintained the original registers of stonework, shingles, and roof, and all but duplicated the details (the brickwork, for example) of the earlier chimneys. An even later addition was done in the 1960s, when the house had become a home for the elderly. It is now owned by Salve Regina University and not generally open to the public *(see Entry 25 in this Tour for other Salve Regina buildings).*

31

31 MRS RICHARD GAMBRILL HOUSE (VERNON COURT) (1898-1901) CARRERE AND HASTINGS

492 Bellevue Avenue

This house, designed by Thomas Hastings of the New York firm and aptly described by architectural historian Vincent Scully as "a sophisticated essay in esoteric taste," fuses elements from numerous French and English sources. Rising up four stories to the ridge line of its hipped roof and screened by a tall masonry wall, Vernon Court seems more crowded on its narrow site than other large *fin de siecle* houses. Elaborate formal gardens were originally laid out to simulate those created by Henry VIII for Anne Boleyn at Hampton Court. On the exterior, its repeated elements of windows, shaped dormers and tall chimneys, and glazed terracotta trim, while numerous, are generously spaced to convey a handsome sense of dignity. Its main hall features a sinuously curving staircase with elaborate metal balusters ascending from a quadrangle of four highly variegated stone columns. Although the historical design sources for the Gambrill House are similar to those used by McKim, Mead & White and others, the cleaner expanses of stucco walls on Vernon Court moderate the often visually insistent ornament found on other large "cottages." Today, with many of its Allard *et fils* interiors intact, Vernon Court is open to the public, housing the National Museum of American Illustration.

32 CORNELIUS VANDERBILT II HOUSE (THE BREAKERS) (1895) RICHARD MORRIS HUNT, PLAYHOUSE (1886) PEABODY & STEARNS

Ochre Point Avenue

Bellevue Avenue may be the best-known street in Newport but The Breakers is arguably its most renowned building. Although in style and grandeur it can be most closely associated with the Bellevue Avenue extravagance of Marble House, Rosecliff, or The Elms, this late Richard Morris Hunt design is sited at the southern end of a phalanx of large houses (including Hunt's own Ochre

32

Court) that are actually several blocks east of Bellevue and perched along the elevated coastline of Easton's Bay in what is essentially an extension of the Upper Cliffs neighborhood whose development began a generation earlier.

The Breakers was the name of an already existing, large wood-frame house, designed on this site by Peabody & Stearns, that Cornelius Vanderbilt purchased in 1885. Emphatically different from the structure we see today, the house Vanderbilt purchased from its owner, Pierre Lorillard, consisted of an irregular series of shapes, projecting gables, a tall tower, and textural surface ornament that reflected an 1880s infatuation with the Queen Anne style. This earlier house was destroyed in 1892 by a devastating fire; all that remains from the Lorillard era is the freestanding playhouse, also by Peabody & Stearns, to the north—an under-sized one-and-a-half storied gabled confection with outsized embellishments and mannered columnar carvings that gives some sense of the earlier Breakers' sensibility. Vanderbilt commissioned Hunt to design a new house—part summer palace, part family seat—on the same site, passing over both Peabody & Stearns and George Post, who was working at the time on Vanderbilt's mansion in Manhattan.

Hunt, who was by the early 1890s considered to be the dean of American architects, had already introduced a number of influential styles to the American architectural vocabulary over his long career. His design work culminated in the elaborately palatial residences of the late 1880s and early 1890s, for which he and Newport are so widely known. He had produced numerous other houses for the extended Vanderbilt family, becoming in a sense their "court" architect. For the new Breakers, Hunt produced a number of different designs (drawings of which still exist), including one version with a French aspect and another, similar

The Breakers is arguably the most renowned building in Newport.

to what was eventually constructed, in the style of a sixteenth-century Genoese Renaissance palazzo.

Cornelius Vanderbilt clearly intended his mansion to surpass in size that of his younger brother Willie (Marble House), which Hunt had just completed on Bellevue Avenue. The Breakers, with its seventy rooms, does just that and appears to be even larger on its relatively confined thirteen-acre property. Beyond sheer size, Hunt and Vanderbilt assert the Breakers' status as family seat with Vanderbilt symbols, initials and images connected to the family, everywhere visible in the multitude of sculptural details. The sober balance achieved by Hunt's composition may, since he knew his client well, have as much to do with the older Vanderbilt's stern personality and rectitude as it does with classical source material.

In addition to these concerns, Hunt was, not surprisingly, charged with designing a more-fireproof building that employed such innovative technical features such as the Guastavino tile vaulting used for the porches, a heating plant removed from the main house, steel-frame construction, and the novelty of both gas and electric power.

Despite the overall symmetry of his palazzo conception, Hunt adds variety where none might be expected. Each elevation of the rather neutral-toned Indiana limestone is interrupted by significant features such as the porte cochere projecting from the entry side, the circular depression of the laundry court off the service wing, and the two-story trellised bay overlooking the formal gardens. One could argue that the grandest classical elevation of all is on the seaside, where we find the symmetry of two wings, projecting toward the cliffs, connected by a triple-arched mosaic tiled loggia on the first floor and the doubled rhythm of arched voids above. Hunt's knowledge of classical design is underscored by his use of the Doric order below surmounted by the Ionic on the second story. It should be noted, however, that the monumental bulk of the house is lessened by the sculptural push-pull of setbacks and projections on every side and by the relief surfaces using a vocabulary of Renaissance forms.

The interior of the house features a central hall (a possible nod to the wooden version of such a central space that was part of Peabody & Stearns' earlier Breakers, but more likely based on Hunt's own use of such a space in the nearby Ochre Court). This great hall is a clear, rational core rising vertically off of open rooms of various shapes and functions. While there are precedents for the hall, the effect here is more monumental; the walls are supported by broad spans of tripled arches and grand Corinthian pilasters set on tall bases running up to a garlanded cornice more than two stories above. Beyond the architect's spatial dexterity, what is meant to engage our attention, is the luxurious combination of variegated stone, detailed carvings, gilded surfaces, and elaborate metal work at a larger-than-life on scale. As in all the large houses, many others were brought in to manage individual aspects of the interior design—including the Parisian firm of Allard *et fils* for the public spaces, as well as Ogden Codman, Jr for the more intimate bedrooms upstairs. Hunt maintained overall control, however, seamlessly blending the many individually distinct and overpowering elements into a unified but stirring experience.

Almost simultaneously with the building's completion, Hunt unexpectedly died in July of 1895. Cornelius Vanderbilt himself spent very little time in his glorious cottage after suffering a stroke the following year that left him debilitated until his death in 1899. One of the Vanderbilt daughters, the Countess Széchényi, opened the house in 1948 as a benefit for the newly organized Preservation Society, under whose aegis the house is maintained and open to the pubic today. Newport's houses completed in the grand manner, such as The Breakers, are buildings open to a wide variety of interpretations. For some, such as Vincent Scully, they express fairytale pretensions. They are glorious excesses of the nouveau riche, pseudo-princely stage sets for the self-styled aristocracy of a new American class—the captains of industry. Recent reinterpretations point out that The Breakers also reflects a wide range of cultural shifts in the varied aspects of its design and

impact: the evolution of Newport's landscape; the immigration of foreign artisans to execute its ornament and décor; the rise of architecture as a profession and that profession's relationship to powerful clients; the implementation of novel construction strategies and technologies that approach modern building practices; and the emergent community of servants who oversaw daily life in these large residences. In sum, the grand mansions mirrored the desires and values of their age. Social theater, old world fairy tale, or imperious architectural accomplishment, they continue to exert an enormous presence. As the architectural historian William Jordy once wrote of these extravagant buildings, "Newport simply would not be Newport without them."

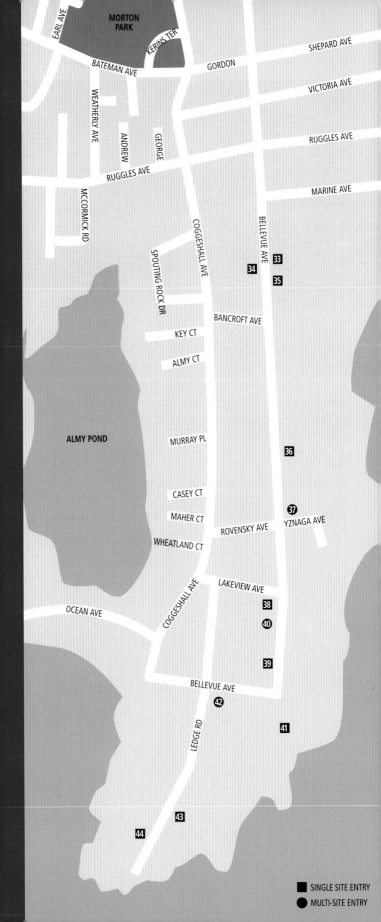

33

33 TESSIE & HERMAN OELRICHS HOUSE (ROSECLIFF) (1899-1901) McKIM, MEAD & WHITE

548 Bellevue Avenue

With a name playing up its cliffside site and the renowned rose gardens of a previous house on the site (owned by George Bancroft a foremost Rosarian), Rosecliff is one of Newport's most famous grand cottages, although from the Avenue it appears rather small and low as it sits far back on its manicured lawn. The grandly arcaded first story is stretched upward with what only seems to be a half story with square attic style windows (it's actually a full story). A classical ambience infuses all the elements of the elevations — engaged iconic piers, arched windows, relief swags, and oval panels—rhythmically arranged to create the pleasing cadence of a French-derived aesthetic. The entire image is derived from the royal garden pavilion of the Grand Trianon at Versailles. Here it is cloaked in white glazed terra cotta, Mrs Oelrichs' favorite color.

Given Rosecliff's architectural heritage, its rooms are decorated by the appropriately chosen Parisian firm, Allard *et fils*. These are arranged in an H-shaped plan with the long connecting wing containing the grand space of the ballroom, its largest public room (42 by 72 feet). Here the Oelrichs hosted lavish events for their social circle. It is no accident that Stanford White chose to place the ornate heart-shaped staircase in the hall through which the ballroom is reached. Although it too might have been based on French models, it created a stage-like effect upon which Tessie Oelrich could make a grand entrance down its sensually curving flight that duplicated the flowing train of her ball gown. Perhaps more than any of Newport's houses, Rosecliff defines the sense of social theatricality that is the primary function of so many Gilded Age houses.

As a property of the Preservation Society of Newport County, Rosecliff is now open to the public.

The elaborate social rituals of this summer colony were played out in elegant ballrooms.

34

34 PEMBROKE JONES HOUSE (SHERWOOD)
(c. 1885, 1906-1908) HOPPIN AND KOEN

553 Bellevue Avenue

Pembroke Jones and his family were summer colonists from North Carolina who were known for hosting elaborate social events. When he bought an extant house from the Havermeyer family, he enlisted the New York firm of Hoppin and Koen to transform it into a stage set for such parties. While the overall effect of their transformation immediately calls to mind the White House, a closer look reveals the kinds of eighteenth-century English overtones clients wanted and that inform both this design and that well-known presidential mansion. The relatively flat expanses of blank wall punctuated with Adamesque window compositions, sculptural rondels, and the bold monumental porticoes on both the front and rear all make the Georgian allusion clear. Hoppin returned about eight years later to add the southern wing, an arcade-walled ballroom that echoes the same stylistic features. He later completed Edith Wharton's house, "the Mount," when she left Newport for Lenox, in the same style.

35 DANIEL PARISH HOUSE (BEECHWOOD)
(1852-1853) CALVERT VAUX AND ANDREW JACKSON DOWNING,
BALLROOM ADDED (1888-1890) RICHARD MORRIS HUNT

580 Bellevue Avenue

The result of a collaborative team effort of Calvert Vaux, who designed the house, and Andrew Jackson Downing, who developed the grounds, this house features a symmetrical main block with primary arch-topped openings. The entrance is essentially a rusticated triumphal arch projecting from a cross-gabled bay that frames the simple geometry of a somewhat small circular window. This house had, from the beginning, two primary elevations, the one to the east labeled on the architect's drawing "Front Facing the Sea." Two superimposed porches, defined by triple arches opening onto the seascape, originally made this elevation seem even more

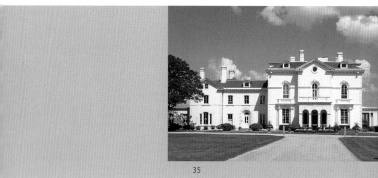

35

like a "Florentine" palazzo, as it was then categorized. This dual orientation toward the street and toward water views informs many of the later large-scale houses along Bellevue Avenue.

Most of Vaux's original scheme and detailing are still here, but the house had to be completely rebuilt by the architects in 1856 after a fire destroyed the three-year-old building. The crescent dormers were the major change on the second design, probably reflecting a novel French taste just beginning to influence American architects.

Nearly thirty years later Mrs Caroline Backhouse Astor purchased the house and had Richard Morris Hunt add a ballroom. This was important for two reasons: it not only altered Vaux's seaside elevation but also became a feature that every large house owner wanted in their own "cottage," at least partially in emulation of this social doyenne. It is important to remember that Ward McAllister's memorable nickname for the elite of New York society, "The 400," was based on the capacity of Mrs Astor's New York ballroom. Such elegant ballrooms and their entry halls were the primary architectural space in which the elaborate social rituals this summer colony became known for were played out on a grand scale that was unimaginable a generation earlier.

36 ALVA & WILLIAM KISSAM VANDERBILT HOUSE (MARBLE HOUSE) (1888-1892) RICHARD MORRIS HUNT, CHINESE TEAHOUSE (1913) HUNT & HUNT, CHINESE TEAHOUSE REBUILT (1981-82) DONAL SIMPSON ASSOCIATES

600 Bellevue Avenue

One of Richard Morris Hunt's most visually stunning designs, Marble House combines a very orderly, grandly formal exterior with a series of magnificently decorated rooms that surpass each other in the concentrated visual and tactile pleasures of their effects. The end result is a "jewel box" effect. Hunt's design for William Vanderbilt's mansion in Manhattan had evidently so pleased his client that Vanderbilt commissioned him to design a

36

special birthday present for his wife, Alva. According to Hunt, Alva Vanderbilt became involved in every aspect of its design. Money being no obstacle, the result from the master architect was the luxurious Marble House.

Sited like so many of Newport's big cottages on a relatively small lot, Marble House achieves monumentality through the grandiose scale of the piers and projecting entry colonnade on the front elevation. Echoes of the White House may be the most obvious American reference but Alva was also particularly fond of the Parthenon—going so far as to insist that Hunt use Tuckahoe marble, known for its whiteness, so that her Bellevue Avenue house, like the ruins of the Parthenon, could gleam in the moonlight. The fluted Corinthian columns of the entry porch and the attached piers to either side support a complex entablature of classical moldings and details that are topped with a balustrade running along the top edge of the entire building. Hunt adroitly contrasts the uniform color and relative shallow relief on much of the white marble exterior with the bolder shadow effects created by the porch and heavy cornice. A centered balance is achieved by the projecting porch—particularly as framed by the rise of stone railings at either side of the entry drive.

The intensity of ornament, for which this house is best known, is evident on the exterior with a swagged frieze over the front entry and on the rear spandrel reliefs that suggest the four seasons in the French manner. On the north side of the house, more low reliefs symbolize the female attributes of industriousness and wisdom held in high esteem by Alva Vanderbilt, who would later become a prominent supporter of the suffrage movement.

Hunt's masterful abilities are readily apparent on the interior where the elaborate materials, ornament, and spaces are orchestrated in a profusion of colors and opulent trappings. He also had to coordinate the various schemes of different interior design firms brought into the project by Mrs Vanderbilt. To the left of the entry hall is the dining room, where Corinthian pilasters

surround the space—echoing their monumental counterparts on the entry front. Instead of the simple white marble of the exterior, these are iterated in a dark pink Numidian marble whose highly energetic variegations, when combined with the room's bronze gilt capitals, wall sconces, and intricate ceiling with heavenly mural, create a complex setting whose nearly claustrophobic overload of effects makes dinner an otherworldly event. In no other Newport interior does the Gilded Age sensibility of royal European architecture seem so overpowering.

The Gilded Age is the perfect metaphor for the Gold Salon, located across the entry hall. Instead of the fiery red tones of the dining room, here everything glitters in auric tones: gilded walls, mirrors, glazing, and bronze sculptures. We sense here the French inspiration of Versailles and its Galerie des Glaces and try to imagine the radiant effect that light from scores of candles in the two huge chandeliers would have had on Hunt's resplendent space. The French connection is underscored by the room's interior designers, Allard *et fils*, who worked for Hunt on many of his best-known interiors.

Other rooms reveal period influences from different times and places. The plan of the house is a long rectangle running along Bellevue Avenue, with two wings projecting off the rear to form a more protected seafront terrace. The southern such rear projection is for the Gothic Room, adjacent to the Gold Salon. In contrast with the previous two rooms, this room originally had decoration derived from late-medieval sources; its stained glass, tapestries, and paneling make it appear somewhat dark. It was designed by Gilbert Cuel, who came from France to work for the Vanderbilts, and was intended to house Alva's collection of Gothic art (he also

Marble House was used as a benefit and convention site for the Women's Suffrage Movement.

designed several other spaces here, including Alva's bedroom). Still other, less public, rooms reflect décor from the period of Louis XVI and the rococo era. In addition to their luxurious level of craftsmanship, these disparate rooms are informed by the French character of their inspiration. As if to assert a fitting architectural lineage, Karl Bitter, Hunt's in-house sculptor, created two portrait busts to embellish the landing on the main stairwell. One is of Jules Hardouin-Mansart, the seventeenth-century architect at the court of Louis XIV, the other is of Hunt himself.

Despite its dominant European imagery, the house was later called the "climax of the American Dream" by Cleveland Amory; it was opened with a lavish housewarming in August 1892. The dream did not last long for William and Alva, however, as they were soon to be divorced. Alva remarried their erstwhile friend, Oliver Hazard Perry Belmont, and moved into Belcourt, also designed by Hunt, a few doors down the Avenue *(see Entry 38 in this Tour).*

After 1909 Alva, who by this time owned both residences, allowed the mostly boarded up Marble House to be used as a benefit and conference site for the Women's Suffrage Movement. In 1912, she called on the firm of Hunt and Hunt (the successor firm to Richard Morris Hunt run by his two sons, Richard and Joseph) to design a Chinese Teahouse at Marblehouse, near the cliff's edge. The Hunt brothers traveled to China, visiting several cities—including Peking and Shanghai—before developing several proposals that were pastiches of Chinese and Japanese architecture. Although first used for lavish entertainments, the outbuilding languished after Alva's death in 1932 and was in a ruinous state by the 1980s.

The Preservation Society of Newport County acquired Marble House after the death of a subsequent owner, Frederick Prince, in 1963; gifts from Prince and Vanderbilt were used to acquire the house and its furnishings. It was the Preservation Society that brought in a crew of craftsmen and restoration experts to rebuild and restore the tattered Chinese pavilion under the direction of Jeff Staats, Donal Simpson Associates, moving it somewhat

37

away from the sea edge of the property for its own protection and thereby saving what may be the most exotic part of the unparalleled American fantasy known as Marble House.

37 EDWARD C. KNIGHT HOUSE (CLARENDON COURT) (1904) HORACE TRUMBAUER

620 Bellevue Avenue

MRS GEORGE WIDENER HOUSE (MIRAMAR) (1914) HORACE TRUMBAUER

650 Bellevue Avenue

Horace Trumbauer, who had earlier designed The Elms for Edward Julius Berwind, built these residences for two other fellow Philadelphians. Although both show his indebtedness to historical sources, one — Clarendon Court — is based on the reticent formality of grand English houses from the eighteenth century. In fact, its details and the flush-set stone blocks of its planar elevation very nearly replicate a design by Colen Campbell for Hedworth House in Durham, England—a place that art historian James Yarnall notes was ironically torn down just as this house was being constructed on Bellevue Avenue. It is a building informed by classical geometries that can be seen in the upper window pediments, the proportion of columns and openings, and the relationship of each element to the others. Although it may well have been unintentional, the effect of Trumbauer's work is a kind of homage to Newport's own eighteenth-century architect, Peter Harrison, who was inspired by this same vocabulary of forms from his own era when he translated his knowledge of English design into the wood-and-brick buildings of colonial Newport.

If Trumbauer's design of Clarendon Court is one of academic rigor and calm repose, his work on Miramar a decade later seems overwrought. This is a relatively small house whose front is congested with ornament and detail, all of it displaying French rather than English eighteenth-century sources, a connection

38

underscored by its setting among formal gardens. Where the broad surfaces of Clarendon Court evoke a quiet grandeur, here the business of rusticated blocks, oversized windows, and sculptural reliefs crowding the elevation on Miramar diminish the house's presence, pushing its appearance closer to a large pavilion than a stately residence. Although the family of Mrs Widener had employed Trumbauer as their architect for years, such design features may have mattered little to her. While this house was being built, her husband and son died in the sinking of the *Titanic*.

38 OLIVER HAZARD PERRY BELMONT HOUSE (BELCOURT, BELCOURT CASTLE) (1891-1894)
RICHARD MORRIS HUNT, ALTERED (1908) JOHN RUSSELL POPE, ADDITIONS, DUDLEY NEWTON

659 Bellevue Avenue

Built by Oliver Hazard Perry Belmont, son of the famous financier Augustus Belmont, as a kind of medieval French hunting and sporting lodge, Belcourt was designed by Richard Morris Hunt with medieval references throughout. Part of its originality lies in Hunt's combination of styles: English half timbering and French-style masonry work that appear to merge different early ideas as evident from the drawings. Here, too, Hunt's other design work with picturesque wood framing and his later, more formal elevations and historical references all collide in one of his last works.

Belmont was an accomplished equestrian, he founded Belmont Raceway in New York and its famous Belmont Stakes, and much of the first story on the main wing to the north is occupied by the

*Much of the first story
is occupied by the
immense and elegantly
furnished stables.*

immense and elegantly furnished stables with the main living space above. Most impressive is the ribbed vaulting of the Gothic-style ballroom—with one end wall filled with a huge fireplace, a visually confusing miniature-scaled sculptural castle set atop the crenellations of its mantle. Although such amenities must have suited Belmont, they probably seemed peculiar choices for the architect who created the Breakers and Marble House during these same years. Still, no less an architectural observer than Julia Ward Howe pronounced Belcourt "a most remarkable house," although a more recent critic, James Yarnall, has termed it an "antimansion." Nonconformist might be a better word, as Belcourt's peculiarities—from its unconventional exterior finish to such interior planning indiscretions as the placement of the master bedroom directly off the public ballroom, a shocking architectural affront to polite society—were probably more in keeping with Belmont's personal demands than with Hunt's intentions.

An arched gateway to the south leads to a much-compressed garden court, hemmed in by the lower, turreted stable and service wing and all but overwhelmed by the scale of the half-timbered residential wing. There are more French references in the steep mansard roofs punctuated by copper-framed oval dormer windows. The busy polychromy of heavy, rusticated granite quoining, brick-arched doors and windows, and iron grillwork— a range of materials and shapes not always successfully unified in Hunt's composition—leave an unresolved lasting impression. Perhaps only the more uniform expanse of the slate roofs helps unify the dissonance of his design.

Belmont's wife Alva probably has the distinction of being the only Newporter to have resided in and owned two Bellevue Avenue mansions—first with her husband, William Kissam Vanderbilt, in Marble House, and then, following their divorce, across the way at Belcourt, which Oliver Belmont gave to her as a wedding present in 1896. She toned down the masculine touches on the original sporting lodge and, after Belmont's death, brought in other architects to convert a tack room into a dining room and

39

add other living spaces. Despite these renovations, she shuttled back and forth between Marble House and Belcourt, using both residences for her social entertaining and for gatherings in support of her favorite cause, the Women's Suffrage Movement.

39 EARL P. MASON HOUSE (QUATREL) (1853-54)
THOMAS TEFFT, ALTERED (c. 1900) OGDEN CODMAN, JR

669 Bellevue Avenue

40 1870s HOUSES

Southern end of Bellevue Avenue

Toward the ocean end of Bellevue Avenue is a cluster of distinguished houses, most of which date from the 1870s but one of which, Quatrel, dates from the earliest years of the Bellevue development.

Quatrel was designed in 1853 by Thomas Tefft, the Providence architect, for Earl P. Mason, a businessman and banker from that city. Tefft often employed Italianate elements in his residential work but here the plain stuccoed walls are topped with a short mansard roof crossed by the wide flare of a flat-arched gable. Built only a few years after the opening up of Bellevue Avenue, this originally was a more isolated house site (and one of the first on the inland side of the street). Although owned by a Rhode Islander, it should be noted here that any traveling between Providence and Newport would have been by sailing or steaming down the bay, with the island much less accessible than today.

Surrounding Quatrel are several houses from the 1870s, many of which show the influence of Richard Morris Hunt and the style he helped popularize. One of these, the Beeches at 647 Bellevue, dates from 1871 and was built by George Champlin Mason, Sr for New Yorker Moses Lazarus, the father of poet Emma Lazarus ("give me your tired, your poor, your huddled masses…."). While the Beeches retains the old-fashioned convention of a mansard roof, the nearby G.T. Brayman House at the corner of Bellevue and Rovensky Avenue (1875) is more overtly decorated with ele-

40

ments suggesting newer architectural fashions. Its ornate, con-toured brackets, tall turrets, and wonderful striped gable ends — delightfully suggestive of tenting — make it a new-fangled orna-mental cottage.

A few doors down, at 665 Bellevue, is the earliest house in this group: the J.T. Gibert House by Richard Morris Hunt (1869-70). Built a few years after Hunt's Griswold House *(see Tour Six)*, it clearly shows the architect continuing to explore the use of struc-turally expressive stick-style elements and extensive porches. The connection between the two houses is not just visual, however, as the property was owned by J.N.A. Griswold (who commissioned Hunt to design this house intended for resale). Griswold was at the time much involved in real estate developments in this part of town, owning as he did large tracts of Newport Neck. He relied, as did others, on the natural coastal beauty of Newport's south-ern landscape to attract new summer residents to the area. One indication of just how appealingly untouched this island land-scape must have been is that Martin Johnston Heade, one of the most renowned American landscape painters of the era, owned property just behind the Gibert House in 1876 (although he moved to Florida a few years later and it was never developed during his ownership).

Finally, at the corner where Bellevue turns west, is the James T. Rhodes House (1874-75). Although it, too, dates from the 1870s, its Gothic tracery under the eaves hints at an even earlier date, and its large cubic wings were added or enclosed only later.

41

41 FREDERICK WILLIAM VANDERBILT HOUSE (ROUGH POINT) (1891) PEABODY & STEARNS, ADDITIONS, RENOVATED (1922-23) HORACE TRUMBAUER

680 Bellevue Avenue

Rough Point, on a magnificent weatherbeaten site, owes stylistic debts to other nearby mansions. Like an earlier house by the same firm, Vinland, its horizontal mass is composed of rough stone walls, although here they are built of a lighter-colored stone. But if Vinland is gathered under a dominant gable with the focal point of a bold archway, the more reticent and balanced elevation of Rough Point has modestly projecting cross bays suggesting the architectural syntax of Tudor or Elizabethan Revival houses. Built for the youngest of four Vanderbilt brothers, this house, like those for Cornelius II and William Kissam Vanderbilt, was gigantic in size. Unlike the Breakers and Marble House, however, Rough Point is discretely set back from the street behind walls and a planting design originally laid out by the Olmsted firm.

Its size is also more human scaled by the cross wings and the cant of its service wing, as well as the relatively small entryway leading into a two-story English-style oak-paneled hall that serves as the spatial hub for the other first-floor rooms. In the hall, heavy ceiling beams, a baronial-size fireplace fitted with massive fire dogs, and the colorful pageantry of wall banners, all emphasize the medieval character of the original Peabody & Stearns' design.

A later set of renovations and additions, including the solarium that overlooks ocean views, were carried out by Horace Trumbauer with a more Francophile classicism. Trumbauer's

*The late tobacco heiress
Doris Duke had a lasting
impact on Newport's
architectural heritage.*

arched windows, lighter colors, flowing spaces, and shifted proportions suggest the influence of changes in interior design fostered by Edith Wharton and Ogden Codman, Jr.

Today the house holds an eclectic, personal collection of art, furniture, and even closets full of clothing and other accessories, all documenting the later residency of the house's most famous owner, the late tobacco heiress Doris Duke. When only thirteen years old in 1925, she inherited the house from her father who had purchased it only a few years earlier. Beyond her ownership of this house, her phenomenal wealth, and her tabloid reputation for eccentricity (camels were even kept on the Rough Point grounds!), she had a more lasting impact on Newport's architectural heritage by establishing the Newport Restoration Foundation in 1968, which rescued over eighty historical properties with funds almost entirely from her. Although the Foundation sometimes treated the buildings a bit like life-size

DORIS DUKE had a reputation for eccentricity—even keeping Princess and Baby, camels acquired in a deal for a used 727 jet.
SOURCE: *Daniel Forster Photography*

42

doll houses — moving them to other lots and altering their interiors — her support not only saved the structures themselves but maintained the urban quality of many eighteenth-century streetscapes in central Newport. Just as important, her support helped shift preservationist attention from the famous late-nine-teenth-century mansions toward the significance of more modest colonial architecture.

42 ROCKHURST DEPENDENCIES (1889, 1891) PEABODY & STEARNS, RENOVATED (1990, 1996, 2005) DORIENNE WEST FARZAN

700 Bellevue Avenue and 38 Ledge Road

Although the large house known as Rockhurst no longer exists, these three delightful structures—two gate houses and a carriage house—still define the outer street perimeter of the property. The gatehouses are beautifully restored today, and the carriage house is partially reconstructed by architect/owner, Dorienne West Farzan. This trio suggests the engaging way that architects extended the visual surprise of varied shapes and inventive, inter-locking compositions to small structures. The round towers, polygonal roofs, high chimneys, and enchanting carved and tex-tural ornament all evoke the image of picturesque rusticity aestheticized through a trained architectural sensibility.

43 SAMUEL G. WARD HOUSE (LAND'S END) (1864-65) JOHN HUBBARD STURGIS, RENOVATED (1893) OGDEN CODMAN, JR

42 Ledge Road

As its name implies, this was an outpost, near the southern extremity of the island and close to a picturesque old stone boat-house, long gone but which was a popular destination for Newporters who ventured down Bellevue to the rocky shoreline to fish, boat, or just rusticate. The severe planes of the first story are weighed down by the dark cap of its roof, shaped in gables,

43   44

gambrels and even a more exotic variant called a "turtleback" roof sheltering the prominent central bay. This last element helps organize the diffuse composition that mostly echoes the horizontality of the landforms on its site.

Although originally commissioned by the wealthy Bostonian Samuel Gray Ward, after 1889 it became best known as the residence of Edith Wharton. Some of its current exterior composition is the result of renovations commissioned by Wharton, who brought Ogden Codman, Jr in to work on the house in 1893. Although now much altered, this was one of the houses where Wharton and Codman developed their refreshing and new interior design aesthetic intended to open up and clear out the dark, claustrophobic ambience of much nineteenth-century interior décor.

44 JOHN RUSSELL POPE HOUSE (THE WAVES)
(1927) JOHN RUSSELL POPE

Ledge Road

The low, brooding mass and organic materials of this house compliment its siting: hugging a wave-lashed rocky coastline. Designed by the architect as his own house and built on the foundations of the Lippitt's Castle, its half-timbered details and weathered surfaces call to mind an isolated English seaside retreat, somewhat worn by the elements and settled with age. For all its ambient rusticity, Pope's original interiors were in a more gentrified, Georgian Revival style. It also holds another, more dubious distinction of being one of the first large houses in Newport to be converted to condominium units, back in 1981.

8. OCEAN AVENUE

The southern part of Aquidneck Island, also known as Newport Neck, is a land mass abutting Rhode Island Sound, extending farther west than the rest of the island and thus providing the town of Newport with its sheltered harbor. Its natural prospects—a landscape of ponds, ocean coves, and rocky formations—have long made it one of Newport's most spectacular attractions.

The thoroughfare of Ocean Avenue (known in the local vernacular as "Ocean Drive" or, more simply, "the Drive") traces the outline of this eroded coast as it swoops down from its intersection with Bellevue Avenue on the east and heads toward Brenton Point, providing vistas of the sea and across to the neighboring island of Conanicut (Jamestown), as well as farther southwest toward Point Judith. Until the late nineteenth century, this area was a remote rural outback for Newporters that contained few buildings and only a handful of farms and landowners.

The increased access to this southern tract brought about by the creation of Bellevue Avenue in the mid-nineteenth century changed the use of this landscape from agricultural to recreational and residential. Leaving the hurried, urban townscape behind, visitors in carriages and on horseback marveled at the stunningly unspoiled and raw natural environment. It became a popular day trip destination for birding, hunting and fishing, and swimming.

Starting in the 1880s, several large landowners began dividing their holdings through sales or developments, which opened up opportunities for architects to create large new homes—some of them on a scale and with acreage unimaginable along most in-town streets. As a kind of roughhewn extension of the tailored and gated landscapes of Bellevue Avenue, here architects and clients seemed happier to coexist with their natural surroundings, using the powerful land forms, rocky outcroppings, and ocean-side inlets to help define the ambience of their oversized summer lodges. This area was thickly settled only very recently and even now enjoys more open zoning than the residential areas of the town itself.

continued on page 299

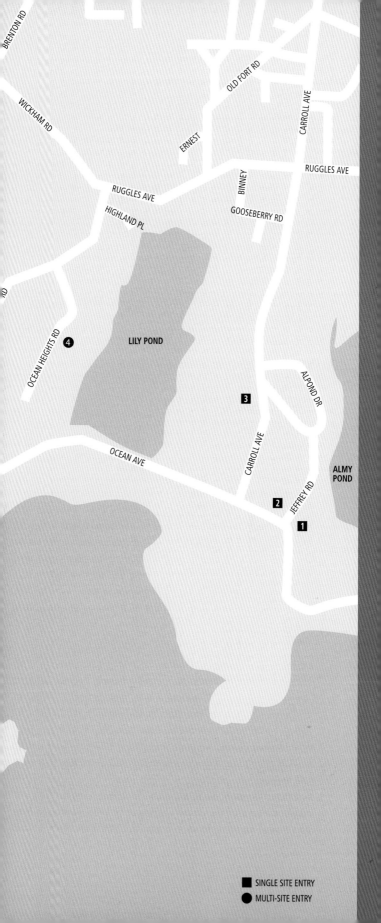

BRENTOM RD

WICKHAM RD

OLD FORT RD

ERNEST

CARROLL AVE

RUGGLES AVE

RUGGLES AVE

BINNEY

HIGHLAND PL

GOOSEBERRY RD

RD

OCEAN HEIGHTS RD

4

LILY POND

ALPOND DR

3

CARROLL AVE

OCEAN AVE

ALMY POND

JEFFREY RD

2

1

■ SINGLE SITE ENTRY
● MULTI-SITE ENTRY

1   2

1 **WILLIAM S. MILLER HOUSE (HIGH TIDE)** (1900)
   WARREN AND WETMORE

   81 Ocean Avenue

2 **STUYVESANT & MAMIE FISH HOUSE (CROSSWAYS)** (1898) DUDLEY NEWTON

   Ocean Avenue at Jeffrey Road

Here, at the start of Ocean Drive, are two very different solutions for large-scale houses that typify the range of designs in this neighborhood — some gently echoing the rustic landscape and others more forcefully imposing themselves upon it. In the first category, Warren and Wetmore have given us in High Tide a stuccoed mansion whose arcade of compass-topped windows and high-pitched shingled roof allude to the understated design of French country villas. The prominent second-story balcony above the bowed front elevation suggests that an excellent view may be had. And indeed, the elevated house site, on this highest seaside outcrop, does afford a stunning panoramic view of the small coves and rocky peninsulas that comprise Aquidneck Island's picturesque coastline where it meets the magnitude of the Atlantic Ocean.

In the second category, local architect Newton, with the Fish House on the next corner, has erected a temple-fronted Colonial Revival mansion that ignores rather than echoes its natural environment. Even the peculiar window work in the huge pediment, which makes an ocean view possible, is a much later addition not original to the house. While Newton's later design work is often filled with outsized details and overscaled elements, the monumental portico here might have been inspired by the fact that this was home to Mamie Fish, an imposing sovereign of Newport's turn-of-the-century high society. With the well-known bon vivant Harry Lehr as her partner, Mrs Fish often hosted

3

exorbitant dinners and grandiose parties at Crossways that were made all the more status-affirming by the house's eminent site and its grand colonnade.

3 KISSEL HOUSE (BLACKBERRY HILL) (2000)
NEWPORT COLLABORATIVE ARCHITECTS

211 Carroll Avenue

The recent change in ownership of two large tracts of land on the rises overlooking either side of Lily Pond created the opportunity for the design of numerous residences. Spread over the east side of the pond are several buildings forming a family compound that are informed by the kinds of picturesque forms found on earlier houses in this area. One of these that is visible from the street is Blackberry Hill, which engaged gabled and turrets, echoing the ever-popular Shingle Style vocabulary. On the other side of the house, facing both pond and ocean, architect Mohamed Farzan has wrapped the large gabled block with a columned porch whose high cascade of wooden steps has the dual function of ready-made outdoor seating. Two large dormers, nearly cross gables, also face southwest, with one scooped out into a sheltered balcony overlooking the ocean.

4

4   OCEAN HEIGHTS

VERBENA (1999) STEVE LAURIN
HOWE HOUSE (1996) WILLIAM BURGIN
SLUTSKY HOUSE (2006) NEWPORT COLLABORATIVE ARCHITECTS

On the western side of the pond, an area known as Ocean Heights was opened to development in the late 1990s. Here three gigantic residences sit in a row near a ridge, the southernmost one over-enlarging traditional shingled forms, the second playing with vertical windows, piers, and roofline seemingly derived from the Prairie School, and the third more nestled in its site, with square towers peeking up through the bank of trees.

OCEAN DRIVE, view towards Gooseneck Pond and Green Bridge, c. 1880.
SOURCE: *Collection of the Newport Historical Society*

5

6

5 EDITH BURNET POMEROY HOUSE (SEABEACH, THE NUNNERY) (1895-96) OGDEN CODMAN, JR, (RENOVATED 1980) RICHARD LONG

Ocean Avenue at Hazard Road

An early tentative design by Ogden Codman, Jr, with a set of elements—the compass-topped arcade of windows, pedimented gable, and dentil trim — hinting at the young architect's interest in Federal-period sources. When built, the house had a stucco covering and is best known for eliciting the biting remark made by Codman's sometime friend and collaborator, Edith Wharton, who held that one of the worst things for an architect was to "build a mud hut and mistake it for the Parthenon."

6 IRVING TOMLINSON HOUSE (SALT MARSH) (1929-1930) DERBY, BARNES AND CHAMPNEY

75 Hazard Road

The planar-stuccoed forms here recall late Victorian-era English models like C.F.A. Voysey, M.H. Baillie Scott, and Edward Luytens. It's a rarity along the Drive—a modest-sized house that turns its back on the coast to face inland. Its choice of perspective is made clear by the tall multi-paned window in the double-storied living room (also borrowed from those same English precedents), affording a view worthy of East Anglia: over a bucolic marsh through a screen of elongated reeds.

7   8

7 F. FRAZIER JELKE HOUSE (EAGLE'S NEST)
(1922-24) ALDRICH AND SLEEPER

222 Ocean Avenue

8 226 OCEAN AVENUE (MOONWATCH) (2000)
NEWPORT COLLABORATIVE ARCHITECTS

9 LUCY WORTH JAMES HOUSE (NORMANDIE)
(1914) WILLIAM DELANO

228 Ocean Avenue

These three and the following sequence of four houses displays the design vocabulary—from understated to fanciful—that has given Newport Neck its architectural character. Most of these houses respond to their environment with textural surfaces, historical references, and orientation to provide views toward Rhode Island Sound. Ranging from several early-twentieth-century firms to three locally well-known contemporary architects, the designers here employ varied options—rustic revivals, elegant historicism, modified Modernism, and even Post-Modern experimentation—to engage their clients and their sites.

Eagle's Nest reflects a shingled Colonial Revival vocabulary that is displayed discreetly on coastal ledges. Landscaped by the Olmsted firm, the provincial French materials and forms of Normandy can be glimpsed from the road through the rustic tile-roofed, brick-gatehouse arch. Between the two houses, Mohamad Farzan designed Moonwatch to swirl around a visitor with the flair of its dynamically curved roof. And yet its total effect is contextual, with shape, detailing, and surface treatments successfully suggesting a house that has been there for generations.

9

10

10 TUCKER-CHASE HOUSE (BELLE RIVE) (1992)
WILLIAM BURGIN

244 Ocean Avenue

Belle Rive, despite the wonderful effect of a rocky ledge that flows from its foundation, stands apart from the contextualism of its neighbors. This tall, broad structure is marked by the bold staccato arrangement of well over a dozen dormers, projecting bays, and the open shed of its entry arbor — all roofed by triangular gables. This was a house for two related families, its doubling announced by two other gabled forms: the large twinned dormers above the entrance. A traditional sensibility informs this eccentric composition but is intentionally channeled into a quirkier, energetic syncopation of distinct parts that is never quite coherent despite the unifying factor of its pleasantly green and smooth masonry surface.

LILY POND, 1963
SOURCE: *Collection of the Newport Historical Society*

11   12

11 HARRIS HOUSE (OCEAN HIGHLAND) (1992)
CHARLES D. FICKE

255 Ocean Avenue

On the other side of the road, the Harris House takes a different approach. Despite its elevated site on a high ledge, this large house tones down its physical presence by employing the temperate forms and broader planarities of an English country house — forms not unlike those employed on the smaller Tomlinson House nearby. Nearly invisible from the road (but adding to its sense of being an English seaside manor) is a quaint-looking, glazed conservatory that projects out from its southern side.

FISH CATCH AT NEWPORT, Postcard, c. 1890
SOURCE: *Collection of Newport Historical Society*

13

12 V.Z. REED, JR HOUSE (SEAFAIR) (1937)
WILLIAM MACKENZIE

254 Ocean Avenue

Seafair, also sometimes called "Hurricane Hut" because of the 1938 storm that swept through its lower story not long after it was built, was the last of the large-scale pre-war summer houses. The historicism of its design—a French chateau with high pitch roof and semi-circular plan—positions it at the tail end of the revivalist idiom begun in the mid-nineteenth century. More interesting, perhaps, is how its architect set the building far back on its lot, creating the illusion from the perspective of its roadside entry that its relatively small shell is monumental.

13 JEROME C. BORDEN HOUSE (BAY HOUSE)
(1917) ANGELL AND SWIFT

274 Ocean Avenue

Across the Green End Bridge sits the Borden House, which was built in the early twentieth century by Angell and Swift. They attempted to modernize the shingle tradition with a horizontal composition recalling the hipped-roof, layered mass, and thick piers of early Frank Lloyd Wright designs. As such it also possesses the distinction of being the last building discussed by Vincent Scully for his chapter on the Shingle Style in his and Antoinette Downing's mid-century survey, *The Architectural Heritage of Newport, Rhode Island.*

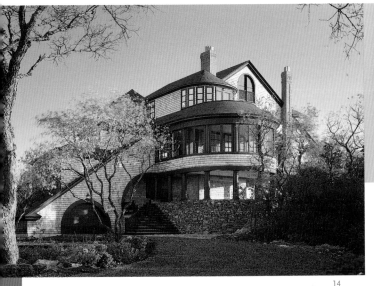

14

14 DAVID HUNTER HOUSE (SEABRIGHT) (1987)
WILLIAM BURGIN

146 Brenton Road

Barely a generation ago one could look inland from Green End Bridge and not see any buildings nearby. While the pond has recently been ringed with a grab bag of heavy-handed houses, Seabright stood nearly alone when it was built as one of the earliest designs in the late-twentieth-century Shingle Style revival. It still stands apart from its newer neighbors in how it more sensitively reflects both its historical and natural contexts. Designed by Burgin (while still in partnership with Jim Estes), this massive house literally bulges out toward the ocean with its curved, triple-storied layering of porch, glazed bedroom, and balcony focused on the bounding horizon to the south, somewhat reminiscent of a ship's conning tower. From the inland side, a dominant gable and an engaged tower with a weathered shingled skin confirms the late-nineteenth-century references, albeit enlarged here to gigantic size.

15 ALBERT H. OLMSTED HOUSE (WILDACRE)
(1900-1901) IRVING GILL; LANDSCAPE DESIGN, OLMSTED BROTHERS

310 Ocean Avenue

THE PLAYHOUSE (1926) IRVING GILL

294 Ocean Avenue

One of the most visually distinct houses along the coast, this was designed by the California-based early modern architect, Irving

Gill. Low and spreading as it rambles across the ledges above a salt water cove, the materials of this house seem to come from the site itself—particularly the rubble foundation and the rough stone walls that penetrate into the interior of the house to form its hearth and then erupt through the roof as chimneys. Despite such heavy masonry work, Gill is careful to open up the walls as much as possible—even creating a number of pocket windows that disappear into the wall itself, thus erasing any division between the interior spaces and the natural environs. While the organic, vaguely Asian-inspired shapes and rooflines here are not typical of Gill's later, proto-modern work, it is just this type of symbiotic connection to the natural world that informs all his mature work (an interest clearly propelled by the milder weather of his adopted home in California). On the interior, undecorated hardware and planar trim details such as flush baseboards and simple balusters are more in keeping with his progressive, modernist aesthetic.

Seeing as this was a house for the brother of Frederick Law Olmsted it is no surprise that the original planting scheme by the Olmsted firm is still preserved in a photographic and written record. Gill had professional connections to the landscape design firm and they were probably instrumental during the first years of the century in bringing him a small number of East Coast commissions, three of which are on Aquidneck Island.

Almost 25 years later, in the waning years of his career, Gill returned to the nascent orientalism and rustic stone work of Wildacre for the adjacent Playhouse. Originally added to the main house as a combination boathouse (and possibly car shed), it comes replete with a charming dovecote wall facing the salt water cove. It has now been turned into a separate residence.

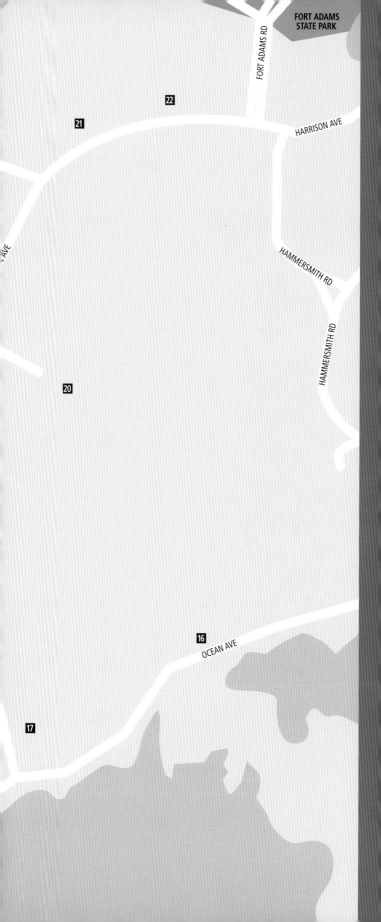

FORT ADAMS
STATE PARK

FORT ADAMS RD

22

21

HARRISON AVE

HAMMERSMITH RD

HAMMERSMITH RD

AVE

20

16

OCEAN AVE

17

16

17

16 JOSEPH R. BUSK HOUSE (INDIAN SPRING)
(1889-1892) RICHARD MORRIS HUNT

335 Ocean Avenue

More organic than most of Hunt's work, the Busk House literally seems to grow out of its boulder-strewn site. Irregular coursed-masonry walls stretch across the brow of the hill to take optimum advantage of the ocean view. The porch fronts most of the main story, its shingled roof seeming to flow down between the heavy masonry towers anchoring the composition at either end. Although Hunt used both dressed and rusticated stone blocks on earlier buildings in Newport and elsewhere, these are not the typical decorative and historicist forms for summer cottages popular in the rest of Newport. Hunt's work, while growing in size here, has not yet achieved the cultivated Europeanized quotations of his final career phase. Instead, this house seems most informed by its remarkable site and parallels the powerful forms and unique designs of another highly regarded architect who had only recently died, H.H.Richardson.

As usual, Richardson' work seemed to be blazing the architectural path for other architects and patrons to follow. By the early 1890s, William Ralph Emerson had designed two houses for Providence clients in the same beefy masonry *(see Wyndham Entry 27 and Roslyn Entry 28 in this Tour)*; by 1894, Peabody & Stearns had designed the rather severe composition of the Guan M. Hutton House (Shamrock Cliff) on nearby Ridge Road, which also features rubble course-masonry. Instead of the Richardsonian Romanesque, however, this house echoes an Irish country estate — with the squared towers of a medieval castle keep suitable for its owner, an Irish diplomat.

18

17 HARRISON AVENUE HOUSE (2006)
RONALD F. DIMAURO

Off intersection of Harrison Avenue and Ocean Avenue

Another large house (but much more recently built and a short distance west of the Drive) is sited quite differently. Although its street address is Harrison Avenue, this building can best be seen from the coastline road. While this is a very large house with several outbuildings, its demure siting, so far back from Ocean Avenue, reduces its visual impact so that it sits comfortably and privately amidst a low landscape that has changed in only a short distance from rocky hills to reedy marshes, with a creek to one side and a screen of taller trees as a backdrop. The inventive play of the gable work on this house is evident in two end wings set at right angles to and framing the undercut porch of the central block. Variations on a theme here include the large gables on the right that are layered with the front one opened up to a porch with exposed decorative posts and trusses, while the somewhat smaller triangle is embellished with the traditional Palladian window motif. The entire composition is topped toward the center with a roof platform whose balustrade evokes a form from a different era, the "widow's walks" found atop ship captains' houses. A final maritime flourish is provided by the rigged mast and yardarm employed here as a flagpole.

18 25 WINANS AVENUE (1990-92) ARCHITECTS UNLIMITED
SHEA RESIDENCE (1989) JIM ESTES

Winans Avenue

Two adjacent houses on Winans Avenue couldn't be more different in their opposite approaches to design. At 25 Winans Avenue, the multicolored abstract planes and lines of the composition made up of industrial materials are derived from early-twentieth century European Modernism, so that it is somewhat like a late variant on the de Stijl architecture of Dutch architect, Gerrit Rietveld. Probably

19

in an attempt to catch the water view, the composition here becomes too vertical for both its site and in departure from its modernist references. (The tallness of the building, in fact, led to zoning regulations limiting the height of structures in Newport.) The tubular metal railing suggests the decks of a cruise ship and the glazed aerie nestled into the top of the building presents an elevated vantage point from which to take in the panoramic view. The overall effect is visually jarring, with industrial materials, abstract planes, and polychromed surfaces creating a sense of haughty isolation rather than habitable hospitality.

Unlike this immodest Europeanized abstraction, the Shea house next door is barely visible through the foliage along the street. Appearing like a cluster of vernacular one-and-a-half-story sheds, its weathered shingles and simple geometries seem as if they predate the development of this entire subdivision. Its composition of understated small masses with irregular window openings backs up to Winans Avenue but opens out on the other side with a terrace and larger windows to frame a more natural southern exposure—publicly modest but well suited to the privacy of its owners. Some details—such as the rudimentary, carpentered shutters hinged to drop down from a variety of mullioned windows—seem to underscore its indigenous character. Elsewhere, however, in the intentionality of subtle scale shifts and in the more explicit skewing of square windows that form diamond-shaped openings (some of which are then tucked under the triangular gable junctions), Jim Estes, who was one of the first local architects to champion a more contextual, organic style, signals that this is a more contemporary, professionally designed building.

20

19 PROFESSOR ALEXANDER AGASSIZ HOUSE (CASTLE HILL) (1874), RESTORED (2001) NEWPORT COLLABORATIVE ARCHITECTS

590 Ocean Avenue

Best known historically as the summer home of the noted Harvard naturalist Alexander Agassiz, this house is picturesquely perched so as to overlook the bay (and to echo, in its siting, the interests of its resident marine biologist). Elements such as exposed brackets and struts reflect designs of the earlier 1870s, while broader-shingled forms reflect those popular in the following decade. The first-floor interior is largely intact and, as in so many houses of the 1860s and 1870s, has dark wood paneling and a grand-sized fireplace. Renovated as an inn, the house recently underwent a thoughtful restoration (guided by Robert Leach of NCA) reviving its nineteenth century character and replacing its prominent turret which had been lost in an early twentieth century gale. Today, with other large, similarly sited houses on the highlands across the way in Jamestown, it helps to form an architectural frame flanking the East Passage as it spills into the Atlantic.

20 NEWPORT COUNTRY CLUB (1894)
WHITNEY WARREN

264 Harrison Avenue

This was one of the first buildings designed by Whitney Warren after his return to the States from training at the Ecole des Beaux Arts in Paris. In a wonderful series of watercolors that still exist for the clubhouse, he composed an originally Y-shaped building with the yoke of the Y facing Harrison Avenue and providing the main elevation of the clubhouse (the stem of the Y was a covered piazza destroyed during the 1938 hurricane). Despite its windswept seaside site amidst a golf course and (what was) a polo field, everything about this building is cultivated, urbane, and Francophile. The high pitched roofline and arcaded windows of

21

the wings gather toward a central, elegant, vertical pavilion whose oval debout windows and double-storied entryway are set between monumental, engaged pilasters with Corinthian capitals all informed by seventeenth-century French royal taste. The result is more luxurious lodge than mundane clubhouse.

The building's size and site work hand-in-hand as the young architect makes the relatively modest dimensions of the clubhouse look much more grand by setting it back off the road, without other scale references nearby, just far enough to achieve the affect of monumentality but not so far to make it appear diminutive.

The watercolors suggest brick and stonework, though the building was in fact constructed of wood and shingles. The classical forms work at this scale and distance even though they are fabricated of wood, not masonry. For all his youth, Warren's successful design was chosen in an architectural competition over those of 50 leading architects. What a storybook way to start a career!

This was where the first U.S. Open was held in 1895 on the original course laid out by Scotland's well-known William F. Davis. Expanded to 18 holes in the early twentieth century, it was remodeled by Donald Ross in 1915. (Most recently, in the summer of 2006, it hosted the U.S. Women's Open.)

Hailed by William Jordy as a masterpiece among American country clubs, this design helped establish Warren's reputation for an elite clientele. It rapidly led to such notable commissions as the New York Yacht Club (1899) and New York's Grand Central Terminal (1903-1913), the train station done for the Vanderbilts, who must have first encountered his work here in Newport.

22

21 JOHN AUCHINCLOSS HOUSE (HAMMERSMITH FARM) (1888-1889) R.H. ROBERTSON

225 Harrison Avenue

This commodious summer residence sits on a colonial farm planted in 1638-39 by one of the first English settlers — who named Hammersmith after his ancestral home in England. The mass of shingled surfaces is juxtaposed with a large, welcoming, light-framed porte-cochère. The picturesque composition by this New York architect incorporated, mostly at the corners, the sculptural protrusions of bays, turrets, and attenuated conical capped tower all unified by the layered roofline. This was the architectural language that by the late 1880s had become stylistically de rigueur in Newport summer houses.

Hammersmith gained national recognition in the early 1950s when Senator John F. Kennedy began visiting Newport, brought there by Jacqueline Bouvier, daughter of Janet Auchincloss. In the early 1960s the Auchincloss home became the summer White House as President and Mrs Kennedy continued summering in Newport and extended the tradition set by President Eisenhower, whose summer retreat was virtually next door on the grounds of Fort Adams.

22 JAHLEEL BRENTON II HOUSE (BEFORE 1720)

203 Harrison Avenue

One of the earliest existing structures in the area, this property — with its open fields and pastures — is one place where the agrarian beginnings of settlement on Newport Neck can still be sensed. This low, gambreled structure sits on an impressive stone-and-brick foundation vault, not unlike that in the basement of another early structure, the Wanton-Lyman Hazard House on Broadway. As its modest scale might imply, this was not the primary house on this site but was instead intended for a tenant farmer on the Hammersmith estate, the Brenton family's farm property originally established during the first years of English settlement.

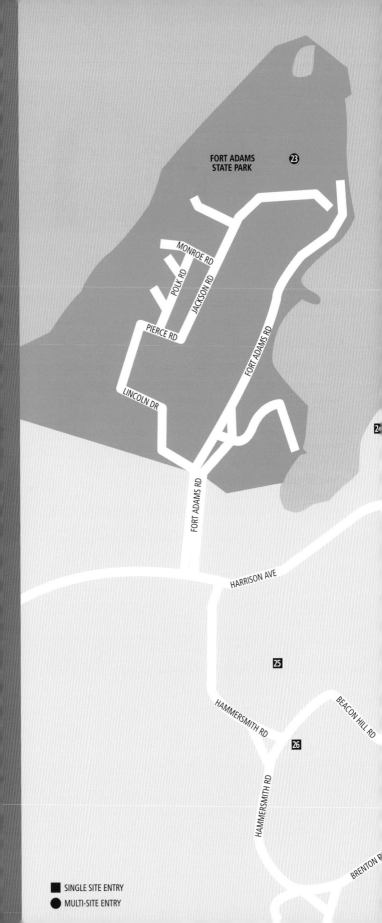

FORT ADAMS
STATE PARK

23

MONROE RD

POLK RD

JACKSON RD

PIERCE RD

FORT ADAMS RD

LINCOLN DR

24

FORT ADAMS RD

HARRISON AVE

25

HAMMERSMITH RD

BEACON HILL RD

26

HAMMERSMITH RD

BRENTON R

■ SINGLE SITE ENTRY
● MULTI-SITE ENTRY

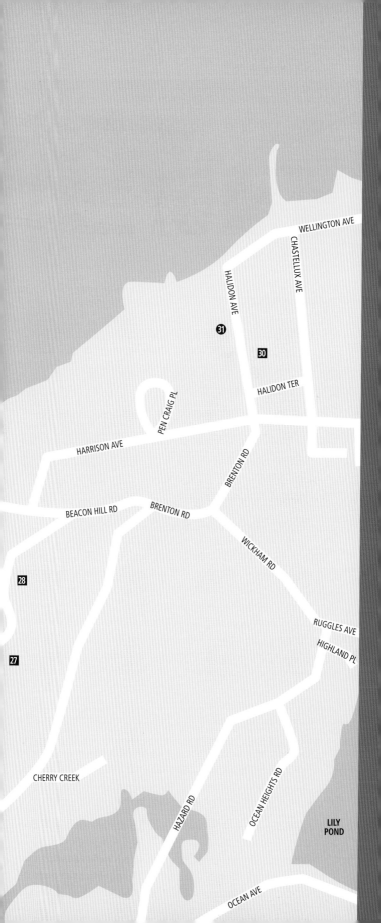

23

23 FORT ADAMS (1824-1857) SIMON BERNARD AND LIEUTENANT COLONEL JOSEPH G. TOTTEN, ALTERED, ADDITIONS (LATER NINETEENTH CENTURY), RESTORED CASEMATE (2000) NEWPORT COLLABORATIVE ARCHITECTS

Fort Adams Road

SAIL NEWPORT BARN (1999) MOHAMAD FARZAN

60 Fort Adams Road

EISENHOWER HOUSE (1873-1874) GEORGE CHAMPLIN MASON, SR

1 Lincoln Drive

Guarding the east passage and southern entrance to Newport Harbor, this extensive, 130-acre military complex dates back to a small late-eighteenth-century fortification. In what is very rare among such installations, Fort Adams, named after the second president of the United States, encompasses in its many features the entire spectrum of nineteenth-century military engineering ideas. This was one of the largest installations built under the modern or so-called "third system," with a perimeter wall running almost three quarters of a mile in a pentagonal shape. Great walls of granite scarps, brick vaults, and shale-and-earth fill were meant to absorb any incoming fire. Although it is impossible to see in its entirety (except from the air), the vast structure clearly dominates its peninsula with layers of redoubts, bastions, and separate auxiliary structures such as a prison, munitions storage, and mule barns still extant and surrounding the parade ground protected by the enceinte. The major entrance into the interior, facing the inner harbor, is a high stone-and-brick portal distinguished from the surrounding walls by a segmental arch.

Before returning to Harrison Avenue, notice the small boat barn at the waterside used by Sail Newport, a non-profit educational sailing organization for youths. Although it looks like what it is—an unadorned, utilitarian dockside building with a ramp and big

wooden doors for ease in storing equipment and a ridge of clerestory windows for natural lighting—it was primarily conceived by volunteer architect Mohamad Farzan to be erected efficiently by volunteers working under a tight schedule and budget.

To the right, set back on a rise and facing Harrison Avenue, is Eisenhower House, so called because Ike and Mamie Eisenhower used it as their summer residence during his presidency. Newporter George Champlin Mason, Sr designed it in 1873-1874, with the mansard roof, broad porch, and ornamental bracket-work typical of his work during the period. It was constructed as the commanding officer's quarters for the fort.

24 EDWIN D. MORGAN HOUSE (BEACON ROCK)
(1889-1891) McKIM, MEAD & WHITE

147 Harrison Avenue

The high rocky knoll now dominated by the Morgan House was the site of a fire-lit signal in the colonial era and later became a popular locale with nineteenth-century American landscape painters such as J.F. Kensett, Worthington Whittredge, and others seeking the sublime in nature. Although its completion was delayed for several years by the considerable engineering chal-lenges presented by the site, this is one of the earliest of the monumentally scaled houses for which Newport became known in the 1890s.

The best view of the house is from the entrance road to Fort Adams. Here, on its western side, the dramatic distinction between the classically inspired entry elevations and the rough stone walls that seem to tumble down the hillside can be clearly

Every room off the oddly-shaped entry hall has a different geometry.

24

seen. Two projecting wings to either side of the central entry form a protected, three-sided atrium-court and their gabled ends present what Richard Guy Wilson has characterized as "the prim and proper Ionic order which greets the visitor." This elevation is clearly juxtaposed in mass and effect with the rest of the house as the one-story entry level of white colonnades cascades down into the textured stonework of the terraces and dark ashlar columns of the other sides, creating a visual tension also noted by Wilson. While the entry composition is most reminiscent of Roman sources, there are evocations of Jeffersonian America here as well in the combination of Palladian forms, native fieldstone walls, and both eighteenth-century French and Colonial Revival interiors.

For this house, as with many of their large houses of the era, mostly under the direction of Stanford White, the firm procured interior furnishing and entire surface finishes from historical European houses. McKim, Mead & White here allow the given shapes of these rooms and the varied interior functions to inform and influence the plan and its ultimate exterior shape. Every room off the oddly shaped entry hall has a different geometry—oval reception room, octagonal dining room, polygonal chambers, curving staircases, and a living room with a bow of windows looking toward the harbor. The irregular topography of the site is even subtly acknowledged in the placement of the rooms on different levels.

The carriage house, whose tile roof and brick wall backs onto Harrison Avenue, was for many years the studio of Felix deWeldon, the sculptor of the Iwo Jima Monument in Washington, D.C. It was sympathetically renovated into a private residence by Charles D. Ficke in 1994.

The grounds, with a dramatic entry road bridging a deep ravine between Harrison Avenue and the house itself, were landscaped by the Olmsted firm.

25   26

25 SWISS VILLAGE (1920-24) ATTERBURY, PHELPS AND TOMKINS, (2004) MADISON SPENCER ARCHITECTS

75 Beacon Hill Road

26 JAMES B. GUBELMANN HOUSE (GREYWALLS) (1986) WINDIGO ARCHITECTS

Beacon Hill Road

Bounded by Hammersmith, Harrison Avenue, and Beacon Hill Road are a set of rough masonry buildings all but invisible from the road. This is a fantasy recreation of an alpine farm that never was, reminiscent of the diversion of a Petit Hameau created for Marie Antoinette at Versailles. While its most visible part is the peculiar rustic entry gate, the tiled turrets, arched bridges, and terraces were meant to evoke, along the rural winding carriage paths popular with summer colonists of an earlier era, the pastoral delights of Europe. Ironically, this old-world setting today houses a high-tech farm and laboratory that collects and cryogenically archives genetic samples of rare animal breeds in the hope of preventing their extinction.

Look up to the right and you will see a more contemporary approach to this rugged countryside: Greywalls. Barely visible through the leafy trees are the rather mannered verticality of chimneys and steeply pitched roofs of a residence perched atop one of the highest ledges on the island. This, the architect's own house, was designed in response to the steep topography of its site as a virtual tree house broken into somewhat separate pavilions and connected by walkways.

27

27 ROSA ANN GROSVENOR HOUSE (WYNDHAM)
(1890) WILLIAM RALPH EMERSON

36 Beacon Hill Road

WYNDHAM CARRIAGE HOUSE (MANDEMAR)
(1890) WILLIAM RALPH EMERSON, (2006) NEWPORT
COLLABORATIVE ARCHITECTS

44 Beacon Hill Road

28 WILLIAM GROSVENOR HOUSE (FAIR OAK, ROSLYN) (1901) WILLIAM RALPH EMERSON

26 Beacon Hill Road

29 GEORGE GORDON KING HOUSE (EDGEHILL FARM) (1887-89) McKIM, MEAD & WHITE

31-35 Beacon Hill Road

By the late nineteenth century larger landowners were beginning to divide their holdings, which opened up this neighborhood to new construction. These three houses are part of a sophisticated suburban development, planned by John Charles Olmsted and Frederick Law Olmsted in the 1890s and known as the King-Glover-Bradley subdivision.

For King's own house, McKim, Mead & White's work suggests French, specifically Norman, sources in its combination of a random stone first story topped by a smoother skin of stucco. Such rusticity was not what they might have produced in town, where Colonial or Federal Revival details might have prevailed.

Based on his earlier work in town *(see Sanford Covell House, Tour Two)* and other shingled beach cottages he created in Middletown, it is hard to believe that the Bostonian Emerson produced such heavy set designs for the Grosvenor houses. Done for

28   29

two related Providence patrons, these reflect a Richardsonian aesthetic in their rusticated stone work, voissoired arches, and ample turrets. With these effects they are more compact versions of Indian Spring, a project that was being constructed at the same time by Richard Morris Hunt out on the southern end of Ocean Avenue.

By the early twentieth century, Wyndham was noted for its fine gardens of both indigenous and imported species that complemented the rocky site. Fortunately, much of the material that caused a major magazine in the 1920s to compare its landscaping to the beauty of a Corot painting still exists today.

Nearby, at 44 Beacon Hill Road, is the 2006 reworking of the Wyndham Carriage House (Mandemar) by Mohamad Farzan of Newport Collaborative Architects. Like the main house, its original rugged stone buttresses and shingle surfaces mesh with the landscape—but its most memorable feature, a corpulent, chamfered tower, is not visible from the public roadside. Farzan replaced a large portion of the roof plane with a bold slope of glass to bravely counteract the dark opacity of the original walls for what is now a private residence.

30 THE CHALET (1866-67) ATTRIBUTED TO RICHARD MORRIS HUNT

35 Chastellux Avenue

THE CHALET STABLE (2002) NEWPORT COLLABORATIVE ARCHITECTS

20 Halidon Avenue

This nineteenth-century house, attributed to Hunt, is sited toward the brow of a hill overlooking the inner harbor (its address is on Chastellux Avenue but can best be seen from Halidon Avenue). It is one of numerous such designs done by Hunt, George Champlin Mason, Sr, and others in the decade after the Civil War that employ a decorative filigree of sawn balusters, balconied porches, and

30

exposed struts under shadowy eaves to conjure the escapist imagery of an exotic European vernacular. While its architect and even its original owner are part of an ongoing historical debate, the terraced effect of this house's many projections seems to perfectly fit its hillside site with sheltered entryway, windows, and overhanging porches affording multiple vantage points from which to view the passing scene while catching salubrious sea breezes.

More recently, John Grosvenor of Newport Collaborative Architects transformed a modest stable set lower on the hill into his own house by partially clothing it in a wrap of vertical boarding and sawn detailing in concert with the decorative flourishes of the original 1860s house.

31 ANNE MARIE BROWN HOUSE (HARBOUR COURT) (1904) CRAM, GOODHUE AND FERGUSON, LANDSCAPING, OLMSTED BROTHERS, KITCHEN AND DINING RENOVATIONS (2004) WILLIAM BURGIN

5 Halidon Avenue

STATION 10 (CA1845) ALEXANDER JACKSON DAVIS, MOVED AND RESTORED (2000) NEWPORT COLLABORATIVE ARCHITECTS

Harbour Court grounds

With tall peaked roofs emphasizing its hillock site overlooking the harbor, this is one of the quintessential waterside residences from the end of Newport's Gilded Age. Designed by Bostonian Ralph Adams Cram for the Brown family in 1904, its sweeping lawns and plantings were created by the Olmsted firm to set off the architect's French-inspired Renaissance Revival massing and forms with an organic landscape of windswept trees and rocky outcroppings.

This is a relatively intimate grand style residence — with a long wood-paneled entry hall that runs across the entry axis and connects the elaborate stairwell on the west with the library to the south. While the waterside is opened with a sheltering veranda on

31

the first story, the south-facing entry is protected from the sea winds by a service ell arching over a broad slype. Elegant trim—including intertwined B's on copper scuppers—and massive doors all assert this to be a baronial residence, while its site, name, and outbuildings remind us that this soon became a kind of elaborate personal port of call for John Nicholas Brown, Jr and his family. Unlike similar residences across town, this house on the high cliffs overlooking Easton's Bay reflects its maritime connection, with boathouse and dockage close at hand and all perfectly suited to residents who would retreat to Newport for the sailing it offered.

In 1987 it was purchased from the three grandchildren of its original owner by the New York Yacht Club, which uses it today as its Newport clubhouse. There have been recent alterations and additions to both the interior and exterior, including a large renovation of the kitchen and dining areas by William Burgin, that are demurely tucked behind the service wing and that echo sophisticated Manhattan restaurants more than the genteel Gilded Age.

The delightful small-frame building just to the right of the entry road is Station 10, the original club building probably designed by A.J. Davis in the mid-nineteenth century. It has led a particularly peripatetic existence, first built in Hoboken, New Jersey and later moved to Mystic, Connecticut where it remained on loan from the NYCC until it was reinstalled on the grounds of Harbour Court in 2000. Although no longer on its original site, it still picturesquely evokes its recreational function with its diminutive size, swooping roofline, decorative eave trim, and stripe-like vertical sheathing all calling to mind informal, temporary structures like the actual tents that are still often pitched on the Harbour Court lawn for special parties.

9. FIFTH WARD & SOUTHERN THAMES

For many Newporters, this neighborhood, known as the 5th Ward represents the real city. Its name survives (although the fire wards that once determined the city districts no longer exist) along with the sense of a neighborhood where residents know each other and often share common ethnic backgrounds, holidays, and familiarity with social institutions such as St Augustine Church, Rogers High School, and the Ancient Order of Hibernians.

Originally known during colonial times as the "court end of town," this area was in fact outside the town proper and marked the beginning of the more undeveloped landscape south of the harbor *(see Tour Eight)*. Although Thames Street stretched down to this area, there were only a handful of buildings south of Pope, Dennison, and Extension streets by the end of the 1840s. When small wood-frame structures were built, they were often constructed by local house-wrights, some of whose names can still be found written on interior timbers (such as G. Knowles who produced the tiny wood-and-brick walled cottage at 19 Extension Street just after 1850). Dense construction came in the later nineteenth century with immigrants arriving from Ireland who settled here and staffed the big houses a few blocks up the hill on Bellevue.

The southern Thames Street corridor connected the old town with the 5th Ward , and provided daily services and jobs for the locals from the fishing industry and mills to, later, the power companies and light manufacturing that were located along the working wharves.

Today the area is better known as an extension of the central tourist district, a transformation that began in the early 1980s with artsy souvenir, and T-shirt shops and restaurants replacing what were once corner grocery stores, butchers, and local eateries. This in turn began attracting the bustle of a tourist promenade and an affordable market for out-of-town homebuyers. Such realities have not generally proved beneficial for the architecture of the area, which is now under constant commercial and realty pressure to change but is not protected by the historic district regulations governing other areas of the city.

◄ JOHN CAREY, JR GARDENER'S COTTAGE

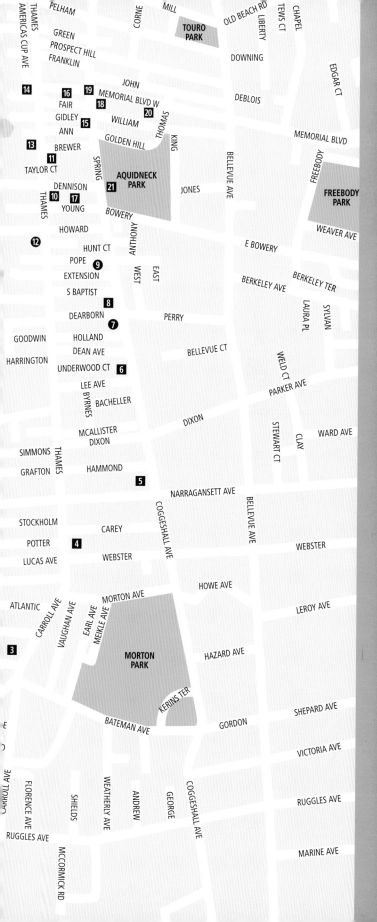

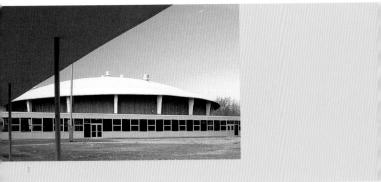

1   WILLIAM S. ROGERS HIGH SCHOOL (1955-57)
KELLY & GRUZEN, (2001) NEWPORT COLLABORATIVE
ARCHITECTS

Wickham Road

When Rogers High School was moved from Broadway to the outskirts of town, this most futuristic of Newport's public facilities
was constructed in the mid-1950s. The site, called Battery O'Shea,
was a former World War II-gun emplacement that lies close to the
rustic terrain of Newport Neck. Here, the New York firm of Kelly
& Gruzen designed a suburban high school campus. Set behind
ample parking lots are ten separate buildings, including a "goo-
gie"-shaped gymnasium and a huge auditorium whose sculptural
roof looks like part of a large prop left over from the 1950s Sci-Fi
movie classic, *The Day the Earth Stood Still*. These stand-alone
elements are connected by covered walkways and windowed cor-
ridors. Much here hints at the influence of the International Style
—walls of plate-glass panels set between machined metal frames,
multi-colored knee walls, flat roofs, and pavilions raised up on
tall pylons. Like most explorations of Modernism in Newport,
this too was met with local resistance. But today, despite a much-
needed 2001 renovation that toned down the brasher color
scheme, it remains one of the quirkiest and best representations
of mid-twentieth century American architectural taste.

2   5TH WARD FIRE STATION (1986) JOHN SMYTH

Old Fort Road

This modest building was designed with a gently Post-Modern
intentionality, one that attempts to blend in rather than overwhelm. Details here represent rather than replicate historical
forms such as the thin latticework of the central see-through
cupola and the very Newport-gable-on-hip-roof line at the
southern end.

2   3

3 **ST AUGUSTINE CHURCH** (1911-1912) MATTHEW
SULLIVAN

Carroll Avenue at Harrison Avenue

Built at the same time as its cross-town sister, St Joseph's Church
on Broadway, St Augustine's is the result of the call for expanded
worship facilities to serve the growing Roman Catholic population that was rising due to immigration. Rather than the
Italianate forms of St Joseph's, St Augustine's employed another
historical idiom for its mostly Irish congregation. What looks to
be Romanesque on the exterior, with its central round arch portal and its row of arcaded windows above, was stylistically called
Byzantine at the time of its construction. Then again, the glazed
yellow brick and constrained limestone trim also hint at an early-
twentieth-century planarity that is ultimately subsumed by the
historical references. Once inside, the Byzantine reference is more
emphatic with the brightly patterned truss ceiling, painted walls,
and the luminous effect of the largest program of stained glass
windows (43) in Newport.

4 **SMALL SCALE HOUSING** (c. 1880s-1910)

672-676 Thames Street and adjacent side streets

The 5th Ward and southern Thames Street are filled with modest
residential structures of which this somewhat intact row is typical. Along the small-scale streetscapes of the 5th Ward itself, these
tended to be separate, small porch-fronted cottages, many with
tiny front yards, decorated (if at all) with wood trim and similar
to those found elsewhere in the city (for example, on Pond Street
off Broadway). Although the results, derived as they are from contractor plans and published patterns, can sometimes be
unremarkable and numbingly consistent, there are variants, such
as 672 Thames, whose flat-topped knee wall above the porch suggests a rural storefront rather than a residence. These small
cottages were often built as rental properties between the 1880s
and the early years of the new century and differ from previous

housing solutions in the southern part of the city *(see Entry 12 in this Tour, the John D. Williams Tenement).*

5   JOHN CAREY, JR GARDENER'S COTTAGE (1876)
STURGIS AND BRIGHAM

523 Spring Street

When he built this residence for a staff member on the estate of John Carey, Jr, Boston-based John Hubbard Sturgis was already well regarded in certain patronage circles, having designed over a half-dozen Newport houses in the 1860s. While some of these (such as the Frederic W. Rhinelander House, 1863-64, 10 Redwood Street) reflect French aspects such as mansard roofs and standing oval windows, Sturgis seems to be moving in a very different direction with this small Gardener's Cottage. The big spindle posts, spinning wheel trim, coved wall, and heavy pilastered chimney (as well as some interior details) are all harbingers of the Colonial Revival, perhaps inspired by the national Centennial being celebrated that year. This cottage may have had a broader influence, seeing as it was published in that early professional journal, the *American Architect and Building News*, the year it was built.

6   ROBERT P. LEE HOUSE (c. 1834)

465 Spring Street

The construction of a stone house such as this, with its random-course square-faced granite blocks and flush stone lintels, was made possible by the availability of trained masons who began working on Fort Adams in the 1820s. While not large, this house presents a severe, forthright image to the street with its fortress-like walls and the compositional equilibrium of central entry, hipped roof, and twin chimneys. Preservationist Antoinette Downing noted a resemblance to some stone houses of the same date in New Bedford, Massachusetts.

There have been later alterations, including the enclosed front porch and its current use as a funeral home, but the Lee House is perhaps best known as the local boyhood home of Henry and William James in the 1860s. It was clearly Henry's recollection of a quieter, mid-century Newport he encountered around this house that led this famous American author to critique what the town had become by the turn of the century (in *The American Scene*, 1907).

7 THOMAS GALVIN COTTAGE (c. 1845)

417 Spring Street

MICHAEL A. McCORMICK HOUSE (c. 1870, c. 1895)

31 Dearborn Street

This small board-and-batten cottage once stood amidst the wonderfully landscaped lot of the Thomas Galvin Nursery, whose owner resided here. Plantings, trellises, green houses, and tree rows stretched down toward Thames Street and along Spring in a kind of living advertisement. These are now sadly gone but were at least hinted at until the late twentieth century when several housing units were added close to the original cottage. Galvin, owner of both nursery and house, became one of the wealthiest Irish-born businessmen in town by supplying the growing summer colony with gardening and landscape services after establishing his business in 1845. His son, Thomas Jr, carried on the tradition and became one of the better-known local landscape gardeners of the next generation, perhaps best remembered for his later work at the Newport Casino.

The house was said by Vincent Scully to be most historically notable for its "exploitation of creative techniques in wood"—by which he meant its surface of crisp, clean lines expressed in milled lumber as boards, battens, and stickwork. In this he closely followed the published theories of Andrew Jackson Downing that, in the 1840s, called for an American cottage style. Here the striations

8   9

of battens not only seal the gaps between vertical sheathing boards but were meant, per Downing's vision, to be an exterior expression of the vertical framing elements within. Galvin's cottage, with its well-planted lot, also hewed to the Jackson dictum that "architectural beauty must be considered conjointly with the beauty of landscape." Being a landscape gardener himself, such sentiments must have held great appeal for Galvin as he planned his house and nursery.

Just to the rear, at 31 Dearborn Street, stands the Michael A. McCormick House (c. 1870 and c. 1895), a residence altered about a generation after its construction by the implementation of idiosyncratic Colonial Revival and shingled details, like the peculiarly rounded front bay. McCormick was an important 5th Ward councilman, a leader in the Irish-American community, and a well-known local building contractor who probably carried out the revival renovations in the 1890s.

8   EMMANUEL CHURCH (1903) CRAM, GOODHUE & FERGUSON

415 Spring Street

This is an English-style stone church set amidst the densely built-up wood-frame housing stock of this neighborhood. Its buttressed, random block walls press up against both street and sidewalk, not unlike the effect of an old church in some ancient European town crowded against generations of buildings. It visually overpowers most other nearby structures, except at the corner of Dearborn and Spring Streets where a lower side aisle reduces its height and its lot placement allows for a small park-like space that is almost a reminder of an ancient country churchyard. The firm, noted for its interest in revival forms, chose to design a side-aisled, side-entry nave with a stout buttressed tower expressive of an architectural language that compliments its Anglican service. This church was funded by Mrs John Nicholas Brown as a memorial for her recently deceased husband. She immediately went on

to commission the firm to design a summer home for herself and her young son, John Nicholas Brown, Jr, resulting in the French-influenced Harbour Court a year later *(see Tour Eight)*. Later, in the mid-1920s, the son, having studied at Harvard under medievalist Arthur Kingsley Porter, would team up with the same Boston firm to produce the great Gothic chapel at his alma mater in near-by Middletown, St George's Preparatory School.

9 **SALMAR NUBIA HOUSE** (c. 1800)

21 Pope Street

NEWPORT GARDNER HOUSE (c. 1810), REBUILT (c. 1850)

25 Pope Street

BACCHUS & PAUL OVERING HOUSE (c. 1810)

29 Pope Street

ROBERTSON HOUSE (1992) JEAN BURRITT ROBERTSON

41 Pope Street

Although they are not much to look at architecturally today and have been altered from their original forms, these buildings are remarkable for their importance as surviving structures of an earlier enclave of African Americans set on the edge of town. In the early years of the nineteenth century, some of the leaders of that thriving community lived here, relatively isolated from the heavily populated streets farther north. Newport Gardner was one of the most influential African Americans of his era—he was a literate civic leader who was involved in every aspect of community life. A music composer, teacher, and blacksmith who had earlier helped found the African Humane Society during the first years of manumission in 1780, and who was one of the founders of the first African church in the city, the Union Congregational

It must have granted distinction to its owner in a town possessing few high-style Federal brick mansions.

10

Church, Gardner owned his house, whose size and modesty are typical of other surviving African American residences from the period. It was here that he organized the African Benevolent Society in 1807 with his friends, Salmar Nubia and the Overings, who lived a few doors away.

A delightful new addition to this old street is the Robertson house, a narrow, one-bay residence. Despite its diminutive size, it has a strong visual presence. This is due to the balance struck between reduced dimensions and the size of its pleasantly familiar classical elements. Here is a temple-fronted building with deep pedimented gable, paneled trim, a frame of side and transom lights around the entrance, and Attic-style windows that acknowledge but never give into the Lilliputian proportions of the lot.

10 SAMUEL WHITEHORNE HOUSE (1811), ALTERED, CUPOLA ADDED (MID-NINETEENTH CENTURY), RESTORED (1970-74)

416 Thames Street

This three-story brick Federal block was one of the last of the big houses built along Thames Street before the era of industrialization. It was constructed for one of the last in a long line of merchants who placed their houses facing their waterfront business interests. Its hipped roof, four corner chimneys, and — most of all — its crisp geometry of shaped windows, modillion blocks under the eaves, and trim elements that barely break the wall plane must have seemed very fashionable in their day. This house, built with profits from a variety of Whitehorne concerns (including a bank, an iron foundry, a distillery, and most likely slave trading as well) must have granted distinction to its owner in a town possessing few such high-style Federal brick mansions. Whitehorne kept the house until he entered bankruptcy in 1843, at which time it was sold. The cupola, with its Italianate windows and fancy bracket work, was added around 1850.

11

On the interior, a four-room plan is bisected by a central hall divided by a low flat arch that echoes the elliptical fanlight above the front door (there are similar forms framing niches in other rooms). This form has in turn been used in the bow of the front portico as a curved entablature is set over Doric columns. But the entryway and portico are both replacements for materials that were removed in the nineteenth century when a set of store fronts were inelegantly added to the front of the house. These were taken down when both interior and exterior were completely renovated in the early 1970s by the Newport Restoration Foundation, which continues to operate it as an historic house museum open to the public. It notably contains numerous examples of Newport furniture, including some by the famous Townsend and Goddard families.

11 FRANCIS MALBONE HOUSE (c. 1758)
ATTRIBUTED TO PETER HARRISON, (1867) DUDLEY NEWTON, (1996) NEWPORT COLLABORATIVE ARCHITECTS

392 Thames Street

This fine Georgian mansion is a surprising pre-Revolutionary War survivor along this stretch of Thames Street, although at one time there were several dozen such colonial merchants' mansions in the area. It features a hipped roof capping a brick block rising off a sandstone foundation that is fronted by a classically inspired doorway—the beginning of the same traditions that mark the later, similarly scaled Whitehorne House *(see Entry 10 above)* a short distance away. The doorway surround is a variation on the patternbook source by James Gibbs that Harrison used for his

12

Touro Synagogue portico. While a double-belt course of sand-stone still remains, the heavy window caps have been cut off flush with the brick surface, making the planarity of the block even more emphatic. Much remains on the interior as well. The plan is typical for its time, with four rooms divided by a large hall whose stairwell turns at a landing lit by a compass-headed window at the rear. These kinds of features can be found in wood-frame houses of the same date (i.e., the Vernon and Hunter houses). In an era of few architectural drawings, this may be due to either the hand of the same architect or the talents of the same housewrights working on the projects. Amazingly, in this case we know that car-penters Samuel Greene and Wing Spooner were involved in the construction, just as they were on other Harrison buildings such as the Redwood Library about a decade earlier.

The Malbone House does not stand alone on its site. In 1867, Newport architect Dudley Newton designed a small gabled dependency in what must surely be one of the earliest applica-tions anywhere of the Colonial Revival. This was intended as an office for the architect's physician father. Much more recently, Mohamad Farzan of NCA designed a large double pavilion whose scale and detailing are in keeping with the main house. It was erected toward the rear of the property, to enhance the function-ality of the complex that is now used as an inn. These new, interconnected pavilions suggest, in their symmetry and shape, other colonial sources from further afield such as the brick man-sions of Tidewater, Virginia. Finally, this connecting structure between the old and the new transformed the existing terraced garden into a private urban courtyard.

12 NEWPORT STEAM MILL, AQUIDNECK MILL, NEWPORT & FALL RIVER RAILWAY COMPANY BUILDING (1831, 1865, 1903)

449 Thames Street, Howards Wharf and vicinity

JOHN D. WILLIAMS TENEMENT (c. 1835)

405-411 Thames Street

Several buildings on the old wharves along the harbor front belie the common perception that Newport was in economic decline in the early nineteenth century and benefited little by the industrialization that was occurring elsewhere. Yet today only a few artifacts still remain of the bustling rough-and-tumble activity evidenced by smokestacks, shot towers, factories, and tanks. The best-preserved relic of this working waterfront is the cluster of buildings now used by the International Yacht Restoration School at 449 Thames Street.

The most architecturally impressive of these is the early three-story Steam Mill that translates the shed roof and tower of traditional wood-frame mills into muscular masonry walls made up of hefty granite and slate blocks. Like other mills along the waterfront *(for example, Entry 4 in this Tour, the nearby Perry Mill)*, it sat along the wharf with its short end towards Thames Street. Its tower at one time possessed a more elaborate cupola and cap. The popularity of such stone work evidently relates to the influx of masons and materials into Newport for the enormous Fort Adams construction campaign just across the harbor in the second quarter of the nineteenth century. Newport's lack of powerful rivers meant that its mills needed another source of power. Here, as its name implies, the energy for this and most other Newport textile mills was initially provided by steam. Extending from the western end of the Steam Building is the four-story Aquidneck Mill Building (from 1865), with its evenly spaced flat-arch windows, that attests to manufacturing successes spurred on by the needs of the Civil War during that decade.

13

Sitting at a right angle to these two is the Newport and Fall River Street Railway Company Building of 1903, which in a single interior space housed the power plant of boilers, turbine, and generators that powered Newport's trolley system. This has a more elegant cadence of monumental windows set between pilasters and arches, which like the sheet metal cornice, echoes classical motifs. It is now the main hall for the International Yacht Restoration School, where the manual skills that were once so vital to Newport's maritime industry are happily kept alive through its mission of teaching about, restoring, and building classic boats.

Elsewhere along the wharves, 5 Goodwin Street, which hails from around the same date as the Steam Mill, with similar rough block walls, is a much-altered mill building that once belonged to the Richmond Manufacturing Company. By the 1890s it was converted to residential use, a harbinger of what would come to be the fate of several industrial buildings along these wharves in the later twentieth century.

These industrial plants were sometimes accompanied by housing for the workforce — such as the John D. Williams Tenement (Brown and Howard's Wharf and Thames Street, c. 1835) whose clerestoried form stretches along Thames Street. This Greek Revival block, which may or may not have originally had at its ground level vitrined storefronts, was company-sponsored housing for the labor force at the nearby harborfront mills.

13 THE NEWPORT ARMORY (1894) EDWIN WILBUR

365 Thames Street

The heavy stone material and fanciful forms echo this building's origins as an enclosed military drill hall replete with conical towers, machicolated parapets, and small archery windows. No moat or drawbridge here, but a big stone arched entry and massive

14

doors do give the effect of a fortified keep. This is presented on the two-story street elevation that fronts a lower one-story hall stretching along the pier. Built by neighborhood contractor M.A. McCormick, this was one of three such armories constructed in Rhode Island in the 1890s with state funds. Newport troops left for World War I from this armory and it was used for more than half a century as intended, with almost no alterations. In the 1960s, '70s, and '80s it served as a press center during the heyday of America's Cup races held off Newport, and has more recently been turned into retail space for antique dealers.

14 PERRY MILL (c. 1831) ALEXANDER MCGREGOR, ALTERED (MID-NINETEENTH- AND TWENTIETH-CENTURY), CONVERTED AND RESTORED (1984) NEWPORT COLLABORATIVE ARCHITECTS

337 Thames Street

This four-plus-story textile mill was built by Alexander McGregor, the Scot immigrant who oversaw stone work on Fort Adams and went on to construct numerous buildings around town using a vocabulary of Greek Revival forms. As built by McGregor, the original roofline featured a long gabled shed interrupted by strips of monitor windows along its length and topped by a tower set a few feet back from the front elevation; the storefront windows are a later alteration done before the 1880s when a low row of offices stuck onto the front of the mill was removed. By the early twentieth century the gabled shed was severely trun-

15   16

cated a few feet above the third-story windows, turning it into a
flat roof, only to be replaced (in a restoration based on early photographic evidence) during a 1984 conversion led by John
Grosvenor when the building was developed into a timeshare and
retail center. This work was made possible under newly developed
state and federal preservation laws that provided tax relief for certain readaptive use projects. Just as the construction of the mill
helped turn around Newport's depressed nineteenth-century
economy, this restoration cum conversion signaled the shift of
southern Thames Street toward another economic revival centered around the late twentieth century boom in tourism.

15   **27 GIDLEY STREET** (c. 1800)

16   **J.D. HIDLER HOUSE** (c. 1885) J.D. JOHNSTON
     28 Fair Street

17   **SCHECHTER RESIDENCE** (1986) NEWPORT
     COLLABORATIVE ARCHITECTS
     34 Young Street

Although southern Thames Street has long been a commercial
dockside, it is sprinkled with interesting residential structures
both old and new along a number of the small side streets. Three
of these, situated only a few lots off Thames Street, represent the
broad spectrum of architecture that can be seen by walking up the
hill to the east of the main thoroughfare.

At 27 Gidley Street is a typical five-bay Federal period house from
about 1800 with an attractive classicizing doorway surround and
decorative fanlight. Although there were eighteenth century residences built in this neighborhood, this one was probably moved
to this site before 1900 where it was then restored in the last quarter of the twentieth century.

The J.D. Hidler House at 28 Fair Street is a quirky rendition of
mid-nineteenth-century elements. It reads like one huge bay with
its dominant polygonal form projecting off a rear block and

This house reaches above three stories to gain views of the harbor.

17

pulling the mansard roofline toward the street. The facets of the polygon are extended up into the bay and each is crowded with a window whose gabled brow adds a play of light and shadow across the dark slate of the mansard. It was constructed by J.D. Johnston, the architect-builder, but may have been influenced by the designs of another Newport architect, Dudley Newton, which often show a similar idiosyncratic sense of scale.

Finally, another interesting play on earlier house forms can be found the 1986 Schechter Residence. Here, architect Glenn Gardiner drops one tall rectangular block into the center of the two-and-a-half-story composition and extends it out over the stoop into a shallow reminder of an entry porch. This rectangular inset reaches above three stories to gain views of the harbor but manages to fit into its neighborhood context by balancing the vertical rise with the strong horizontal of the deep roof eave. The hipped roof, the vertical stack of windows to the right, and the geometric planarity of triangular bay, roof, and main block all echo both the local Shingle Style of the 1880s as well as the slightly later, Chicago-based formulations of Frank Lloyd Wright.

18 ST MARY'S ROMAN CATHOLIC CHURCH
(1848-1852), SCHOOL (1865) PATRICK C. KEELEY

250 Spring Street

Although this impressive church was begun in 1848 and completed some three years later, it housed Rhode Island's first Roman Catholic parish, established two decades earlier in 1828 and initially dedicated to St Joseph. The architect, Patrick C. Keeley, was a fitting choice—he was Irish, Roman Catholic, and had built several churches in the New York area as a Brookyln resident. Quite a few earlier buildings were adapted or constructed for this parish's use (including one on Barney Street where an early Irish cemetery still exists) but at mid-century this bold sandstone building was meant to visually confirm that the congregation was a thriving, well-established part of Newport life. This is underscored by the

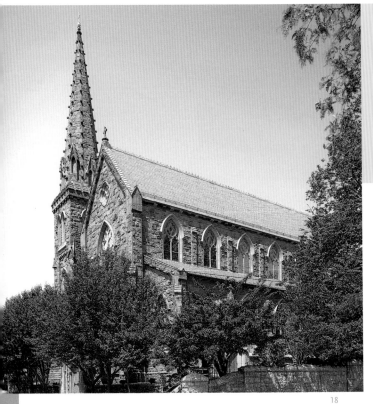

18

fact that by the late 1840s it counted some 600 members out of a total city population of 9,000.

Keeley chooses here, as he does in other designs both earlier and later, a brownstone, late-Gothic-styled structure — a predictable mid-century set of forms and an idiom particularly popular with the hierarchy of the Roman Catholic Church. A sculptural porch crowned with a figure of Mary, Our Lady of the Isle, at its apex, projects a human-scaled entrance toward Spring Street, but this church's most memorable impression is made by the dominant forms of its 125-foot corner tower with a crocketted spire as well as the soaring verticality of its main nave.

The rough-hewn, random-course work is related to that of a medieval-styled residence of the same date, Malbone Hall across town. Here, however, we know from church records that some of the men from St Mary's volunteered their time, as a kind of tithe, to cut construction costs. And who were these volunteers? Some were Catholic families that summered in Newport and made financial contributions to its erection, but other volunteers were full-time residents who volunteered their labor (many of these men had ties to the construction of Fort Adams). The priest of St Mary's notes in the first baptismal register that "St Mary's congregation started with Fort Adams," making clear that the

19–20

population of manual laborers who immigrated to work on the construction of the fort became the historic core of Newport's Irish-Catholic community. They influenced St Mary's and the course of Newport's architectural history with their physical work, construction skills, religious values, and sheer numbers.

After the Civil War, Keeley returned to Newport to design another stone structure: a Victorian-era Gothic-trimmed school that would serve the needs of the growing Catholic population.

St Mary's is perhaps best known today as the site of the 1953 marriage between future President John F. Kennedy and Jacqueline Bouvier, whose family summered at Hammersmith Farm.

19 MEMORIAL BOULEVARD (1946, 1966)

The swath of this twentieth-century thoroughfare, with its four-lane width split by a wide park-like median on its eastern end, forms a visual dividing line between the older colonial neighborhoods to the north and those areas — southern Thames, the 5th Ward, and the Drive—largely developed later. Although its construction sadly entailed the elimination of several smaller streets and buildings that included, in part, an African American enclave, the Boulevard does function effectively to move traffic from the harbor side to the beachfront.

Back in the early twentieth century, a planning report by the Olmsted firm proposed an earlier version of such a road as a radical solution to Newport's clogged waterfront: a new limited-access, multi-laned highway that would run across the head of the harbor and then head over the hill toward Easton's Beach at the eastern edge of town. It would have entailed massive destruction of the working wharves and surrounding residential streets, and thus was never built as envisioned. The road we see today was eventually constructed in several stages. The divided highway reaching over the hill to the beach was part of a post-World War II urban redevelopment plan, constructed in two campaigns some twenty years apart. The first of these, the eastern leg, created what was originally called Memorial Boulevard in honor of the city's World War II military dead. Another memorial was appended to its name in the early 1950s when a modest bronze figure of the Italian explorer Christopher Columbus was added at its intersection with Bellevue Avenue. Then, as late as the 1970s, and despite more consternation about such destructive redevelopment, its last leg (the stretch called America's Cup Avenue) was completed, realizing, at least in part, the function if not the form called for in the Olmsted plan of more than fifty years earlier.

20 PUERINI'S ITALIAN SPECIALTIES (1920), ALTERED (1994-2006) MARY MEAGHER

24 Memorial Boulevard West

For a town so well known for its restaurants, this genre of building has produced little in the way of interesting architecture. Admittedly, many occupy older houses with few changes to their exteriors, but here on the Boulevard one commercial block from the 1920s has recently been the site of more innovative alterations. Over the course of more than a decade, the simple, square brick block has seen changes such as the addition of small plate windows and interior alterations; but the most dramatic has been the new construction on its uphill side. The boxy rectangularity of the original building is extended and slightly set off by the higher elevation of the addition. The balconies and terrace framed by the new work are traced in an outline of hefty posts and beams all painted a semolina yellow; darker, aubergine-colored panels between the yellow elements visually recede. The effect is that of a ruin, or rather a remnant of an existing el whose structure has been exposed by stripping away wall fabric rather than having been added anew. Colors are important here as the dusky yellow also helps lighten the bulky dimensions of the elements and ties it to the trim color on the earlier block.

21

21 NEWPORT PUBLIC LIBRARY (1969) ROBINSON GREEN BERETTA, (2001) THOMAS BEEBE

290 Spring Street

The Newport Public Library, called the People's Library, was housed in the nineteenth-century Edward King House set far up the slope of the grassy hillside until the late 1960s—when a new library was designed adjacent to Spring Street. Strangely, this edifice never addressed the street itself but faced instead the grassy lawn and parking lot. Adding to this unfortunate design choice in response to the topography of the site, the public entrance was on the second level, accessed by a long staircase so that it appeared unapproachable and uninviting to passing pedestrians. Within only a few decades, the library collection and programming had outgrown this "new" facility.

Fortunately, the present library building adds new, more user-friendly spaces and corrects many of the shortcomings of its predecessor. The big broad main entrance on Spring Street is clearly something its predecessor never had: a welcoming street-level entry. Its eye-catching white frame spans the space between hefty brick pylons. The interior has generous spaces, some dedicated to functions such as computer access that didn't exist when the preceding library was constructed. The most dramatic interior change is the result of much more glass—both as windows and room dividers—pleasantly admitting natural light even as it allows for better visual security. If there is a whiff here of the Prairie style in the hipped roof, overhanging eaves, and emphasis on horizontal planes, it may be because this congenial building was designed by noted Chicago architect Thomas Beebe. It happily feels connected to the street and the surrounding neighborhood in ways that Newport's earlier library buildings never did and so finally befits its nickname of the People's Library.

TOUR ONE *continued from page 21*

of 1739, which served as the administrative capital of the English colony situated close to the spring; and the Brick Market of 1773, which sits at the head of Long Wharf where its east-west axis crosses Thames Street and divides into Broadway and Touro Streets. Such economic and commercial activity around the square and along neighboring streets reflected Newport's vitality and its role as an important east coast port city, a center of trade and artisanal production. Taken together with the nearby residential structures, it all affirmed Newport as a self-sufficient, thriving seventeenth- and eighteenth-century town.

Although some of this centrality has been lost, Washington Square and its environs still look and feel like a town center. Despite attempts through the years to create newer centers (such as the "uptown" Bellevue Avenue district of the 1870s or the Disneyland approach of Queen Anne Square from the 1970s), Washington Square remains the only such civic space that has grown with Newport over the entire course of its history.

TOUR FOUR *continued from page 81*

For all this development in the North End, there is still evidence of its earlier history as a kind of rural outback. The North End boasts one of the earliest structures remaining in Newport: the late seventeenth-century Elder Bliss House. And not far from this are a wonderful eighteenth-century Revolutionary War earthworks redoubt; Malbone House, a major mid-nineteenth-century mansion; and the site, at the end of Bliss Mine Road, of a camp set up for Italian immigrant stone carvers when they came to work on Marble House and other Bellevue Avenue mansions at the end of the nineteenth century. Today if you walk along Vernon and Fenner you can even find several granite posts with an "N" on one side and an "M" on the other, signifying the municipal boundary between Newport and Middletown.

TOUR SEVEN *continued from page 179*

the 1880s and one lot further south, the Casino announced the arrival of a new sophisticated taste in decoration and ambience. Although its entry arch ran alongside the Avenue, it might just as well have been built astride Bellevue as a kind of gateway to the Gilded Age. Passing through the arch, the mundane noise and traffic of the townscape falls away and the building embraces you with its fanciful architectural references and visual pleasures. It is still the best introduction to the late-century Bellevue social environment.

As you walk or drive along Bellevue, the change from the tight warren of byways in the colonial town to the scale and greenery of the Bellevue streetscape is visually striking. Many of these houses sit on verdant lawns and landscaped properties. Later their images would evoke baronial halls and princely villas but the earlier houses clearly conjure up a more idyllic and rustic countryside. As time went on, as with most suburban developments, the character of the place found itself increasingly altered by the number and density of new homes being erected. The final result of this development is not unlike the character of an early suburban tract.

While some of these houses have found new institutional uses (the headquarters for the Preservation Society, a conference center for Salve Regina University, several private museums), a surprising number are still in private hands. Thanks to the efforts of a handful of organizations led by the Preservation Society of Newport County, key buildings have been saved. The character of this Gilded Age enclave has been maintained as a reminder of the exuberant and ostentatious architectural responses to an America undergoing rapid change due to immigration, industrialization, and urbanization.

TOUR EIGHT *continued from page 245*

In the last generation, after seeing a decline in the decades surrounding World War II, this area has once again experienced a surge in large residential building and thus contains a large number of contemporary residential designs. With this recent building boom, exurbia has morphed into suburbia, not quite crowded with buildings but far from its original pristine isolation. Here and there, one can still sense the grandeur of the earlier, wilder landscape, but this has more recently been supplanted by a different kind of outcropping: everywhere there are new, very large buildings. Some are wonderfully creative and contextual, but others call attention to themselves as much as they do to the natural beauty of their environs.

Ronald J. Onorato, a graduate of Rutgers College, received his Doctoral degree from Brown University. Besides his experience as a museum curator in Rhode Island, Massachusetts, New York, and California, and his teaching at a number of colleges, he is currently Honors Professor of Art History at the University of Rhode Island where he has been on the faculty since 1977. He also serves as a commissioner on the Rhode Island Historical Preservation and Heritage Commission and on the State Historical Cemeteries Commission. The author of numerous books, articles and museum catalogues, he has written and lectured on an eclectic variety of 19th- and 20th-century American and contemporary art and architectural topics. He is a long time resident of Newport.

Eva Anderson and **Colin Murphy** are principals of **Symbio Design,** an award-winning firm specializing in communications design solutions for diverse corporate, institutional, and government clients such as General Electric, Harvard University Art Museums, and The Nature Conservancy. Anderson, an MFA graduate of Rhode Island School of Design, was a team leader on the *PPS/AIAri Guide to Providence Architecture*. She has taught at Rhode Island School of Design and Clark University, and is nationally recognized for her design and her work on environmental issues. Murphy combines a Rhode Island School of Design education with an MBA. He has won awards for design has extensive experience in interactive and web-based communications. He has been a guest lecturer at Brown University on interface design and has taught at Rhode Island School of Design.

Warren Jagger, an architectural and commercial photographer, is a BFA graduate of Rhode Island School of Design. His clients include nationally known architects, interior designers, hotel groups and developers, major corporations, and government agencies. With photographs published in periodicals ranging from *Interior Design* and *Architectural Record* to *Rhode Island Monthly*, his books include *Most Admirable: The Rhode Island State House* and *PPS/AIAri Guide to Providence Architecture*. He is the owner of Warren Jagger Photography, Inc, with a studio in the Jewelry District of Providence.